THE JEROME L. JOSS
COLLECTION OF AFRICAN HEADRESTS
AT UCLA

SLEEPING BEAUTIES

BY WILLIAM J. DEWEY

WITH CONTRIBUTIONS BY

Toshiko M. McCallum on Asia

Jerome Feldman on Oceania

Henrietta Cosentino on Mr. Joss

FOWLER MUSEUM OF CULTURAL HISTORY ● UNIVERSITY OF CALIFORNIA, LOS ANGELES

This catalogue and associated exhibition
were supported by funding from the following:
    Ahmanson Foundation
    National Endowment for the Humanities Challenge Grant
    Manus, the support group of the
        Fowler Museum of Cultural History

Fowler Museum of Cultural History
University of California, Los Angeles
405 Hilgard Avenue
Los Angeles, California, USA 90024-1549

Printed and bound in Japan by Nissha Printing Co., Ltd.

Library of Congress Cataloging-in-Publication Data:
Dewey, William Joseph
    Sleeping beauties: the Jerome L. Joss collection of African
headrests at UCLA / by William J. Dewey: with contributions by
Toshiko M. McCallum, Jerome Feldman, Henrietta Cosentino.
        p.   cm.
    Exhibition catalog.
    Includes bibliographical references.
    ISBN 0-930741-27-7 : $40.00
    ISBN 0-930741-28-5 (pbk.) : $27.00
    1. Wood-carving — Africa. Sub-Saharan — Exhibitions.
2. Headrests — Africa. Sub-Saharan — Exhibitions. 3. Headrests —
East Asia — Exhibitions. 4. Headrests — Oceania — Exhibitions.
5. Joss, Jerome L. (Jerome Lionel), 1909-   . — Art collections —
Exhibitions. 6. Headrests — Private collections — California —
Los Angeles — Exhibitions. 7. University of California, Los Angeles. Fowler Museum of Cultural History — Exhibitions. I. McCallum, Toshiko M. (Toshiko Miyabayashi), 1943-   . II. Feldman,
Jerome, 1944-   . III. Cosentino, Henrietta, 1941-   . IV. Universi-
ty of California, Los Angeles. Fowler Museum of Cultural History.
V. Title.
NK9788.75.D48   1993
736'.4 — dc20   92-82945
                                                         CIP

CONTENTS

ACKNOWLEDGMENTS

While many collectors build specialties within more generalized holdings, few have pursued this with the commitment and enthusiasm of Jerome L. Joss. His substantial collection of headrests — primarily from Africa, with smaller groupings from Asia and Oceania — is a promised gift to the Fowler Museum of Cultural History

and will be a major asset to our collections. These headrests fill a niche which was only modestly occupied until now. They also significantly broaden our material from east and southern Africa.

It has been a genuine pleasure playing a small role in the development of this collection. Jerry has proven to be much more than a benefactor. He is a friend and colleague who in the selection of all his acquisitions has consistently kept the goals of the Museum and its best interests clearly in mind. He has built a collection that will be of lasting value to future generations of students and scholars and to the Los Angeles community as a whole. His generosity is greatly appreciated and his friendship highly valued.

The headrests themselves are a superb study in the marriage of form and function. Many represent African art and design at their finest. Although most are only four to six inches high, they are highly expressive sculptures with a monumentality of their own. Headrests have typically been seen as modest objects with a simple function — to support the head during sleep. While some are also used as stools in public areas during daytime, most are usually hidden from view in the interior spaces of a home. This accounts for the relative absence of context photographs of their use.

We are fortunate in having Dr. William Dewey to bring these intimate objects out into the light. He is one of the few scholars to probe the complexity of headrests as an integral part of his field research and to elucidate the social, spiritual, and political dimensions of them. Since his Shona material is unique, it is featured here as a case study that should serve as a model for further work on this genre. Unfortunately it may be too late to conduct comparable studies in many cultures. We are grateful for Dr. Dewey's serious approach to this subject and for his enlightening essays.

I would also like to thank Toshiko McCallum for her insightful paper on the Asian section of the collection. She previously authored *Containing Beauty: Japanese Bamboo Flower Baskets* for the Museum and here again she brings her characteristic clarity to a difficult topic.

Likewise Dr. Jerome Feldman deserves our appreciation for his contribution on the Oceanic segment of the collection. He too is a former visiting curator at the Museum and was principal author and editor of *Eloquent Dead: Ancestral Sculptures of Indonesia and Southeast Asia*. Dr. Feldman has frequently served as an informal consultant on the Joss Indonesian collection and his expertise has consistently enhanced our understanding of this material.

Very special thanks go to Paulette Parker, who has served multiple roles in organizing, researching, and cataloguing the collection. Her attention to myriad details kept this publication and accompanying exhibition on track and made everyone's job easier. It has been a joy working with Paulette over the past several years as Jerry's various collections expanded into new and exciting areas.

Henrietta Cosentino, Senior Publications Editor at the Museum, changed roles for this volume and wrote the biographical profile of Jerry that illuminates his interests in African art and in collecting. As always her writing is engaging and lively as befitting her subject.

Leslie Jones edited this volume with care and diligence. Her energy under difficult deadlines ensured the successful completion of the project. Thanks also to Judith Herschman, our librarian, for her organizational and editorial contributions in the final stages. Publica-

tions Director Daniel Brauer worked closely with Judith Hale and Barbara Kelly of UCLA print communications to develop lively yet thoughtful design that serves as an appropriate complement to the objects themselves. Staff photographer Denis Nervig took the splendid photographs that fill this book.

David Mayo created an innovative exhibition design to emphasize the aesthetic qualities of the headrests with-

out obscuring their functional roles. The rest of the museum staff (listed at the back of this volume) performed with accustomed professionalism. I would like to single out Owen Moore and Fran Tabbush for handling logistical problems beyond the norm. Final thanks must return to Jerome L. Joss for making all this possible.

Doran H. Ross
Deputy Director

What's the hidden link between a Sealy Posture-pedic mattress and a carved African headrest? The first answer, of course, is Jerome Lionel Joss, who four decades ago invented the name of the former, and more recently devoted years to collecting the latter. Is it mere coincidence that both are the furnishings for sleep? With a twinkle in his eyes, Jerry confesses he has wondered the same thing himself. "Maybe a subliminal connection..." he proposes: "Sleep has been a sort of theme in much of my professional life."

To a friend, it seems this mysterious connection might have as much to do with dreams as with sleep. It certainly involves Jerry's lifelong ability to comprehend humble needs (a good night's sleep), unpretentious objects (headrests), and the ordinary habits of attention that determine how and what people see. These particular attributes made Jerry Joss a gifted advertising man, and more recently, an acute observer and collector of non-Western art. They are enhanced by his commitment to sharing, and by his determined humanism.

Jerome Lionel Joss was born March 21, 1909, in Minneapolis, Minnesota, the eldest child of Gertrude and Harry Joss. His mother's family, the Goldenbergs, had immigrated from Russia to Minneapolis in the late 1880s, when Gertrude was seven. His father's parents had arrived in 1881 from the town of Ninestadt at the German-Lithuanian border. After struggling as homesteaders in the bitter cold of Manitoba, they fled south to the relative tropics of Minnesota. (Jerry once asked, "But Grandpa, Why Minneapolis? Why not someplace

Jerome Lionel Joss

warm??" To which Grandpa had replied, "But Jerry, what immigrant knew about California in 1881?!").

Jerry recalls the elements of a secure and ceremonious childhood, shared with his sisters Adele and Rita: Kindergarten and elementary grades at the Sumner School, and Hebrew classes after school at the Talmud Torah. Friday dinners at his paternal grandparents' home with the aunts and uncles. For Jerry, a paper route. A short-lived career with the violin "because every Jewish family wanted to have a young Heifetz. But I had no ear, and besides I didn't practice...." He was more interested in marbles, the major sport of the era for elementary school kids. Jerry not only played well, he amassed a collection of agates and carnelians that won him a Blue Ribbon. His "collector's genes" were already showing.

High school years were even busier, as Jerry's tremendous entrepreneurial energies found outlets. Involvement with the North High paper, the *Polaris*, consumed most afternoons. Starting as a reporter, he soon discovered the business department interested him more, and wound up as advertising manager of both the weekly and the annual.

In 1927, after graduating from North High, Jerry entered the University of Minnesota; but in 1929, with the onset of the Great Depression, he was forced to drop out and take a full-time job running a small army-navy surplus store upstate. After two years he was able to go back for his degree. When he returned to the university, he entered the first class of an experimental multi-disciplinary program called "University College," in which students charted their own programs of study. By this time, Jerry already had an idea that his future lay in business — either advertising or merchandising. His courses, however, ranged widely, including economics, journalism, psychology, and anthropology. He was especially interested in the latter. Nevertheless, he had to turn down an intriguing invitation to join a group of graduate students for a nine-month-long anthropological field trip in Africa; financial constraints made it impossible. (Later in life he was to return to that particular road not taken.)

Jerry Joss at his home in Sherman Oaks, standing by a carved door panel from Indonesia.

Much later, so it happens, these same Goldstein sisters, having retired to Los Angeles, bequested the proceeds of their Westwood house to establish a modest museum of textiles, costumes, and decorative arts at the University of Minnesota, on the St. Paul campus — the small but well-appointed Goldstein Gallery. When Jerry learned of this, in 1989, he donated his collection of Roman glass to the Gallery; at the same time he established an endowment for a graduate student in textiles.

Although he missed the fieldtrip, Jerry had adventures of his own when he embarked on his most unconventional course of study. Rayon had just come on the market and Jerry wanted to explore the possibilities — probably heeding the words of his maternal aunt Celia, whose perpetual query, "What are you gonna do when you grow up?" was typically followed by: "I hear there's a wonderful field in textiles." The textile class at the University of Minnesota was taught by two sisters, Harriett and Vetta Goldstein. When he presented himself for the first session, and the sisters were shocked: "Why, this is a course for home economics students!" It had always been an all-female class. The Goldstein sisters ended up developing a seminar just for him; eventually, it became a standard in the School of Business.

Jerry graduated in 1933 and set out to make his way in advertising. It was the depths of the Depression; jobs were far from the asking. Jerry tried the ad agencies first, and got hit with the age-old catch-22: "Come back when you have experience, kid." Undaunted, he decided he would accept a job in sales if necessary. He set off by foot down State Street, that boulevard of venerable department stores in Chicago's Loop. He started with Marshall Fields and worked his way down, finally arriving at Morris L. Rothschild, clothier. There he was able to talk his way into an entry-level job as stock boy for the decidedly unprincely salary of $14.50 a week. Soon he was working half-time on advertising copy, and within three years he had risen to Assistant Advertising Manager. He was a young man going places.

In 1936 Jerry was offered a job in the Schwimmer and Scott Advertising Agency, which specialized in broadcasting. Radio, still in its infancy, offered limitless commercial possibilities, and Chicago was the major hatching ground for most of the early radio soaps and other varieties of drama.

Jerry, brought into the agency because of his background in garment business, took on the account of a small-time local clothier, Morris B. Sachs. Jerry put him on a major radio station via a weekly regional amateur hour that reached into Wisconsin and Indiana. Once a month it was devoted to children; Steve Allen and Mel Tormé were among the child talents to be heard on the show. Morris B. Sachs prospered.

On behalf of his clients, Jerry also cultivated serious radio drama. One early project was a series based on *The War Years*, Carl Sandburg's four-volume tome on the Civil War. Jerry worked directly with the author to adapt the script, which was aired on Mutual Broadcasting Company, and sold to local retailers. Another project involved actor Marvin Miller, who did dramatic readings sponsored by Coronet Magazine, an account handled by Schwimmer and Scott. Miller went on to be known as "The Millionaire" on the popular weekly television drama of the same name.

In 1939, as Hitler's armies marched through Europe, Duffy Schwartz, of radio station CBS-WBBM, asked if Jerry would volunteer as Deputy Director for the Treasury Department's Bond Division for the state of Illinois. They were asking celebrities to do war bond commercials, and Jerry was to place public service announcements with the radio stations. This brought him in contact with stars such as Bob Hope and Marion Anderson. One day he got a call from his counterpart in Hollywood: they were having "trouble" with Marlene Dietrich. She wanted to do pitches for war bonds and industrial plants, but no one could provide scripts that satisfied her. Marlene was to be in Chicago, at the Ambassador East, for three days. Would Jerry help?

Jerry remembers looking at the actress as she sat in her hotel suite, minus her makeup and false eyelashes — a plain woman in a simple cotton dress, someone you wouldn't look twice at on the street. But she had a powerful presence. Like nearly everyone in the industry, Marlene was "into" Astrology. "Jerome, do you believe in the stars?" No! he exclaimed, pointing out that Hitler was a believer.

In 1942 Jerry was drafted into the Armed Forces. After a stint at Camp Hood he was sent to Adjutant Generals school in Classification, and thence to New York, Washington, D.C., and Hollywood. His major assignments were in radio, where he was responsible for "de-lousing" (combing out the commercials), and inserting in their place announcements on "conservation" of soldierly health and equipment. The idea was, take care of your equipment and it will take care of you!

When victory was proclaimed in Europe, Jerry returned to his old job at Schwimmer and Scott. His first major project was to develop a radio quiz for the Sealy Mattress Corporation, which had been a faithful client in the late 1930s. "Calling All Detectives" offered an 8-minute mini-mystery, followed by calls to random listeners for the jackpot question. Soon it was the most popular show in that time slot, and before long it went syndicated. In 1947 Jerry was asked to take charge of Sealy marketing — not just the mid-Western account, but the national one. He had moved to the Grey-North Advertising Agency, which was better able to handle a national account. Sealy was determined to overtake its competitor, Simmons.

Jerry understood the longing for a good night's sleep and the agony of a bad one. He knew the repercussions of bad mattresses: insomnia, pain, and crippled posture. Sealy was developing a new spring system which would give the back firmer support; orthopedists were consulted in the process. *Firm* bedding was the key concept, and this in turn inspired the slogan for the ad:

Jerry Joss with Earl Bergman, President of the National Sealy Corporation, and bathing beauty, at a national sales meeting in the 1930s. This photograph captures the ethos of the times.

"Posturepedic" — a word that subliminally captured the dual notions of marvelous bearing and medically certified good health. The ad was a hit, and Sealy took the market by storm, soon overtaking its competitor in the mattress business.

Jerome went on to mastermind other award-winning campaigns. In the latter half of the 1950s he was recog-

nized at least five times by the Chicago Art Directors for variety of television commercials — including one for Purex Corporation's Sweetheart Soap, one for Sealy Posturepedic, and one for Carling Brewery. In the late 1950s, all of America still shared an infatuation with cartoons. One of the great favorites was the nearsighted Mr. Magoo, wont to address tirades to his own doorhandle — a sweet, bumbling elder, lovable in his endless comic frustration. It was Jerome's inspiration to borrow this character on behalf of Carling Beer. He worked with Jim Backus (the voice of Magoo) and the animators to produce animated commercials. A 1958 film won the Chicago Art Directors Award. Another one produced in 1959, earned him a Cannes Film Festival award. It was the very first Cannes award granted for a commercial.

By the time Jerry retired and moved to Los Angeles in 1971, he had accumulated many honors and awards. One career was over. Another was yet to begin. Finally, now, he was able to indulge interests long ago kindled but never developed. First, he turned to travel. His initial journey, in 1971, took him around the world including much of Africa. His group traveled from Cape Town to Cairo, often on roadless terrain where tires lasted only 5,000 miles, and they encountered amazing sights, such as elephant migrations. It was the first of many trips for Jerry, and the start of his special love affair with Africa, which he has continued to visit frequently. He mentions with reverence the two greatest moments of his travels: one, his sight of Murchison Falls in Uganda; the other, his first view of Mopti on market day, with its swirl of people and goods, the magnificent women swathed in regal costume, all set on the banks of the River Niger, in Mali.

Jerry Joss in Ach Zhiv,
during the
1989 excavation.

As Jerry traveled he began to admire and purchase the artistic creations of African artists. At first they were tourist pieces. Then, in 1977, he met Helen Kuhn. His first vision of the Kuhn collection amazed him with its beauty and breadth, opening his eyes to the world beyond tourist art. He was now smitten with collecting. Throughout the 1980s, under the mentorship of Helen Kuhn and Irwin Hersey, and with strong encouragement from Doran Ross, he began building his collections, concentrating on Africa and Indonesia. Gradually he developed special interests — most notably, his treasured headrests. "I started collecting like a drunken sailor," says Jerry.

At the same time, he nurtured philanthropic interests. All were guided in one way or another by his own deeply felt Jewish secular humanism. A founder and benefactor of Hebrew University of Jerusalem, for several years he funded the giving of an annual award to the person, regardless of nationality or religion, who had done most to show positive improvement in Israel's image in the western world. One year, the prize went to Bill Moyers for his PBS report on a flower-raising kibbutz in the north of Israel. Founded by Dutch and Danish Protestants, it was and is a model of cross-cultural cooperation and tolerance, values that Jerry most deeply believes in.

Perhaps dearest to his heart is the archeological excavation at Ach Zhiv, in what was Phoenicia, on the Mediterranean shore about three kilometers south of Israel's northern border. Excavations begun there in 1942 had later been abandoned. In the years 1988-90, Jerry sponsored renewed excavations through Hebrew University's Institute of Archaeology; he also participated in the actual digging. Most dramatic was the discovery of an underground burial chamber dating back almost three millennia and containing dozens of burials as well as pottery vessels, jewelry, and ceramic figures from the eighth to ninth centuries B.C. — all significant new clues to the mysterious culture of the ancient Phoenicians.

In the course of his involvement with Hebrew University, Jerry visited Israel frequently. During his travels there he managed to accumulate a collection of oil lamps ranging in date from the time of biblical Abraham to the fifteenth-century Islamic era. These he donated, in 1989, to the Mid-Eastern Studies Center at the University of Minnesota. At the same time he set up an endowment for a graduate student to do research in this area.

These and other charitable activities constitute what Jerry sees as his legacy. He has already donated some 150 scripts from his early days in radio and television to the UCLA Film and Television Archives. As for his art: "I feel it is my mission to be caretaker of these things for a short time," he says. "Then I want them to go to a museum where they will be available to a lot of people." Wooed by many prominent institutions, he finally chose the UCLA Fowler Museum of Cultural History because it is "one of the most important museums of its kind in the country, with holdings of great geographic breadth and individual quality. Also, it is becoming an outstanding national center for museum research and scholarship. This is important because no matter what the objects' aesthetic qualities, it is scholarship that will ultimately help people understand the cultures of the people who made them."

Pausing to muse on this, Jerry returns to the idioms of advertising. "If you watch the way people walk through a museum, you'll see it's like ... a soundbite in a commercial. People pass objects as if they were billboards — fast ... except for the scholars." You have to know how to catch their attention, what to say.

Even without interpretation, though, Jerry's headrests catch your attention in surprising ways. Many are ingenious, some sinuous, all sensual, and it is easy to understand how one could become obsessed with such furnishings. Imagine the heads that have rested on these objects. Here, the Egyptian monarch from the eighteenth dynasty, buried with his head laid on alabaster. There, the tenth-century Chinese noblewoman, saving her elaborate hairdo on a cold ceramic pillow that is filled with glowing charcoal to warm her neck in the dead of winter. Or perhaps an Asmat headhunter from Irian Jaya, his head resting on the decorated skull of an ancestor. And nearby (in our imaginary exhibition), the Shona diviner from Zimbabwe who will sleep tonight on a handcarved wooden pillow in hopes of summoning the spirits to his dreams.

All this is embedded in Jerry's legacy of headrests. From his first legacy, in the creative world of advertising, to his second, in the realm of African and Asian arts, he has explored the simple concept of firm bedding — around the world, through time, and into dreams. With this loving collection of headrests, he awakens our aesthetic attention, helps us see culture in new ways, and even sets us to dreaming.

Henrietta Cosentino

Africa

I

AN INTRODUCTION TO AFRICAN HEADRESTS

WILLIAM J. DEWEY

In the Marungu and Uguha [the southern and northern Tabwa lands within Zaire], the natives' monumental coiffures do not do well in contact with [sleeping] mats, the beads break and the horns [of woven hair] are deformed. Since one cannot redo the edification of these coiffures every day, those wearing them preserve them by sleeping with their necks lying on little wooden supports. Some of these pillows are very simple, with a small horizontal piece of wood mounted on a single foot, the whole thing being carved rather simply from the same block of wood. Others, though, are very well carved. The magical medicines (dawa) attached to the pillow ... probably bring agreeable dreams to the person sleeping on the pillow (Jacques and Storms 1886:107).[1]

African headrests, as a distinct type of object, have increasingly become the focus of attention for many scholars, collectors and museums.[2] Roy Sieber deserves much of the credit for this intensified interest. His 1980 exhibition and catalogue, *African Furniture and Household Objects*, pointedly set out "to whet the viewer's and reader's appetite with a sampling of traditional, utilitarian, often splendid but essentially modest objects" (1980:13). This catalogue intends to tantalize the viewer and reader even more with the physical and intellectual beauty of headrests. Here daily use serves to closely link art to the cycle of its owner's life.

This catalogue and exhibition are not intended to be definitive surveys of African headrest styles and meanings, for some geographic areas are not represented. Nevertheless, the remarkable collection that Jerome Joss has assembled eloquently displays the range of forms produced on the African continent. The collection is all the more amazing considering that it was assembled in approximately ten years. Jerome Joss' generosity in donating his collection to the Fowler Museum of Cultural History and bringing it to the attention of the broader public through the publication of this catalogue will, it is hoped, encourage further scholarship and appreciation of headrests in general.

There is considerable emphasis in this catalogue on what some may consider pedantic formal issues of style and distribution patterns. However, this approach is a necessary prerequisite for understanding the use and meaning of the headrests. For too many years the art of

eastern and southern Africa (the source of most of the Joss examples) has been under-represented in scholarly publications, museums and private collections. Much of what has been written, particularly in general surveys of African art, greatly simplifies its use and meaning. Misattribution of headrest origins is also a problem. The general tendency to focus on figurative sculpture and masks (now, thankfully, changing) also makes it understandable why there are still so many unanswered questions concerning headrests, which are primarily non-figurative.

Another aim of this catalogue is to emphasize the context in which the headrests are, or were, used, and their importance as declarations of status and conduits of the spirits. Obviously not every headrest has a symbolic meaning and not every owner used headrests for reasons other than sleeping. Because social, political and religious uses have largely been ignored, however, I have chosen to emphasize them whenever sufficient scholarship is present. In their original contexts the uses and meaning of headrests are often as subtly rendered as their visual beauty is subtly communicated to the viewer's aesthetic sensibilities. There is obviously still much to be discovered.

The label "headrest" is used in preference to other common terms such as "pillow" and "neckrest" because I believe it more accurately describes how these objects are used. From my research I discovered that some Shona sources felt the "rest" could be placed at the back of the neck, but the majority said that the rest was placed under one ear and along the side of the chin to support the whole head. This seems to have also been the pattern for

Zairean headrest,
cat. 48,
see also p. 60.

other parts of Africa.

The usual reaction of Westerners (and contemporary Africans who no longer use headrests) is that wooden headrests must have been very uncomfortable to sleep on. It must be remembered that Africans traditionally slept on sleeping mats rather than mattresses. A wooden headrest is not much harder than a mat on the ground. Headrests are not part of the Western tradition and the ease of using an implement does depend on what one is used to. Even in our own culture, however, there are similar objects, such as inflatable neckrests for traveling, and it is common practice to put one's arm under one's head if no pillow is available. Eugene Burt, who has worked in East Africa where pastoralists continue to use wooden headrests, notes that it

> is not as uncomfortable as many people assume. In fact, Africans say that nerves in the head are slightly numbed by the pressure of the headrest producing a pleasant, tranquilizing effect that leads to deep sleep. Of course, a headrest user can lie only on his back or side (1985:16).

Not all the illustrated examples from the Joss collection are, strictly speaking, headrests. While some African groups, such as those in southern Africa, do make headrests only for sleeping purposes, others, particularly in West and East Africa, make multifunctional objects that can be used for sitting or sleeping. These are designated in the catalogue as headrest/stools when it is documented that they were used in both fashions, but in other cases there is insufficient evidence to make such a distinction. A few very low stools are also included either to make a comparative point or to clarify what is known about a type of object that in the past has often mistakenly been called a headrest.

History

The oldest known headrests of Africa are from ancient Egypt. They first seem to appear around the time of the Second or Third Dynasty of the Old Kingdom, that is, around 2600 B.C. (Petrie 1927:33). Later African headrests are often compared to those of ancient Egypt, with the implication, either implicitly or explicitly stated, that Africans derived their forms from the ancient Egyptians. Sieber has pointed out that it would be better to speak of "early Egyptian parallels—they cannot properly be called prototypes, for there is no evidence to show that the direction of influence was not from Africa to Egypt" (1980:107; also see Dewey 1991a:93).

The ancient Egyptian headrests were often placed in tombs and the wooden examples were primarily preserved because of the dry desert atmosphere. Other ancient African examples were for the most part not so lucky, soon falling victim to the wetter sub-Saharan climate or the prevalence of termites. Despite a lack of evidence for early sub-Saharan headrests, Flinders Petrie, the noted Egyptologist, asserts:

There seem to have been two introductions of the idea into Egypt, one in the Second-Third Dynasties, another in the Seventeenth-Eighteenth Dynasties. In the latter, there is no question of strong African influence; and by the portrait of Zeser, the Third Dynasty has been supposed to be of southern origin. It may be that the head rest, so characteristic of Africa at present, was twice introduced into Egypt from African sources, coming first with the fluted columns of the step pyramid age (1927:36) [See the Joss catalogue examples, cat. nos. 1-2].

In sub-Saharan Africa there are a few types of ancient headrest that have been preserved, but none are as old as the ancient Egyptian examples. In the dry sealed caves of the Bandiagara escarpment of Mali, Rogier Bedaux has found wooden headrests interred with the communal graves of the people who have come to be known as the "Tellem." These date primarily from the eleventh and twelfth centuries A.D. and then disappear by the fourteenth century (Bedaux 1974, 1988) [See Joss catalogue examples, cat. nos. 93-95].

In central and southern Africa there are also tantalizing bits of evidence pointing to the ancient existence of headrests. As explained in more detail in Chapter 2, gold sheeting has been recovered from the twelfth-century site of Mapungubwe along the Limpopo River. This ornamentation is believed to have adorned a wooden headrest, long ago disintegrated. There is also evidence that the practice of sheathing headrests with metal may have continued during the times of Great Zimbabwe and the successor states in the area during the thirteenth through seventeenth centuries A.D.

In the Upemba Depression of Zaire an example of a ceramic headrest from the Kisalian period (late eighth through thirteenth centuries A.D.) has recently come to light. Apparently found at Sanga by the missionary W. F. P. Burton in the 1930s, together with other pottery of the same age, it was sent to the University of the Witwatersrand in Johannesburg with other collections of Luba material culture. Burton noted that "the pillow could scarcely be used by a living person. It is too fragile ... (and) must have been molded ... specially to be interred with the dead" (Huffman 1992:fig. 32). Since this headrest was taken out of its archaeological context it will never be possible to date it definitely. No similar object has as yet been found in excavations in the area (Hiernaux et al. 1971; de Maret 1985; Nenquin 1963), but it nevertheless is an intriguing bit of evidence.

In West Africa,

> headrests were reported by early European travelers in the Senegambia and the Gold Coast where they seem not to have survived to the present. For example, Loyer, reporting on Issini (Assini) on the Gold Coast in 1701, states "they have only a few Stools, about a Foot high, which, in the Night, serve them for Pillows" (Sieber 1980:108, citing Loyer in Astley 1745-47, II:437).

An engraving of a Ghanaian coastal scene by Pieter de Marees, dating from 1602, also appears to show a man carrying a headrest (Cole and Ross 1977:13, fig.

15), although the object actually may be a headrest/stool.

Materials

Wood is the primary medium of headrest manufacture in sub-Saharan African but other materials have sometimes been employed. Occasionally some have been carved of ivory (e.g., Falgayrettes 1989:76, 77 illustrating a Luba example; Dewey 1991:fig. 134 showing a Shona example; Sweeny 1935, 1:472 illustrating a Lega example). These however are very rare and must have been reserved for persons of high status. Ceramic examples are also quite rare. Among the few known are Sieber's illustration of an example from Chad (1980:124) and the previously-mentioned ancient example from the Upemba depression of Zaire. Examples carved of stone are known from ancient Egypt, but no examples from sub-Saharan Africa have been seen in any of the literature. Metal in the form of wire, nails or strips applied on wooden headrests is somewhat common but headrests entirely made of metal are very rare. The only sub-Saharan examples known are the iron headrests of the Tellem. Bedaux (1974, 1988) describes these fourteenth-century examples as "votive," presumably because they could not have actually supported the weight of a head. But if these headrests were only intended to support the skull, which does not weigh very much, perhaps they were functional.

Style and Ethnicity

The study of headrests also reveals some interesting things about style and ethnicity. The nature of ethnicity has been receiving considerable attention in various disciplines including art history. This is not the place to review theoretical considerations, but it is important to remember that ethnicity is not a static entity. Identities are negotiated within particular historical frameworks, and can be modified or changed by several factors, especially the nature of interactions between peoples: warfare, political domination or incorporation, shared social and religious institutions, colonial intervention. The way in which artistic style interacts with ethnicity is also variable. Sometimes style coincides with ethnic boundaries and art is part of the mechanism for maintaining these boundaries. At other times style seems to have nothing to do with ethnic divisions and instead is contingent upon such things as pan-ethnic political boundaries, the geographical extent of religious and social institutions, and the range and mobility of artists and patrons. While art historians will continue to use ethnicity as one aspect of understanding art, it is important to define more accurately what ethnicity means within particular historical settings and to seek a greater understanding of the motivations for the people themselves to use and manipulate ethnicity.

A few examples of how artistic style and ethnicity interact can be easily shown using African headrests. Nooter has pointed out that it is difficult to assign too-precise attributions for Luba headrests, since art was often used as a gift to cement political bonds and neighboring groups frequently copied the Luba styles in order to share in their prestige (Nooter 1984, 1991, 1992). Klopper has pointed out that Zulu identity was in part forged by inventing fictitious genealogies to broaden the political base of the ruling elite. "Zulu" headrests with the *amusumpa* or 'wart' motif, therefore, coincide more with the extent of Zulu royal patronage and power than with particular ethnic or clan groups (Klopper 1991). Conner's observations of the Ngoni of Malawi illustrate a different variation of ethnicity and style interaction. There, members of a single ethnic group use headrests of various styles; one is "Swazi-like," another is lakeside Tonga in form, and a third seems an adaptation of a northeastern Shona style. The styles relate

FIG. 1.
Initiated Pokot male with distinctive blue mudcap hair ornamentation indicating his status. Northern Kenya. Note the headrest he carries, indicative of his age and status (see cat. 21).

to the ethnicity of a man or his ancestors before they were assimilated into the Ngoni (Conner 1991).

I have documented that headrest stylistic areas in northeast and southeast Zimbabwe encompass various ethnic groups including Shona subgroups and the Barwe-Tonga and Tsonga of Mozambique (Dewey 1991 and Chapter 2). The motivations and historical circumstances that contributed to the establishment of these stylistic areas have yet to be totally defined. The East African pastoral groups provide some of the most interesting examples because this region is one of the few

areas of Africa where headrest use is still prevalent. There, examples exist of: shared headrest styles among several ethnic groups; stylistic variation of headrests based upon age, status and gender differences within single ethnic groups; and headrest styles that are part of the system of maintaining ethnic boundaries. Hodder's analysis of material culture in the Baringo district of Kenya, where three different groups live,

would seem to suggest that in spite of interaction in trade and marriage connecting these politically-distinct populations, they nevertheless maintain clear distinctions between their material cultures. As Hodder points out (1977:260) such a conclusion is unexpected. After all, these are acephalous societies, without the kind of centralized institutions which would seem to be the precondition of clear-cut political or tribal, let alone material, expressions of identity. In this circumstance Hodder argues, albeit tentatively, that the preservation of a distinct material culture is itself the vehicle of this broader identity, that such consistency is "related to and is perhaps an emblem of the general need to conform with the expectations of the society in which one lives" (Mack 1982:111).

How this correlates with the reasons for sharing headrest styles requires more study, but John Mack's comments are a useful corollary:

It is worth remembering that in a total assemblage of objects it only requires one item, or one apparent minor idiosyncrasy of style so long as it is adhered to consistently, to declare ethnic identity. In any case it is easy to forget that material culture is only one of a number of visual systems through which such identity might be expressed. Among the Lotuxo the age sets within each rain-area have their own distinctive dance movements which are correlated with patterns of drum beat and trumpet rhythms. These too assert identity among people who otherwise share a common system of material culture (1982:129).

Use and Meaning

Headrests are so often described as being used to support or protect elaborate coiffures that the statement has become a truism. Too often downplayed is the purpose of these coiffures and why they need protection. Of course there is the common urge to adorn and beautify, and the hours and even days of labor invested in constructing elaborate coiffures are reason in themselves to protect and preserve the hair with a headrest. However there is another important reason which is often glossed over or ignored. Coiffures frequently declare their owner's age, gender, rank or status, and are often embellished and/or empowered by accoutrements and charms of a magico-religious nature. They then become signs, symbols and potent empowering devices that must be protected.

Many early European explorers in what is now Zaire commented upon the elaborate hairstyles of both men and women. Edward Hore, for example, described in the 1880s how among the "waGuha" of the Lukuga river area

> the hair was encouraged to grow long by every possible aid of combing and stretching over rolls and puffs, which are built up into shapes resembling crowns or turbans, and ornamented with iron and copper ornaments, bands of cowries and beads with terminal points and cones, forming a structure requiring great care to preserve from damage (Roberts 1980:345, citing Wolfe 1971:145).

Several authors have shown how coiffures such as these have been reproduced in the figurative sculpture of such groups in the area as the Luba, Tabwa and Hemba (Nooter 1984, 1990, 1991; Roberts 1980, 1985, 1986; de Grunne 1985; Neyt 1985). They interpret the coiffures in the sculpture as signifying the status or rank of those they depict and even as symbolizing the organizing cosmological structures of that society. Dewey and Childs have established that the practice of inserting iron and copper nails into elaborate coiffures is an ancient one due to their discovery of this practice in an ancient Kisalian period grave (eighth-thirteenth centuries A.D.). These ancient nails have the same shape as more recent Luba examples, as well as the same shape and name as Luba blacksmiths' anvil/hammers. It is claimed that the small nails symbolically lock in the power of people such as kings, who were also the ones said to have introduced the blacksmiths' expertise with iron (Dewey and Childs forthcoming; Dewey 1991b). It is no wonder that headrests were employed to protect these important coiffures.

Among East African pastoralists, coiffure is also primarily an indicator of status (see Cole 1974). Among such groups as the Pokot a young man only is entitled to begin wearing the distinctive blue mudpack that marks him as an adult after he is initiated through the *sapana* ceremony and ritually spears an ox. As his age-set and he rise through the ranks of the hierarchical Pokot society, changes in jewelry, and especially hairstyle and feather decorations for the hair will mark each promotion (Brown 1986).

> Advancement often must be fought for. When elders deliberately delay it, men may wear ornaments to which they are not entitled and spark serious inter-set and even intergenerational warfare. These conflicts are ostensibly over personal ornaments, but actually express a thwarted desire for promotion. They are regulated by the fact that the senior generation must eventually give way (Brown 1986:28).

The headrests of the Pokot are stylistically differentiated according to status as well, and also must be seen as playing an active role in instigating these inter-generational struggles for control of authority.

The role that headrests play in inducing dreams has been highlighted in a recent article by Anitra Nettleton (1990), "'Dream Machines': Southern African Headrests," and in the Fondation Dapper's catalogue and exhibition *Supports de Rêves* or 'Dream Supports' (1989). I have noted this role of headrests among the Shona (Dewey 1986, 1991) and will explain it in more depth in Chapter 2. Many of the Joss collection catalogue entries

also summarize information known about the connection between headrests and dreams for specific ethnic groups. Rather than repeat that information here, I will instead illustrate an example of the connection for the Chokwe, who are not represented in the exhibition.

The Chokwe use a type of divination that they call *ngombo ya cisuka* or 'shaking the basket'. The basket they use is filled with a variety of objects such as plants, seeds, bones and small carved figurines. The diviner shakes the basket and interprets the resulting configuration for a client who is faced with a particular problem. Miniature headrests are regularly included among the carved objects in these baskets. They are called "pillow of dreams" and are said to represent a mechanism for explaining problems, brought by consultants, through dreams (Rodrigues de Areia 1978:40). A recent query to Chokwe diviners confirmed that the headrests still are included in the baskets. One diviner added the interpretation that the headrests were only for use by chiefs. He explained that headrests formerly incorporated a piece of human skull as a magical device to empower the chief. If a sick person was divined for and the headrest came up, he interpreted it as showing that the illness was the result of the patient having inadvertently walked past the place where a person had been sacrificed as part of the chief's investiture ceremonies (Manuel Jordan, personal communication, 1992.)

There is also an interesting connection often made between the incised or raised surface decoration on the headrests and human scarification. Among both the Luba and the Shona both types of decoration have the same name (*ntapo* and *nyora* respectively). This practice

FIG. 2.
Karo males dancing in a
line to celebrate initiation
or marriage. Lower Omo
River, southwestern
Ethiopia. Note distinctive
coiffures and headrests
(see cat. nos. 23-25).

is probably found among many other groups as well but we lack information about their terminology. Arnold Rubin has noted that such scarification marks are seen by their makers as marks of "perfection" on the body, and function as signs that the recipient has become socialized, enculturated and "civilized" (Rubin 1988:14, drawing on ideas from Vogel and Cole). Others have noted that writing and other forms of inscription have also acquired the same name as scarification, and as Roberts (1988) has noted, they are all systems of communication. The linkage of scarification and headrests, however, is even closer than that.

A Shona carver told me that sleeping on a headrest would cause a man to have the incised scarification on the upper platform impressed and transferred to his own face. This would cause considerable amusement when women saw it because women are the only people to have this type of scarification among the Shona. Several Zaire groups such as the Kuba and the Teke make headrests that leave similar marks on the sleeper's face.

The Luba make a similar conceptual link between headrests and scarification. The name of one pattern usually put on the inside of the upper arm is known as *musamo* or 'headrest' because it is the place "where the husband lays his head at night" (Nooter 1991:246 and personal communication, August 1992). Allen Roberts has also pointed out to me that among the Holoholo, women had scarification on their lower bellies and lower backs, and on their left shoulders, which was the shoulder that the husband rested his head upon when sleeping (personal communication, January 1992, citing Delhaise 1908:435-6). The headrest, then is analogous to the wife's shoulder.

Surveying the groups mentioned it is important to note that headrests are claimed by the Shona to be for the exclusive use of men. The situation among the other groups is unknown. The Shona and Luba headrests seem decidedly female in gender. What this means and whether there is a more widespread pattern of association between women, headrests and scarification are questions yet to be answered.

AESTHETICS

Another important point to be made concerns our own aesthetic evaluation of these objects. While we can admire the headrests for their color, patina, subtle curves, elegant simplicity, exquisite abstractions, and so on, we must remember that these are rarely the criteria used by the Africans themselves. African cultures do not usually compartmentalize conceptual categories to the extent that Western cultures do. Thus, an "aesthetic" discussion by an African will often reveal as much about religious, political and social values as about what we in the West see as artistic values.

Sieber cautions that if Westerners do make aesthetic inquiries they must be careful in interpreting any verbal judgments, for he notes that often

> when an African is asked to explain his
> preference for one sculpture over another,
> his reply will be that it is better carved. In
> short, the judgement seems based solely on
> skill. But this term used cross-culturally

may be deceiving; it can mean significantly more than excellence of execution. It includes the degree of success with which a carver can produce a form in the style, size, color and material expected of him by his audience.... In short, skill is the ability to create recognizable, acceptable variations of a shared stylistic, formal, and aesthetic norm.... The definition of skill must be enlarged to include the expectancy of the familiar, which results in acceptance and approval of the familiar and rejection and disapproval of the unfamiliar (1987:14-15).

Susan Vogel has noted that the evaluative words Africans use often have multi-layered meanings, and asserts that

> the moral basis of African aesthetics is
> fundamental, a point the researcher may
> learn quickly and with dismay when he or
> she discovers that one word—and this is
> the case in many languages—means both
> beautiful and good (1986:15).

Paula Ben-Amos, in an excellent review of the approaches scholars have taken in studying African aesthetics, also sees a close correspondence between ethical and aesthetic concerns.

> Looking closely at the reports of aesthetic
> notions among the Yoruba, Igbo, Baule,
> Pakot, Bamana, Chokwe, Wolof and Akan,
> one finds clues that the core of their aes-
> thetics is morality and effectiveness.... [She
> goes on to advocate that] studies of African

aesthetics cannot stop at formal evalua-
tions, or even at understanding something
of associated cultural values, but must also
investigate ethics and ontology, concepts
of goodness and the essential nature of
humans and their world (1989:34-5).

Studies of aesthetic responses to non-figurative arts in
Africa are rare but important. Fred Smith has added
essential information with his examination of Gurensi
aesthetics. In wall decoration a concept of "embellishment" exists but it is used non-judgmentally in an all-or-
nothing manner. He makes the important observation
that in Gurensi society criticism is considered antisocial
and disruptive in nature (1978).

Another important distinction is illustrated by Harold
Schneider's discoveries about Pakot (or Pokot) art.

[The Pokot] distinguish between what is
useful in subsistence or the ordinary act of
getting a living and what is an aesthetically
pleasing embellishment having no subsistence or utilitarian use except as decoration.... This distinction became apparent
during a discussion of a carved wooden
milk pot *(aleput)* which has a projecting lip
carved into the rim. Informants said the
pot was *karam*, a word usually translated as
'good', and which may be used in a wide
variety of situations. When asked to further explain what was meant by 'good',
one informant said that the pot was useful
for holding milk and so was 'good to have'.
This informant further stated, however,

that the lip of the jug was *pachigh*, a word
which had previously been translated by
the interpreter as 'pretty' or 'beautiful' and
which, it was explained on this occasion,
meant 'pleasant to look at' and 'unusual'.
[The lip was a recent invention and super-
fluous to the function of the pot.] ... To
generalize, the thing which is *pachigh*, in
this case, is something pleasant to contem-
plate, strange or new and an embellishment. The pot is clearly not considered
wholly beautiful and the utilitarian part is
plainly distinguished conceptually from
the pretty.

A European has a tendency to generalize beauty to a whole object on which
embellishment had been made, and thus to
fail to recognize the fine distinction that
Pakot make between an object and its embellishments. Furthermore, some things
which the Pakot consider aesthetically
pleasing embellishments were missed,
while some things were considered beautiful which the Pakot would not. Deductively the lip of the milk pot along with the
pot was considered non-aesthetic. This
proved to be wrong, the lip being considered by the Pakot a pretty embellishment.
On the other hand, the headrest was
deductively classified as an object of art
because, although it has non-aesthetic
functions, it is carried about by its owner

FIG. 3.
Bumi man with elaborate
mudpack. Lower Omo
River, southwestern
Ethiopia. These mudpack
coiffures, worn only by
initiated males, also
symbolically proclaim the
courage of their owners
for killing an enemy or
dangerous animal.

like a decorative cane and is polished and decorated. To the Pakot only the gloss and incised or inlaid design are beautiful. A headrest without these is not beautiful in any way (1956:104-106).

In my investigations of Shona aesthetic response, discussions about people's preferences often got no further than "it's better carved." It was only through persistent questioning that people would make choices and/or explain them. This reluctance is partly explained by the very personal character of the objects such as headrests that I asked about. They are not objects normally used in public performances but are family heirlooms used predominantly in private family ceremonies. When they are used in public by religious practitioners or family spirit-mediums they are accoutrements. Perhaps there is little need among the Shona for the "specialized vocabulary for subtle aesthetic dissection" (Sieber 1973:428) that has been found among such groups as the Yoruba and Bamana.

It is interesting, nevertheless, to examine the responses that people did give me (see Dewey 1991 for a more complete explanation of Shona aesthetic attitudes). Criteria for the choice of headrests tended to vary between practical considerations, ritual considerations, and ideas about style. Though most local prototypes are gone, my sources, especially the elderly ones who had seen headrests, picked as their favorites the styles that had been made in their respective areas.

Size was often a criteria given by sources; the larger the headrest the greater the degree of status associated with owning it. Only very elderly sources, who remembered that the headrests were once carried, opted for the smaller, lighter examples and gave portability as a reason. The surface finish or smoothness, the ornateness of the surface chip-carving, and the overall shape and straightness were given as criteria by many sources.

Some sources characterized their choices as the work of an expert *(nyanzvi)*. The most important criteria mentioned was the surface decorations, called *nyora* by most of those I interviewed (the same word used for the cicatrix decorations on women). Carvers said this was the part that took the most time to do. Words used to characterize this aspect were either *chidavado*, which means an attractive or embellished object, or *akanaka*, which is a more general word that can be applied to anything pleasing, right, fitting or good.

The color black was sometimes given as a desirable quality because that is the color liked by the ancestors. One man, for example, declared that the black item he chose "is identical with the needs of my ancestors who like black ... We Duma people use black for praying to our ancestors and even kill black cattle for ceremonies." Some sources equated the circular motifs on the headrests with *ndoro* (conus shell disk ornaments; see Chapter 2) that were used by their ancestors and appeared on their ancestors' headrests. One artist explained that his choice (among a group of headrests) was "identical with what I am doing and was given to me in dreams by the ancestors." The ultimate compliment therefore was that the headrest was either like what the ancestors had had or what they would want. Aesthetic concepts for the Shona thus should be seen as being related to concepts of utility, prestige, embellishment and religion. A dramatic demon-

stration of the importance of the Shona spirit world in matters of aesthetic choice has been documented by Paul Berliner. A possessed spirit-medium was so displeased with the performance of some musicians at a possession ceremony that "the spirit" literally threw the musicians out (1978:202). My own demonstration was provided by Johwani Nyamukapa, a blacksmith-carver. When I questioned him about his choices of the objects I brought, he would merely explain that he had picked them because he liked them and would elaborate no further. When I asked about his fame as an artist in the area, however, he gave the following explanation. He said that he had once been commissioned by a spirit-medium to make some ritual items. When the spirit-medium came to collect the items he was so impressed that he (the spirit-medium) was possessed on the mere sight of the axes and the spirit told those who accompanied him to give Johwani some more money. Possession by mediums occurs only in very controlled, particular circumstances, so the implication is not that the sight of ritual axes triggered possession but that it was triggered by the excellent quality of the axes.

Aesthetic appreciation was expressed most vividly in this Shona case by the judgment of the spirits themselves. The ramifications of this type of belief on issues of style and history are extremely important. Shona axes of the type ordered by the spirit-medium do not seem to have changed in style for hundreds of years. African art has often been characterized as being conservative in terms of resistance to changes in style, but the reasons why this is so have not always been clearly articulated. In the Shona case it became clear to me that what my sources believed the ancestors (or spirits) liked, was what they (the spirits) knew when they were alive. This was to them a morally justifiable explanation for the conservative retention of styles.

DISTRIBUTION

Instead of trying to delineate every group and region where headrests are used, I have organized the catalogue entries of the Joss collection into regional groups in order to give a general survey. Headrests may have been used throughout Africa but from the existing material evidence, historical accounts and current practices we are left with an incomplete picture. We know of their existence in ancient Egypt and the catalogue entries will begin with the Joss examples from there. In more recent times, the three most prominent areas of headrest usage in sub-Saharan Africa have been Northeast and East Africa, Central Africa and Southeast Africa. The catalogue entries will be presented in this order and finally the relatively few examples from West Africa will be presented.

It is often assumed that headrests are primarily used by pastoral nomadic people. While this may be true of contemporary practice, especially in eastern Africa, this is not so for the rest of the continent, where headrests were used primarily by settled agriculturists. There is also evidence that around the edges of the pastoral regions of East Africa there are non-pastoral groups such as the Bari who use headrests. For the most part, however, the cattle- and camel-herding peoples predominate.

The catalogue entries will therefore continue in the East Africa region with those from Sudan and Uganda, then continue with Ethiopia and Somalia. Kenya exam-

ples, which numerically predominate, will be surveyed last.

For the central African area there is still no better survey of styles or map of their distribution than that produced by Joseph Maes in 1929. His basic outline for organizing the area's headrests into three basic types has not been superseded. The Joss collection does not have any of the box-type headrests from northern Zaire but there are a couple of examples from the western area of Maes' second style with curved upper platform and straight supports. The bulk of the Central African examples from the Joss collection are from the southern Savannah region where figurative examples are numerous. Examples will be examined starting with western groups and going to the eastern ones. While all the Joss examples for this region are from Zaire there are also examples known from Angola and northern Zambia that would fit into this scheme.

While headrests are known from Zambia, Malawi, southern Tanzania and northern Mozambique, this band across Africa is not represented in the Joss collection and the literature on headrests here is scant. Perhaps this is an area where headrests were not so common, but more likely it just represents a gap in our knowledge.

The next area of importance to be surveyed is that of southeastern Africa. Examples from southern Mozambique appear first. The Joss examples from Zimbabwe are mostly reserved for Chapter 2, which serves as a case study and offers the most detailed examination of stylistic distribution, usage and symbolism. Finally the Zulu and Swazi area of South Africa and Swaziland will be examined. The other area in Africa where nomadic pastoralists still use headrests is Namibia, where married adult Himba men use them to keep their coiffures protected (see Becker 1975:56; Jackobsohn and Pickfords 1990:112). Unfortunately the Joss collection does not have any of these.

In the West Africa section, the general organizational scheme will be to move from south to north. Akan and Baule examples are from the Guinea Coastal style area, while the Western Sudan style is represented by the Lobi, Dagari, Nuna, Bobo, Tellem and Dogon.

Notes

I am deeply grateful to Jerry Joss for sharing his headrests with me and to Fowler Museum Deputy Director Doran Ross for asking me to write about the collection; also to Research Assistant Paulette Parker for her prompt, cheerful attention to inquiries and thoughtful research.

Special thanks are also owed to many people who shared their expertise with me for the research on this catalogue. In particular, my colleagues at the University of Iowa, Christopher Roy, Allen Roberts, and Richard dePuma, and graduate students Ofori Akyea, Manuel Jordan, and Dana Rush. Others who generously shared their knowledge include: David Binkley of the Nelson-Atkins Museum of Art; Steven Brandt, University of Florida; Michael Connor of Indiana University; James Bellis, University of Notre Dame; Arthur Bourgeois, Governor's State University; S. Terry Childs, Smithsonian Institution; Kate Ezra, Metropolitan Museum of Art; Marc Felix, Brussels; John Johnson, Indiana University; Ivan Karp, National Museum of Natural History, Smithsonian Institution; Sidney Kasfir, Emory University; John Mack, Museum of Mankind, British Museum; Mary Nooter, Center for African Art; Sharon Patton, University of Michigan; Philip Ravenhill, National Museum of African Art, Smithsonian Institution; Doran Ross, Fowler Museum of Cultural History; Raymond Silverman, Michigan State University; and Ernie Wolfe III, Los Angeles.

My 1983-84 dissertation field research in Europe and Africa was generously supported by a Fulbright-Hays Doctoral Dissertation Grant and done with the cooperation of the University of Zimbabwe and the National Museums of Zimbabwe. I also received an Indiana University Doctoral Student Research Fellowship for 1984-85. A subsequent trip to Africa in 1988, focusing on another topic but helpful nevertheless, as a Massachusetts Institute of Technology post-doctoral fellow, was funded by the Getty Grant Program. All this financial aid is gratefully appreciated.

[1] Special thanks to Allen Roberts who brought this quotation to my attention.

[2] This is amply documented by two recent exhibitions and catalogues: *Supports de Rêves* organized by the Fondation Dapper in 1989, which surveyed headrest forms around the world, and *Art and Ambiguity. Perspectives on the Brenthurst Collection of Southern African Art*, produced by the Johannesburg Art Gallery in 1991, which although focusing on a variety of art forms featured headrests from that part of Africa.

1. Headrest.

Old Kingdom Egypt

Alabaster

22.5 x 21.6 cm.

FMCH 90.428

The Joss collection has two examples of the most commonly seen ancient Egyptian headrest types. The older type, which Petrie believes was introduced in the Second or Third Dynasty of the Old Kingdom (c. 2600 B.C.), consists of one or two architecture-like columns (with round base, fluted shaft and square abacus) between the flat base and curved upper platform (Petrie 1927:33, pl. 30, figs. 5, 10, 11). The Joss example, carved of three alabaster pieces fitted together as is the usual pattern, has been estimated to date from the Seventh Dynasty or 2290-2155 B.C. The other example is of a type Petrie believes was introduced in New Kingdom times of the Seventeenth or Eighteenth Dynasty (c. 1500 B.C.). On these the single supporting column is connected to the platform and base with emphatic curves and the base is now noticeably longer than the platform (Petrie:1927:35, pl. 32, figs. 32, 34, 37). The Joss example is carved of two pieces of wood with a mortice-and-tenon type connection, with the addition of side holes for inserting pegs to adjust the height. It has been estimated to date from the Eighteenth Dynasty or 1558-1303 B.C. (see also Falgayrettes 1989:17, 29, 31, 34-5 for similar examples).

The Egyptians liked to sleep in a sloping position, and until the Eighteenth Dynasty most beds were higher at the head than the foot: a foot board prevented the sleeper from slipping down too far.... Nevertheless, beds were comparatively rare and a headrest, a prop of about the same height as the shoulder, was the greatest necessity for a good night's sleep. Egyptians who possessed beds used a headrest as well (Scott 1973; see also her photograph of a reconstructed Egyptian bed and headrest in the Metropolitan Museum of Art, and Romano 1990:32 for a photograph of an Egyptian statue of a woman resting on a bed with a headrest).

The headrests for daily use were normally made of wood while more formal ones were made of alabaster or other stone, and some for royalty, even plated with gold and silver. There is some evidence that a few were cushioned on the sleeping platforms with layers of linen (Baker 1966:45). Headrests were frequently used as burial furniture, with the most famous example being the tomb of Tutankhamun where eight were found (Reeves 1990:180-83).

The ancient Egyptians regarded the head as the seat of life and consequently its preservation was thought to be of particular importance for continued existence after death. It could not, however, function without the help of magic, which could be obtained by various means, one of which was an amulet in the form of a headrest, either model or actual.... A spell in the *Book of the Dead* (no. 166) has been interpreted as attributing to the headrest the power of resurrection (Edwards 1976:162-3).

2. Headrest

New Kingdom Egypt

Wood

16.5 x 29 cm.

FMCH 92.10 A,B

3. Stool, *hegba*

Bongo; Sudan

Wood

10.3 x 24.9 x 10.4 cm.

FMCH 91.68

While many of their pastoral neighbors use headrests, the Bongo, a settled agricultural people, apparently only made small carved stools. The Bongo are not well documented and virtually the only descriptions or illustrations of their material culture come from early explorers. Junkers, for example, illustrates two slightly more elaborate stools of the Bongo (1889 1:498; 2:108). The sculptural core of an upper platform and four legs with out-turned feet is common to all. Schweinfurth also illustrates several (1874 1:283; 1875:Table IV, nos.1-2) and gives this description:

> Hardly inferior to the skill of the Bongo in working of iron is their dexterity in wood-carving. Perhaps the most striking specimens of their art in this way may be noticed in the little four-legged seats or stools which are found in every household, and are called "*hegba*." These are invariably made from a single block, the wood chosen for the purpose being that of the Goll-tree (*Prosopis lanceolata*, Benth.) which is of a chestnut brown, and after use acquires an excellent polish; they are used only by the women, who are continually to be seen sitting on them in front of their huts, but they are altogether avoided by the men, who regard every raised seat as an effeminate luxury (1874:282-3).

Ravenhill (1991:12-13) in describing a similar example from the National Museum of African Art claims that similar forms are made by several groups, "including the Dinka and Bongo." John Mack, however, who has traveled through both Azande and Dinka areas and looked extensively at museum collections, does not feel such attributions are justified. He feels Bongo is a sound provenance but notes that the Museum of Mankind has some similar pieces which are said to be Bari (personal communication, July 1992). Anthony Jack, illustrating another similar example (1991:28-9), notes that the Bongo were decimated in the nineteenth century by the activities of ivory hunters and slavers to the extent that many fled the region and others took refuge or were absorbed by the Dinka and Azande. With such movement of the Bongo it is not surprising that the almost completely vanished material culture has been ascribed to several groups in the area.

Anthony Jack states that the Musée Royal de l'Afrique Central, Tervuren, has examples from Ethiopia and Somalia with forms similar to this example and the one he illustrates (1991:30). All seem to be made of monitor-lizard-skin strips forming a container around the double supporting columns of the underlying headrest or stool. Ravenhill, however, illustrates a similar one ascribed to an undetermined Sudanese people (1991:14-15). John Mack feels these types can be "fairly clearly provenanced as Bari. Clearly we have material in our own collections (Museum of Mankind) from Evans-Pritchard who gives them as such and very likely collected them in the field" (personal communication, July 1992).

The Bari also made another type of headrest which is constructed of bent wood held in place by leather strips (see Sieber 1980:113 and Falgayrettes 1989:51 where the leather is missing). It is interesting that some pastoralists such as the Pokot and Turkana also use wood and leather construction for some types of headrests. That does not mean there was any interaction between them and the Bari, a settled agricultural people of southwestern Sudan, but merely that they use the same types of materials in their own way. Anthony Jack says these leather-bound receptacles were used for holding small valuables or tobacco (1991:30) but there seems to be no other documentation as to any other uses.

4. Headrest/stool

Bari; Sudan

Wood, reptile leather,

vegetable fiber,

iron, brass

20 x 23.1 x 11 cm.

FMCH 87.1508

5. Headrest/stool

Bari; Sudan

Wood, reptile skin?

16.5 x 24.8 x 10.7

FMCH 87.1509

6. Stool/headrest

Madi; Uganda

Wood

19.6 x 38 x 13.7 cm.

FMCH 86.2438

This low stool type is identified by Trowell and Wachsmann as being for women and coming from the Madi group of northwestern Uganda (1953:155, pl. 35E). Several neighboring groups such as the Alur and Acoli also make stools with geometric voids in the side legs, or crossbars running between the legs, in what appears to be a regional stylistic trait. Only the Madi, however, seem to make stools with this triangular type of void. The Madi live in an area just to the south of Sudan in an area on either side of the Nile. They traditionally practiced a shifting type of agriculture, moving as the fertility of the soil became depleted. They also had large herds of cattle at the turn of the century but never accorded the same special attention to the cattle as their Nilotic and Nilo-Hamitic neighbors (Baxter and Butt 1953). Unfortunately there seems to be little or no information in the literature on these elegant stool/headrest forms and their use and symbolism.

7. Headrest?/stool,

eicolong lotuba?

Teso?, Acoli?, Lango?;

Northern Uganda

Wood

31.5 x 15 x 16.5 cm.

FMCH 86.2453

As is the case with headrest types in northern Kenya, this headrest/stool form seems to have been used by several different groups and consequently should be thought of as having a regional style rather than any specific ethnic group designation. The Tsumako people of southwestern Ethiopia make a similar shaped but smaller headrest (Jensen 1959:ill. 15.10). Trowell and Wachsmann illustrate an Acoli (1953:pl. 37I) and a Teso stool (pl. 36B) of Uganda that are similar. Lawrance, describing the Teso of Uganda, however, gives the most information. He illustrates two stools of this type which he calls *eicolong lotuba* (1957:117 figs. 7, 9). While circular stools with three or four legs are more common, "a rarer type is a stool carved from the solid, which has short thick-set legs at either end and a crossbar running from end to end underneath the seat" (Ibid:116). Headrests among the Teso, he claimed, resembled those of the Karamajong but were by then no longer used.

Ivan Karp, who has worked among the Kenyan Teso, remarked that he only observed the circular stools in use, but that there are very important symbolic functions associated with them. Three-legged stools are associated with women while four-legged ones are associated with men. Only adult males who have parented a child and are the head of a household are allowed to own and use a stool. While a man is alive only he is allowed to use it. After his death his first son will inherit it but there are no ancestral associations that are ever implied. The only time a woman may be seated on a man's stool is as the widow at her husband's funeral.

The Teso stool, therefore, symbolizes social independence, for only when the man moves out of his natal home to establish and head up one of his own is its use permitted (Ivan Karp, personal communication, August 1992). Whether the Uganda Teso and the neighboring groups who use this type of stool have similar beliefs is unknown.

8. Headrest

Ethiopia?

Wood, pigment

20.7 x 25.3 cm.

FMCH 91.64

Ethiopia has for too long been excluded from African art historical studies. Given the wide variety of headrests produced there, this is a serious oversight. Raymond Silverman's forthcoming exhibition and catalogue on Ethiopian art is therefore greatly anticipated. He has also informed me that Dr. Girma Kidane is preparing a catalogue of the headrest collection of the Institute of Ethiopian Studies Museum in Addis Ababa (personal communication, June 1992). That, too, is eagerly anticipated. In the meantime a few bits of information are known about Ethiopian headrests but they are unfortunately meager.

Kidane and Wilding note that "among many groups in the south, carved wooden headrests are used to enable one to sleep without interfering with a complicated and vulnerable coiffure. As in many other parts of Africa these neckrests are also used as occasional stools" (1976). With this brief statement, they fortunately include two headrests similar to ones in the Joss collection, cat. nos. 12 and 13. There seem to be a number of variations on this stylistic theme of a gently curving support on a conical base.

Some have smooth surfaces like cat. 11, others have incised designs covering the conical base (cat. 13) or incorporate multiple cones (cat. 2). One type has appendages curving down from the ends of the upper platform to the base of the cone (cat. 14).

Eike Haberland illustrates an example very similar to cat. 12 but with a single conical support, which he labels "Gimma-Galla und Kaffa" (1963:pl. 27, no. 10). Steven Brandt, an archaeologist who has lived in Ethiopia and collected headrests, was told by Addis Ababa dealers that the variety with incised decorations (cat. 13) was from the Gurage area to the south of Addis Ababa by Lake Zeway (personal communication, August 1992). The double conical form (cat. 12) he was told was from the Kaffa area in the southwest (see also Falgayrettes 1989:25 for another example). Pankhurst and Ingrams (1988:128) illustrate two Kaffa headrests from a nineteenth-century engraving with essentially the same conical base and crescent head support shape, while Huntingford (1955:128) declares the Kaffa use wooden headrests of "a familiar Egyptian shape" (perhaps meaning a single tapered column). The distribution of this conical-base type headrest may be in the general area of the Kaffa but this is not at all certain.

The very rectangular type headrest seen in cat. nos. 15 and 16 (also see example in Falgayrettes 1989:43) is said to be from the Sidamo area (Brandt). This blocklike type headrest is typically concave on the top, covered with closely spaced parallel striations and has a small rectangular lug on one side. Cerulli (1956: 127 citing Simoni 1940:128-32) says Sidamo women wear intricate hair styles "which require the use of a headrest when sleeping" while men normally shave their head. He unfortunately gives no other details of style or usage so the Sidamo attribution must be regarded as very tentative.

The other style which Brandt could identify was cat. nos. 17 and 18 which was said to be Kambatta (Brandt). The Kambatta live to the west of the Gurage on the upper Omo river. Haberland illustrates a very similar example as coming from the Sidamo and Arussi (1963:pl. 27, no. 9) who are found to the south and east of the Kambatta, so perhaps this is a regional style. A number of this type of headrest have been appearing in the American market recently. Little has been written on the Kambatta, so until more is published on the art of Ethiopia there is unfortunately no way of confirming the attribution.

Cat. 8, which is perhaps Ethiopian, looks quite similar to one illustrated by Haberland, that he identifies as being Borana (1963:pl. 27, no. 11). Cat. 9 with hemispherical base and flat upper platform seems more akin to the groups of the south and southwest of Ethiopia (see Beckwith and Fischer 1990; Jensen 1959) or to the Turkana or Karamajong, but even this is unsure.

9. Headrest

Ethiopia

Wood, pigment

18.2 x 20.6 x 13.7 cm.

FMCH 91.311

10. Headrest?

Ethiopia?

Wood

18 x 20.3 x 6.8 cm.

FMCH 89.777

11. Headrest

Kaffa area?; Ethiopia

Wood

17.5 x 13.5 cm.

FMCH 86.2431

12. Headrest

Kaffa area?; Ethiopia

Wood

16.6 x 11.9 cm.

FMCH 91.61

13. Headrest

Gurage?; Ethiopia

Wood

17.6 x 17.5 x 6.2 cm.

FMCH 86.2435

14. Headrest

Ethiopia

Wood

16.1 cm.

FMCH 91.571

11

12

13

14

15

16

17

18

15. Headrest

Sidamo?; Ethiopia

Wood

18.7 x 17 x 6.5 cm.

FMCH 86.2461

16. Headrest

Sidamo; Ethiopia

Wood

6.5 x 18.4 cm.

FMCH 92.191

17. Headrest

Kambatta?, Arussi?; Ethiopia

Wood

17.8 x 16.3 x 7.5 cm

FMCH 91.62

18. Headrest

Kambatta?, Arussi?; Ethiopia

Wood

19.7 x 18.5 x 7 cm.

FMCH 91.321

The exquisite formal qualities of Somali headrests, such as this example, combining subtle curvilinear, circular and elliptical shapes with intricate interlace surface ornamentation, make them among the most widely recognized and appreciated African nomadic art forms. It is therefore quite tragic that the current civil war and widespread famine are causing such human suffering and devastation in this area of the Horn of Africa.

This type of headrest with crescent upper platform, small circular or oval base and double flat supporting columns is used by nomadic Somali in both southern Somalia and eastern Kenya. Very similar forms are made by the Boni (Prins 1965) of southeastern Kenya and extreme southern Somalia but these seem to be made with more squat overall proportions and different surface ornamentation. Somali nomads also use another type of headrest with a single supporting column which is cylindrical in appearance (Loughran et al. 1986:54). Whether the distribution of this type coincides with that of the type under consideration or is from the Shabeelle River area, as is implied in Loughran et al. (1986:54), is uncertain. Steven Brandt (personal communication, July 1992) reports that his experience was that both types are found in the same areas. He was told by Somalis that different styles were for men of different status, with the more simple single-columned variety being for young men, the other for elders. The distribution for this double-columned variety includes, according to Allen (1976), the Hawiya and Digil subgroups who live in the southern coastal hinterlands and the Ogaden-Darod subgroups who extend south to the Kenya-Somali border.

The headrests are carved of a very fine-grained, tough but light-weight wood identified by Allen (1976:45) as *hagar* in Somali and by Loughran et al. (1986:55) as *yucub* wood. Acknowledged artists are sometimes commissioned to make them but any man can make his own. A tree branch which has forked into equal sections is selected, the basic shape is roughed out by cutting a hole through the center, then the shapes refined and the intricate surface patterns cut last (Allen ibid.; Prins 1965:189). The wood is usually left its natural color, but Puccioni reports that men occassionally paint theirs red or black (1936:24).

Somali headrests are used by both men and women. According to Lewis (1969:83) the women's are more ornate than the men's. Puccioni, however, describes and illustrates women's headrests that have a different form from the male variety. While the male type, such as this one, have a relatively small base and are thus somewhat unstable to sleep on, the female variety are much more rectangular in form (Pucccioni 1936:24-6, pl. V). While the image that comes to mind is of the nomadic herdsman carrying his headrest with him to sleep on while following his herds, Puccioni reports that they are also used on the constructed raised beds Somalis use in their permanent or portable houses. Somali men carry this variety by slipping a wrist through the central hole. Allen has also observed that herders will sometimes rest by standing on one leg, resting their headrest on their shoulder and twisting their head so as to rest their neck upon it.

Mary Jo Arnoldi (in Loughran et al. 1986:21) notes that

> Men's headrests also function as symbols. Men are charged with guarding the herds at night. The instability of their headrests prevents them from falling into a deep sleep, and the headrest itself has become the tangible symbol of vigillance (Personal communication: John Johnson, 1984). Cerulli noted that the headrest also plays a role in the nuptial ceremonies. It is under the bride's headrest that the groom places the *tubash*, the defibulation price. The morning after the marriage is consummated, women enter the bride's *aqal* to confirm the evidence of her virginity. The bride then lifts the headrest from the marriage bed and takes this sum of money which she uses to purchase an amber necklace, the symbol of her new status (Cerulli 1959,2:92-3).

Adamson observed a similar practice of placing money under the "pillow" of the new bride among the Kenyan Somali (1967:202).

The intertwine or guilloche pattern seen on the base and sides is typical and probably reflects Islamic influence. Images of snakes and scorpions are often incised on the surface of the upper platform. The idea is to portray sources of danger so as to protect oneself. Allen in fact interprets both the figurative items and the guilloche as a "form of shorthand for a prayer" to insure God's protection for the sleeper (Ibid.:55-6).

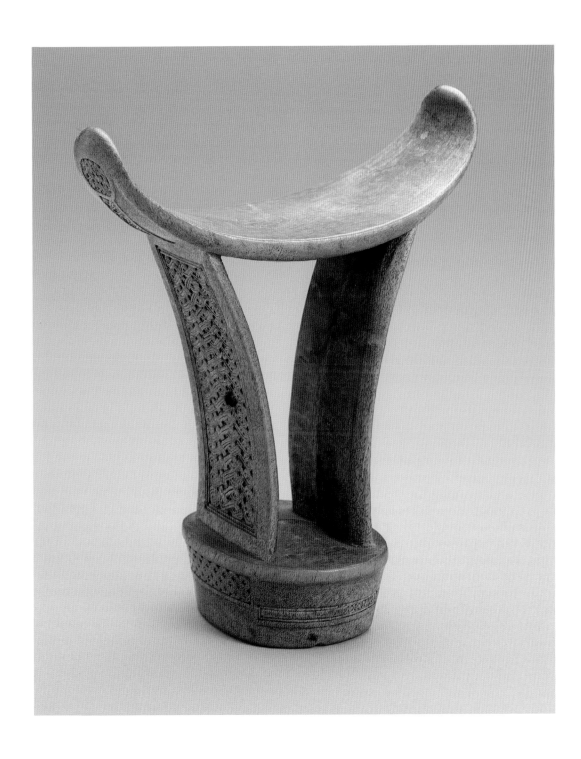

19. Headrest, *barkin*

Somali; Somalia, Kenya

Wood

15 x 18.3 x 6.7 cm.

FMCH 86.2418

20. Headrest

ngachar or *chemperit*?

Pokot? Turkana?

Karamajong?;

Kenya, Uganda

Wood, leather

23.5 x 13.9 cm.

FMCH 89.373

The nomadic pastoralists of northwestern Kenya, northeastern Uganda, southeastern Sudan and southwestern Ethiopia share a number of cultural practices. In addition to their transhumant settlement patterns, moving to new grazing lands with the passing of seasons, most had the custom of wearing elaborate coiffures which are differentiated on the basis of status and or age-grade categories (see Cole 1974; Beckwith and Fisher 1990). Both of these factors made the use of light, portable headrests a necessity. Because of the isolation of these areas and the conservative tenacity of many of the people in retaining their "traditional" ways of life, the pace of change has perhaps not been as fast here as in other areas of Africa. Many are now abandoning the practices of elaborate body ornamentation and coiffures but this remains one of the few areas in Africa where people still carry and use their headrests.

This type of headrest with two slender legs and leather interwoven between has been documented among the Pokot, the Karamajong and the Turkana of Kenya and Uganda. Trowell and Wachsman (1953:pl. 37E) and Jack (1991:30) illustrate Karamajong examples. Sieber (1980:111) and Emley (1927:180) show Turkana examples. Beech (1911:pl. VI), Wolfe (1979:14) and Bockoff and Fleming (1986) illustrate Pokot examples.

21. Headrest

ngachar or *chemperit?*

Pokot? Turkana?

Karamajong?;

Kenya, Uganda

Wood, leather, beads

19.1 x 10.1 x 5 cm.

FMCH 91.59

Among the Pokot there is evidence that the different styles of headrests (of which this style is only one of several) relate to different age and status of their owners.

> The basis of social and political organization is an age-set system which forms the Pokot into a rigidly controlled hierarchical society. Ritual, judicial and political authority rests with the oldest men. Initiation into this system is by the ceremony of *sapana* at which the initiate spears an ox, ceremonially adopts the blue mudpack hairstyle, and is given a headrest (Brown in Bockhoff and Fleming 1986:28).

There is some confusion in the literature (Beech 1911:pl. VI; Bockhoff and Fleming 1986:36, 40) whether this type of headrest should be called a *ngachar* or a *chamaperit* among the Pokot. From the latter source there is also the implication given that the simpler unadorned variety, such as cat. 20, is for use by uninititated Pokot boys, while an embellished and beaded example, such as cat. 21, is reserved for "a young male initiate after his *sapana* ceremony" (Ibid, 36).

It should also be reiterated that while we as Westerners may admire equally the simplicity of form in each of these examples, the Pokot would differentiate between them by their own aesthetic standards. The unadorned variety would be characterized by the word *karam* meaning 'good' or 'useful' while the other would be called *pachigh* meaning 'pleasant to look at' or 'unusual' (Schneider 1956:106).

(left)

22. Headrest/stool?

Pokot? Turkana?; Kenya

Wood, leather, metal

13 x 22.5 cm.

FMCH 86.2443

(right)

23. Headrest/stool

Pokot? Turkana?; Kenya

Wood

18 x 18 x 8.5 cm.

FMCH 86.2451

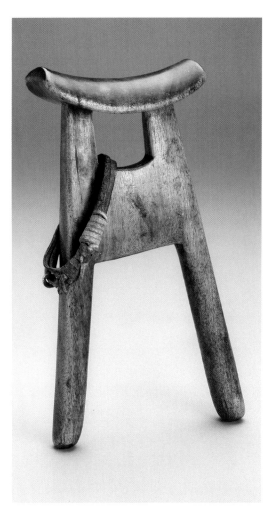

These two-legged varieties of headrest also seem to be a type shared by several East African groups, similar to the pattern of the previous examples. Wolfe illustrates two Kenyan examples with crossbars between the legs (1979:16-17) but gives no attribution to them. Sieber shows two examples of this general two-legged variety: one Pokot (with a crossbar); and one Karamajong (1980:11, 112). In the latter example the legs merge into a single support below the upper platform in the same manner as two examples from the Turkana (Donovan 1988:47; Fedders and Salvadori 1977:n.p.) Emley illustrates another Turkana example with a crossbar between the two legs. He labels it as one of two "Turkana stools, which are used as headrests to prevent the plastered hair from touching the ground while the wearer sleeps" (1927:180).

Caggiano illustrates two context photographs of young Pokot men carrying the two-legged variety. One is labeled "Young Pokot warriors after the *sapana*" (n.d.:5) and the other "*sapana* candidates" (n.d.:24) so perhaps it is a style designating intermediate status among young Pokot men. To confuse matters, however, it must also be pointed out that a similar-shaped object with two legs and a crossbar illustrated by Soper is called *ekicholong loa aberu* or a Turkana woman's stool (1985:133).

24. Headrest

Karamajong; Kenya,

Uganda

Wood, leather

24 x 16 x 10.8 cm

FMCH 86.2429

(left)

25. Headrest

Turkana?; Kenya

Wood, leather

21.7 x 26.5 cm.

FMCH 89.786

(right)

26. Headrest

Turkana; Kenya

Wood, metal

15 x 15 x 7.5 cm.

FMCH 86.2440

This type of headrest with a dome-shaped base, single flat support which narrows in the middle, and a relatively flat upper platform, often either rounded on the ends or figure-eight in shape, is probably the single most common type that is used by East African pastoralists. John Mack has noted that in southeastern Sudan

> The Toposa, Didinga and Larim all use an identical form of headrest with a single central support to which is often lashed a knife and tobacco container. As with the wrist knives, headrests in this style extend to peoples whose material cultures and linguistic and historical traditions do not otherwise show extensive affinity. Thus they occur not only among the Nyangatom and Turkana, whose links with the Toposa are particularly strong, but also among the Murle and more distant Surma-speakers the Mursi, and even among the Cushitic-speaking Hamar (1982:117).

This does not mean to imply that different groups do not make substyles, for they obviously do, but compared to other headrest styles used by the same people this type has only subtle stylistic differences in a rather large stylistic area. Beckwith and Fischer document that this type is used by the Hamar, Karo and Bumi of the Omo River area of southwestern Ethiopia (1990:209, 254, 302, 316-17). Trowell and Wachsman illustrate examples used among the Acoli and Karamoja of Uganda (1953:pl. 37F-G). Caggiano shows Pokot men carrying them (n.d.:8, 24) and many authors have documented their use among the Turkana (Sieber 1980:116; Fedders and Salvadori 1977, 1979:74; Donovan 1988:45, 47; Dyson-Hudson 1973:99). Wolfe ilustrates an example that is very close in style to the Joss collection piece, cat. 24, from the Karamajong (1979:17).

> All of the personal artifacts of the Karamajong are highly stylized ... each style bears its own distinctive name, some having a distinct use and others may be associated with an individual's status. Thus an adolescent male into early manhood would wear a conical type of head-dress as a mark of his age-set and carry a U-shaped stool. On passing through the *asapan* initiation into the succeeding age-set he would take off his conical head-dress and commence the wearing of another type, known as *etmat* in accordance with higher status, similarly he would discontinue carrying his *amakuk* (U-shaped stool) and make himself another different outline, possibly one known as *lokaepanak*. In former times there were even artifacts of particular outline connecting eldership, these included a head-dress known as *pelekwa* or sometimes *eyoliputh* and a stool known as *lokaisekoo*, the latter may still be in evidence (Wilson 1973:83-4).

In all the previously-mentioned ethnic groups, headrests have a similar role of declaring their owner's status. While the degree of status may shift from area to area, the type under consideration seems to generally be the emblem of an adult male who has completed his initiation.

(Left)

27. Headrest/stool

Rendille?; Kenya

Wood

23.5 x 14 x 9.5 cm.

FMCH 86.2452

(right)

28. Headrest

Rendille?; Kenya

Wood

17.78 x 21 cm.

FMCH 89.378

So many of the East African people make headrests/stools from carefully chosen branches, that it is hard to give any attribution to specific examples unless they have been field collected. They are most often three-legged with one side of the branch flattened (e.g. cat. 27 and 28). A few such as cat. 29 are further embellished by their owners with other materials, such as, in this case, the spiraled metal which seems to form a convenient handle.

Those examples seen in Western collections and museums often have acquired lustrous patinas from years of use. While this would suggest they were cared for and cherished by their owners, there is little documentation to suggest whether there is any status differentiation implied by the ownership of these as is the case with some of the other headrests used by the same people. A brief review of published examples and photographs of them in use demonstrates how widely they are used but also leaves the impression that they were an alternate form that any adult male, high status or low, could make and use.

Sieber illustrates examples from the Njemps and Rendille of Kenya and one undetermined Sudan group (1980:107, 109). Hodder writes that in the Baringo district of Kenya, this simple headrest/stool type is used by Tugen, Njemps and Pokot (1977:245). Jensen illustrates examples from the Baka and Banna of southwestern Ethiopia (1959:diagrams 15.3, 15.8). Beckwith and Fisher show a Karo man of the Omo river area of southwestern Ethiopia holding one (1990:305). Krieger illustrates examples from the Shilluk and Dinka of Sudan (1990:figs. 13-14). Fedders and Salvadori have examples from the Kipsigis, the Nandi and the Tugen of Kenya (1979:48, 53, 59). Jones shows a Rendille man of Kenya with one (1984:1932). Trowell and Wachsman show an example from the Teso of Uganda (1953:pl. 36C). Riefenstahl shows a Shilluk warrior of the Sudan using one to protect his elaborate wig (1982:229).

Another variety of headrest/stool uses found, natural forms and elaborates them by carving, to delineate resting platforms and other details. Cat. nos. 31 and 33 from the Joss collection are two excellent examples of this type. Both are said to be from the Rendille but the style is also seen among neighboring groups such as the Borana and Gabra (Sieber 1980:110; Wolfe 1979:18). Their form is often called bovine (or cattle-like) but it should be remembered that camels are the primary animals herded in those arid areas of northern Kenya. In a related style, cat. 32 from the Pokot "is reported to represent the foot of a large beast such as a rhinoceros" (Sieber 1980:116).

29. Headrest/stool

Rendille; Kenya

Wood, metal

36.2 x 22.2 x 19 cm.

FMCH 88.301

30. Headrest/stool

Borana; Kenya

Wood

19 x 34 cm.

FMCH 89.379

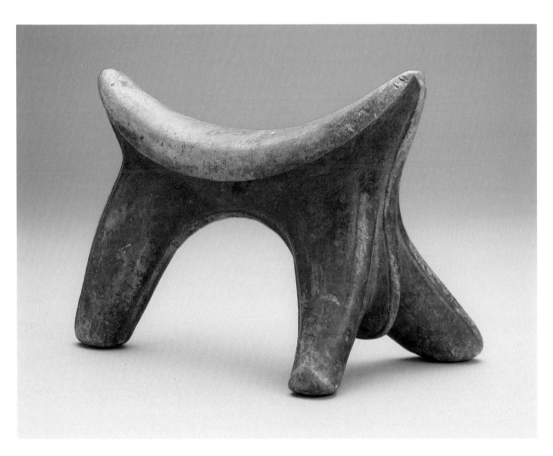

(above left)

31. Headrest

Rendille; Kenya

Wood

16 x 23 cm.

FMCH 89.377

(above right)

32. Headrest

Pokot, Kitale; Kenya

Wood, leather

16.5 x 17 cm.

FMCH 89.380

(left)

33. Headrest

Rendille; Kenya

Wood

18 x 25 cm.

FMCH 89.384

34. Mudcap (headwear)

Rendille? Pokot?; Kenya

Mud, paint, ostrich

feathers, wood,

aluminum, human hair

26.7 x 25.4 x 17.8 cm.

FMCH 89.366

35. Headrest/stool

Pokot; Kenya

Wood

13.9 x 15.2 cm.

FMCH 91.309

This headrest must have been conceived of aesthetically by the Pokot as a *pachigh* or a 'pleasant to look at' and 'unusual' object (Schneider 1956). It adheres quite closely to the usual stylistic canons for Pokot men's three-legged headrest/stools (see Caggiano n.d.:9, 26) but for the fact that the flaring legs each have a curved vertical face to them. This allows the headrest/stool to be placed on its side and rolled with ease. Why this was done or if there was a special function for such an unusual stool is unknown but the conceptual genius of the artist must be acknowledged.

Stylistically similar three-legged men's headrest/stools have also been documented among the Turkana (see Fedders and Salvadori 1977; Soper 1985:133) who called them *amakuk*. Ian Hodder, who has meticulously examined various aspects of material culture in the Baringo district of Kenya (just to the south of the Pokot and Turkana), came to the following conclusion about Njemps four-legged stools:

> The pattern [of distribution] is related to the tribal boundary to the south of the lake. Tugen rarely obtained this type of stool "because they are Njemps stools." The stools symbolize the quality of being a Njemps and they are part of a world view which is "other" to the Tugen. They are used in Njemps ceremonies, and for the Njemps they are associated with men, especially with the deliberations and status of older men. The stools are thus both part of the internal structure of the Njemps world view and a symbol of the Njemps/Tugen dichotomy (1982:54).

While there is no definitive documentation to demonstrate whether the Pokot headrest/stool functioned in a similar way, it is a good guess that it also was an emblem of elder male status.

36. Headrest, *ekomo*?

Yansi? Bokala?; Zaire

Wood, brass wire,

upholstery nails

16 x 15.5 x 9.1 cm.

FMCH 86.2432

The inclusion of metal on cat. 36 probably influenced the original tentative identification of this as a Kota headrest because of the prevalence of metal on the well-known Kota reliquary figures. Based on the form of these two headrests, however, it might be better to ascribe them to the area of the middle Zaire, or on either side of the lower Kasai River. Maes offers the only apparent source providing clues regarding the origin of these headrests (1929:4-6, pl. I). In his important early article on headrests in the Musée du Congo Belge (Tervuren) he attempts to organize Zaire headrest styles into five principal groups based on formal characteristics. For our purposes his inclusion of information drawn from the "numerous invaluable unpublished documents prepared by collectors" (Biebuyck 1985:23) is most fortunate. While the material evidence is meager, he does illustrate several headrests that are quite similar to these Joss ones in his section of the "Middle Congo." Five or six of the illustrated headrests have the same crescent-shaped upper platform, single columnar support, and pyramidal base. Their origins are variously given as Yansi, Teke, Bokala, Bunianga and Mfinu. One example said to be from the Yansi of Busande village on Lake Tumba (Maes 1929:pl. I, fig. 2) also has brass wire wound around the supporting column. N. Sondag collected another similar piece, which was said to have the indigenous name of "ekomo" among the Bokala (Ibid., fig. 8). Several others have the horizontal linear motifs seen on cat. 37. But these motifs are also seen on Teke and Mfinu objects. The metal work on this latter example is also more akin to the Teke and Mfinu (Felix, personal communication, September 1992) so perhaps it is better to ascribe this one to those groups.

The only information as to their usage, unfortunately, was the rather ubiquitous comment, given with the Yansi example, that these pillows were to protect their coiffures. It is hard to ascribe any regional styles merely from the ornamentation of these headrests with brass wire, tacks, and strips of metal, as many people all over Africa embellished their objects with similar metal ornaments. While nothing more definite concerning the use of metal is known in the case of these headrests, it is essential to remember (as so amply demonstrated by Eugenia Herbert in *Red Gold of Africa*, 1984) that copper and copper-based alloys were the prestige metals of most of Africa, rather than gold.

Biebuyck notes (but does not illustrate) that "unadorned but well carved neckrests (the concave top supported by an elongated concave cone) were made in two Yansi villages near the Inzia River (Tervuren, R.G.34998). According to de Beaucorps, who collected them (Tervuren Dossier 715), most neckrests used by the Yansi were purchased from the Mbala" (1985:131). It would not be surprising to find out that this style of headrest was a shared one, exchanged among several of the mentioned groups who lived along these rivers.

37. Headrest, *ekomo*?

Teke? Mfinu?; Zaire

Wood and metal

16 x 17.4 x 7.8 cm.

FMCH 86.2449

38. Headrest

Teke; Zaire, Peoples

Republic of the Congo

Wood, brass tacks

15 x 11 x 9 cm.

FMCH 88.1254

In Maes' 1929 survey of the headrest holdings of the Musée du Congo Belge (Tervuren) at least half-a-dozen Teke headrests are illustrated and described (pp. 4-7, pl. 1). None have caryatid figures like this example but the majority have the same type of curved rectangular upper platform and conical base but with single cylindrical nonfigurative columns providing the support. A figurative headrest very similar to the Joss example, from the Linden Museum in Stuttgart is illustrated in Fagg and Plass's *African Sculpture* (1964:40).

Felix (1987:172) reports that the Mfumu or clan elders who headed the matriclans making up Teke villages had headrests, presumably more elaborate ones like this, as one of their accoutrements of office. Whether the figure on the headrest had a similar protective function to the better-known Teke personal and village "power" figure (see Hottot 1956; Lema Gwete 1978) is unknown.

The figure style is typical of Teke sculpture with its stocky, solid torso with hands to the belly, vertical striations on the face, and crosshatched elaborate coiffure. The attachment of brass tacks or upholstery nails for eyes is unusual but may function to "empower" the figure in the same way that magical and medicinal substances are more often added to the torsos of other Teke figures. Their placement on the eyes may also allude to a magical function of the headrest, allowing the owner to "see" danger through visions or dreams while asleep and vulnerable.

39. Headrest

musawa or *musau*

Yaka?; Zaire

Wood

23.5 cm

FMCH 89.369

The Yaka of southwestern Zaire have produced a great variety of caryatid headrests, with images ranging from humans, leopards and antelopes to houses (see Bourgeois 1984:70-6). It would be tempting to say they are the most inventive or at least display the most varied subject matter of any African people who make figurative headrests. Arthur Bourgeois notes that headrests are apparently falling into disuse for the only headrest he saw in a Yaka village in 1976 had been discarded and damaged and was only being used as a plaything by children. Nevertheless he has been able to provide a wealth of information about their use and symbolism.

[They are] used by traditional male dignitaries but most especially by *kalaamba*, land chiefs and some matrilineal headmen *(lemba)* to support and protect elaborate headpieces or coiffures. As the headpiece of a *kalaamba* functions as a communal charm, it had to be worn both day and night. [See Bourgeois 1982] ... The neckrest was kept in the bed chamber, an inner room of a pitched two-room cabin. They appear to have been personal property rather then heirlooms and may have had personal charms attached [Biebuyck 1985:196 notes that one with charms is illustrated in Maes 1929:pl. VI, no. 18].

Decision-making frequently entailed an elder or diviner "dreaming" on the matter which has implications for this object and its imagery ... Neckrests were made by a traditional carver *n-kaleweni* (Kiyaka) who had in most cases apprenticed under some relative. The item followed the individual artist's style or repetoire of forms. Like in other imagery on masks, faces and figures on neckrests can possibly be read as ancestors-elders manifested in dreams, leopard as a signifier for a person in authority, cabin as the domestic unit, antelope as trickster animal of the forest or savannah. Yet when given carvers were questioned as to the precise meaning of their imagery, uniformly they responded that the imagery was for decoration alone and are traditional forms (Arthur Bourgeois, personal communication, June 1992).

●

(left)

40. Headrest

musawa or *musau*

Yaka; Zaire

Wood

17.6 x 17.5 x 6.2 cm.

FMCH 86.2434

●

(right)

41. Headrest

musawa or *musau*

Yaka; Zaire

Wood

16.7 cm

FMCH 91.298

The Joss collection presents a delightful assortment of form. Cat. nos. 40 and 41 perhaps represent felines with upturned tails. Cat. 44 is some type of quadruped but its very abstract form makes it hard to correlate with any specific type of animal. Cat. 42 may be a buffalo that with its "ponderous and bullish strength" is another symbol of leadership (Bourgeois 1982:30). Cat. 39, an old, well-worn example, illustrates an anthropomorphic form. The typical Yaka upturned nose may have been abraded off. Cat. 43 has been ascribed by Marc Felix as being either a Yaka or an Nkanu example. The Nkanu are the easternmost Kongo people who adopted many Yaka customs when their more numerous neighbors moved into the area. The slight indication of a line encircling the upper face of this headrest, an Nkanu style characteristic although usually more pronounced, may be a point in favor of an Nkanu attribution. Without field collection documentation, attributions in areas like southwestern Zaire where there is such ethnic intermixing can be very difficult.

Cat. 45 may be the most interesting example of all the Joss Yaka headrests. At first thought it would seem to be an imaginative Yaka artist's combination of a traditional animal caryatid with a quaint depiction of a colonial businessman complete with pith helmet and necktie, perhaps intended for sale to Europeans. Bastin, however, has documented that sculptures of a trader seated on the back of an ox are made and used by the Chokwe, Songo and Imbangala. They are called *Nzambi* by the Songo and *hamba wa Cimbali* 'the spirit of the white men' by the Chokwe. "They carry powers and take possession of the person who worships them during a special ceremony ... [Depicted with these figures are objects] symbolizing the wealth that the cult will bring to the person initiated into it" (Bastin 1969:78 and figs. 10-11). Although there is no documentation that the *Nzambi* cult spread into the Yaka area, this headrest seems to suggest that at least one Yaka was perhaps initiated into it and incorporated the symbolism into a headrest so he could dream of the wealth to be acquired.

(above left)

42. Headrest

musawa or *musau*

Yaka; Zaire

Wood

16 x 12.5 x 7 cm.

FMCH 88.958

●

(above right)

43. Headrest

musawa or *musau*

Yaka?, Nkanu?; Zaire

Wood

12.6 x 12.2 cm.

FMCH 89.779

●

(left)

44. Headrest

musawa or *musau*

Yaka?; Zaire

Wood

29.3 x 6.7 x 8.5 cm.

FMCH 86.2420

45. Headrest

musawa or *musau*

Yaka; Zaire

Wood

18 x 20 x 9 cm.

FMCH 87.612

46. Headrest

Holo?, Songo?, Shinji?;

Zaire, Angola

Wood, nail, brass

upholstery tacks

35 x 14 x 8 cm.

FMCH 86.2410

Both of these headrests have been attributed to the Holo with influence from neighboring groups. The Holo are an agricultural and hunting people who live in the immediate area of the upper Kwango river in southwestern Zaire and extend across the border into Angola. To the north their neighbors are the Yaka, Suku, and Shinji while to the south are the people whom they are more closely related linguistically and culturally, the Imbangala, Songo and Chokwe. While no specific information about Holo headrest use or symbolism appears in the literature, some inferences can perhaps be ascertained from the practices of their neighbors with whom the Holo share many customs.

The Chokwe, Yaka and Holo all make headrests with animal caryatids. The animal in cat. 46 with its ears broken off is perhaps a leopard, a common symbol of authority. Yaka- and Chokwe-related people associate headrests with male dignitaries (Arthur Bourgeois, personal communication, June 1992; Manuel Jordan, personal communication, June 1992) so it is probably appropriate to think the Holo may also. Bourgeois reports that the Yaka and Suku use the headrests at night to protect the elaborate headpieces or coiffures of chiefs, which function as communal charms (ibid.). Neyt (1982) notes that the Holo have coiffures inspired by the Suku so perhaps their headrests are also used to protect powerful communal coiffure charms.

The eyes of this animal are coffeebean-shaped with vertical striations under them. Much of Holo art has these features (Felix 1987:36-7) but they are also seen on Songo objects where the striations are called *masoji* ('tears') (Bastin 1969:55). The "tears" scarification is of course also a common feature on Chokwe *mwana pwo* masks.

The other Holo headrest, cat. 47, literally bristles with brass upholstery nails, a common African indicator of status objects. The Janus imagery seems enigmatic but perhaps relates to the

47. Headrest

Holo; Zaire

Wood, hair, brass

upholstery tacks,

sheet metal

13.8 x 17 cm.

FMCH 89.783

(detail on page 5)

Holo Janus heads "called *kisimbi*, which are placed in the houses to protect the inhabitants against evil spirits" (Neyt 1982:45). The bird imagery may in some way be connected to what Neyt calls the "cult of guardian birds ... In the houses, sometimes erected on the roof, these guardian birds are intended to bring good fortune to the inhabitants" (Neyt 1982:42). The Janus configuration of a bird in one direction and a human in the other may also have a protective function or imply cosmological meanings relating to directions and the preferred orientation for sleeping.

48. Headrest

Northern Mbala; Zaire

Wood

14 x 18.5 cm.

FMCH 90.453

Several examples of northern Mbala headrests very similar to cat. 48 are quite well known. There are examples in the collections of the Museum für Völkerkunde, Berlin; the Musée Royal de l'Afrique Centrale, Tervuren; the Museum of Mankind, London; and the Metropolitan Museum of Art, New York (Krieger 1969 3:183; Maes 1929:pl. I, figs. 27-8; Fagg and Plass 1964:102; Sieber 1980:119). All consist of an oval base, a curved rectangular upper platform which is longer than the base, and a compact squat caryatid figure with massive squarish legs. Their feet are flattened on the base and the elongated squared arms hold up the upper platform at either end. All of these examples have a Janus figure but Biebuyck (1985:171) says other examples exist that do not.

The northern Mbala ascription is quite certain as we know that the British Museum example was collected by Emil Torday at Massonge, a northern Mbala area, in 1907 (Mack 1991:34); one of the Tervuren pieces given by M. Arnold and collected before 1904 is described as Mbala; and Frobenius illustrates an Mbala, Mbonga example of the same style in his fieldnotes of 1905 (Frobenius 1985:102).

Felix (1987:102) includes such headrests among a group of objects that are "prestige items." Biebuyck (1985:163) notes that there are differing accounts of what paraphernalia is associated with Mbala chieftaincy, but citing Lumbwe Mudindaambi's accounts (1976) he includes the headrests and says that the intended symbolic message is "that the chief rests on his people (i.e. that he must listen to them)." Whether the Janus headrest caryatids also function to provide clan protection as some larger Mbala Janus figures do (Felix 1987:102) is unknown.

An ascription for cat. 49, the other Janus-figured headrest in the Joss collection, is not so certain. Perhaps it is Teke or Mbala. The Tervuren Janus headrest of similar style to the previous example is listed as being Teke-Nfumu (Maes 1929:7) and an example belonging to Ernst Anspach which very closely matches the slender neck and leg shapes of the Joss example is listed as being Teke, Djoue Plateaus (Duponchael 1980:43, fig. 56). Biebuyck, likewise, feels that some of the Mbala caryatid headrests "show Teke-Wuum influence" (1985:171, citing Cornet 1972:74 and von Sydow 1930:383-7).

49. Headrest

Mbala? Teke?; Zaire

Wood

16.6 x 15.5 x 11.5 cm.

FMCH 91.325

(above left)

50. Headrest

Kuba?; Zaire

Wood

24.7 x 13.5 x 6.5 cm.

FMCH 86.2430

(above right)

51. Headrest

Songye?; Zaire

Wood

22.3 x 12.5 x 10.5 cm.

FMCH 86.2447

(right)

52. Headrest

Kuba; Zaire

Wood

21.5 x 13 x 6.5 cm.

FMCH 86.2456

53. Headrest

Songye? Kuba?; Zaire

Wood

26.5 x 14.5 x 7.9 cm.

FMCH 87.624

Although the Kuba are one of the better-known Zairian groups, there is very little information about their headrests. Maes (1929:2-3) notes that none of the early explorers in the Kuba area, neither Wolf in Wissman, nor Harroy, nor Torday, make any mention of headrests. He concludes that the Kuba did not formerly use headrests and have only recently borrowed the ideas and forms from neighboring groups, in particular the Kete, and adapted the surface designs so that they are typically Kuba. David Binkley (personal communication, June 1982) has pointed out that this idea probably also comes from oral traditions which declare that when the ruling Bushoong sub-group migrated into the area, the Kete were recruited to be the woodcarvers. A more likely explanation for the dearth of headrests mentioned was that the early explorers focused more on the royal arts of the Kuba and ignored the relatively simple utilitarian objects.

Binkley reports that, from his experience in the region, no one makes headrests any more in the Kuba area, and while he was there he did not see any in use (ibid). Maes illustrates more than thirty headrests collected among the Kuba in his survey of the holdings of the Musée du Congo Belge (Tervuren) many of which he personally collected. The Joss example, cat. 52, is of exactly the same style as the majority of those in Maes (1929:pls. III-IV). A flat base usually holds two supporting columns which angle inward at varying degrees to form an hourglass-shaped opening under the head support. The gently curved upper platform is almost invariably covered on top with incised linear and geometric designs. These designs are of the same general style as those seen on other Kuba items such as cups, boxes and raffia cut-pile textiles, and Maes feels they are the distinctively Kuba aspect of the headrests. Frobenius (1987:65) also illustrates two headrests of the same variety seen in the Kuba area in his 1905 and 1906 fieldnotes. Cat. 51 represents an example with a very similar form but with upholstry nails embellishing the ends of the upper platform rather than incised patterns. It may be an example of a Songye headrest. Maes (1929:pl. V, no. 35) illustrates a very similar one said to be Batempa, Songye of the Lusambo area, just to the east of the Kuba area. These may represent a variation of a regional style.

Another Joss example, Cat. 50, has the same type of upper platform with densely packed patterning on its upper surface, but the diamond-shaped central support is unlike any documented Kuba examples. Perhaps it is from one of the many subgroups which were amalgamated into the Kuba kingdom. Cat. 53 exhibits a very different, somewhat enigmatic style. It had been identified as Songye, presumably by previous owner Willie Mestach, a collector of Songye art and author of several works on the Songye, but another example (Walker Art Center 1967:fig. 11) in almost exactly the same style, with the two opposing bracketed supports, was labeled as being collected by Fourche among the Kuba. Was this an example of the Kuba using a Songye headrest as they are known to have done with Songye "power" figures or is it yet another Kuba headrest substyle? Cat. 56 is an example made by the Twa or Pygmy who live among the Kuba. The incised upper platform echoes the other Kuba headrest styles but the figurative caryatids are quite different from Kuba figurative art. Cat. 54 is from the Binji, a group which lives between the Kuba and Songye, and display some of the characteristics of styles of both (Felix, personal communication, September 1992).

(above left)

54. Headrest

Binji; Zaire

Wood

15 x 13 x 7 cm.

FMCH 86.2433

(above, right)

55. Headrest

Lele; Zaire

Wood

13 x 12.4 x 6.9 cm.

FMCH 92.358

(right)

56. Headrest

Twa; Zaire

Wood

23.8 x 9.2 x 14.9 cm.

FMCH 92.464

57. Headrest

by "Master of Beneki"

Nsapo; Zaire

Wood

13.8 x 17 x 11.4 cm.

FMCH 89.365

Although we do not know his name, we can quite easily recognize the style of the "Master of Beneki" who made headrest cat. 57. The style is characterized by a prominent forehead, large semicircular eyes and a small pinched mouth which often almost coincides with the diminutive chin. On headrests, the artist's signature style was also to carve the feet as enormous low relief outlines on the circular base. Other "Master of Beneki" headrests are to be found in museums in Italy, Detroit, Tervuren (Maes collected one in Lusambo; Maes 1929:pl. VII, fig. 11) and Iowa City (Roy 1992:167).

58. Headrest

Nsapo; Zaire

Wood

15.9 cm

FMCH 91.296

The Nsapo were part of the Beneki Songye who in the late nineteenth century were forced to relocate into the Lulua area. In 1888 they followed the Belgian lieutenant Paul Le Marinelle's forces and settled in the Kananga (formerly Luluabourg) area. It is from here that the "Master of Beneki" and his workshop must have operated (Felix 1987:134; Timmermans 1962; Neyt 1981:199).

Cat. 58 is very similar in style, especially the facial features and body stance, but lacks the distinctive flat feet seen on the other example. As this headrest does not have the refinement of carving seen on the "Master of Beneki" examples perhaps it was made by an apprentice in his workshop. A very similar, though unused, headrest was collected by William Shepard for Hampton University around the turn of the century. Where it was collected is unknown, but we do know that Shepard worked in the town of Luebo and in Kuba county just to the west of the Nsapo area. Shepard commented of that headrest in 1911, that "the figure almost always the same, emblematic of rest watches the owner while sleeping to care for him" (Zeidler and Hullgren 1988:139). The only other indication of headrest usage among the Nsapo are Felix's comments that headrests were a status symbol (1987:134).

●

(left)

59. Headrest, *musamo*

Luba?; Zaire

Wood

13 x 14.4 x 9.8 cm.

FMCH 87.615

●

(right)

60. Headrest

Songye?; Zaire

Wood

12.9 x 10.9 x 7.6 cm.

FMCH 91.312

Figurative arts of Zaire have received much more attention than non-figurative arts. The bulk of collectors' and scholars' attention has also gone towards the figurative headrests of Zaire. Non-figurative headrests, unfortunately, have been overlooked even though they are beautiful and worthy of study on their own terms. Their study would broaden our perspective on the arts of particular areas and ethnic groups and contribute to the understanding of figurative arts in those same areas.

These three examples of headrests from eastern Zaire illustrate at least some of the variety produced. There is some question as to what Luba non-figurative headrests look like. Mary Nooter (personal communication, August 1992) related that there are at least as many abstract/non-representative headrests in Tervuren's collections as there are figurative ones. The bulk of them, however, are of questionable provenance (Maesen, personal communication to Nancy Nooter, 1988). Fortunately the University of Witwatersrand Art Galleries has recently published information on the collection of William F. P. Burton. Several headrests he collected in the Luba area while he was a missionary there early in this century are illustrated (University of Witwatersrand Art Galleries 1992:figs. 29-33). All have linear incisions on the sides of their sloping bases, like the Joss example, cat. 59 (and two of the Luba figurative examples seen in this volume), but have quite different supports. This is not surprising, however, for Burton's notes accompanying them indicate that "there are five different designs and different people rest more peacefully on pillows of different design" (Ibid.). One headrest with a chain-like linked column similar to the Joss example is illustrated in Torday and Joyce (1922:39, fig. 24d). It is labeled "baLuba" but whether it is Luba-Kasai or Luba-Shaba is unknown.

The Tabwa? example (cat. 61) has been attributed by Evan Mauer as probably being Tabwa. Although there are none exactly like it in the Mauer and Roberts catalogue, they do illustrate a somewhat similar one with a cutout in the support column (1985:264, fig. 311). Roberts reports that early explorers "found that Tabwa coiffures were the most ornate of those encountered in east and central Africa;... (and) used headrests to protect them" (1986:35 and n. 17). Cat. 60 seems to be a Songye example. Maes illustrates a number of examples with the same type of cylindrical base and rings in the middle of the support column (1929:pls. IV-V) that are labeled as being Songye.

61. Headrest

Tabwa?; Zaire

Wood

19.5 x 18 x 10.5 cm.

FMCH 86.2444

63. Headrest, *musamo*

Luba; Zaire

Wood

14 x 12.4 x 5.5 cm.

FMCH 88.929

62. Headrest, *musamo*

Luba; Zaire

Wood

17 x 9.5 cm.

FMCH 86.1721

The Joss collection has an especially fine collection of Luba figurative headrests containing an array of regional examples, several of which are among the finest known. The movement of artists and prestige objects among the Luba make ascribing too precise a provenance risky especially as there is no collection information for these headrests, but it is possible to place them tentatively in regional stylistic groupings.

Cat. 62 has been indentified as sharing "attributes of a style often identified with the Kinkondja region" by Mary Nooter (personal communcation, August 1992). Felix uses this headrest, or a very similar one, to illustrate what he calls the Lake Upemba style (1987:84, 58, fig. B6). (Kinkondja, one of the larger towns in the area, is on Lake Kisale, just to the north of Lake Upemba.) A very similar headrest by the same artist is in the Buffalo Museum of Science (Buffalo Museum of Science 1969:fig. 362).

Nooter notes that "[cat. 63] does seem to resemble the Shankadi style that has been attributed to the town or village of Basangu" (ibid., 92). Marc Felix illustrates a very similar headrest (except for torso scarification and a double line of dotted scarification instead of the V-shaped one on the forehead) that he puts in the "Sungu style (which) seems to be a later version of the Bena Ngoa substyle, made by the carver Kiloko" (1987:154-5, fig. 11). It should be remembered that the Shankadi area was not a political entity but is a stylistic name Westerners have given to an area. It encompasses a group of independent chiefdoms with a number of related styles, the most famous done by the "Master of the Cascade" (de Maret et al., 1973).

Cat. 64 is from the eastern Luba area where there is a lot of ethnic mixture. The high shaved forehead, arching eyebrows, coffeebean eyes and small delicate mouth, scarification on the belly and lower back, and cruciform hair style are all characteristic of this area. Cat. 65 is also from this eastern region but of a different style area, where the figure and cruciform coiffure is handled in a different way. A Luba headrest with a similar configuration of torso, head and arms is illustrated in Maes (1929:pl. VII, figs. 2, 4). The head of the Joss piece is very round and large and the rectangularly set arms are flat on the sides. On the outer surface these are covered with crosshatching and the human arms, moving from upper to lower extremity, are transformed into furniture. Cat. 66 is from the Zela to the east of the Luba (Felix, personal communication, September 1992).

Many of Mary Nooter's sources remembered that their grandparents had owned headrests but felt that nobody kept them anymore (personal communcation, August 1992). Although headrests were not often mentioned in early accounts of the Luba this probably relates more to the fact that they are such personal objects and not seen, rather than not being important. There certainly is evidence to associate the more elaborate figurative headrests with other more public royal regalia such as stools. Mary Nooter has noted that

> their utilitarian purpose, however, is only a means of supporting their more symbolic messages. Maesen related (personal communication to Mary Nooter, 1982) that when an important person died, and the body was irretrievable, his or her headrest was buried in place of the individual.... He also noted that during the severe iconoclastic upheaval with the Yeke at the end of the nineteenth century, all headrests were burned, while stools, staffs, and other objects were left intact (1984:62-63).

Luba headrests were certainly used by their sleeping owners to help preserve the elaborate coiffures the Luba are noted for. Depictions of some varieties of these can be seen on the figures of these Joss headrests. Nooter has noted that a style such as the Shankadi casade was styled "over a canework frame, it took almost fifty hours to complete, and with the use of a headrest at night, it could last two to three months (Burton 1960:notes to painting no. 8)" (Nooter in Koloss 1990:64). While the coiffures are appreciated aesthetically by the Luba, they are also an integral element of social identify. Nooter notes that "different Luba coiffures and headdresses [are] associated with different status and ranks, and with different moments and events in a person's life, like engagement, marriage, widowhead, or being a fisherman, diviner, chief's messenger or aristocrat, for example" (personal communcation, August 1992).

The very prominent cicatrization seen on headrests cat. nos. 62 and 64 is also important to note in connection with the meaning of the headrest. Scarification is only done on females among the Luba and it both signifies the maturing of a girl into a woman and has an erotic (visual and tactile) purpose to her husband (Nooter 1991:244-7). In the arts associated with royalty and the state there is also a symbolic link between the cultural refinement of the state and the refinement seen in statuary form on the "perfected Luba woman-lover-mother" (Roberts in Roy 1992:236-7).

There is also an interesting conceptual link made by the Luba between headrests and scarification, for the name of one pattern usually put on the inside of the upper arm is known as *musamo* or 'headrest'. Nooter was told this was because it is the place "where the husband lays his head at night" (1991:246; personal communication, August 1992).

64. Headrest, *musamo*

Luba; Zaire

Wood, copper

15.5 x 9.9 x 8.5 cm.

FMCH 91.60

(right)

65. Headrest, *musamo*

Luba; Zaire

Wood

13.97 cm.

FMCH 91.307

(detail below right)

(below)

66. Headrest

Zela; Zaire

Wood

13.9 x 9.5 x 7 cm.

FMCH 86.2421

67. Headrest, *musamo*

Luba; Zaire

Wood

14.8 x 7.5 x 16.7 cm.

FMCH 89.781

This Janus-faced headrest is quite unlike most Luba figurative headrest with single or double female figures. Instead it is more like the Janus-faced objects such as Hemba *kabedja* (Neyt and de Strycher 1975) or some half-figures attached to calabashes (Agthe 1983:110, fig. 95). This latter type has been identified by Allen Roberts as a *kabwelulu* which is used in the magico-religious practice of Bugabo, a protective, and later anticolonial, secret society in southeastern Zaire (Roberts in Roy 1992:234-5). A different type is illustrated by a small Janus charm included in the University of Witwatersrand's recent catalogue of the Burton Collection. Burton, who photographed it described it as "the two-headed and one-naveled spirit who guards against the unwelcome attentions of the dead and the living" (1992:42).

It is therefore perhaps not unreasonable to think one could interpret the meaning of this headrest in a similar manner to what Allen Roberts has done for a Tabwa Janus headrest.

Despite a total lack of information concerning these objects, one can hypothesize that these headrests were used in conjunction with other Janus-faced objects or magic depending on the power of duality, in Bugabo or other contexts ... Where other Janus-faced objects have medicine bundles between the two faces, here the diviner's head is the "little world" where transformation takes place as he dreams, a process facilitated by other sorts of magic and protected by medicine bundles such as *kalunga* horns (1985:35).

68. Headrest

Hemba; Zaire

Wood, metal

16 x 12.1 x 10.2 cm.

FMCH 91.67

(details on pages 6 and 7)

Neyt and de Strycher (1975:51) have identified this headrest as coming from the Kangolo region in the southwestern Hemba area along the upper Zaire River. Felix wonders if there is not some Kusu influence evident as well (personal communication, September 1992). *Singiti* or male ancestor figures are the best known Hemba sculpture but chiefs' stools and headrests do utilize female caryatid figures such as that seen in this headrest. What the females depict is not totally clear. Felix says they represent "female or primal ances- tors" (1987:34). Also it must be remembered that Luba kings attempted to incorporate this area into their territory in the beginning of the nineteenth century (Reefe 1981:131).

Reefe has noted that "sisters and daughters of Luba kings were imposed upon client rulers as consorts or wives, especially along frontiers, and the importance of royal women was emphasized in [stories] ... in the Luba genesis myth. Offspring of unions with client rulers frequently lived at the Luba king's court, and one of their number was likely to be chosen to rule over their father's domain after he died" (1981:133-4). Nooter has noted that this political role of women in part helps to explain the prominence of women in Luba art (1984; other gender-related aspects of Luba sculpture are discussed in Nooter 1991). How these items so closely linked with Luba kingship, such as the stools and headrests, came to be integrated into Hemba arts needs more careful examination. While it is true that Luba kings dispersed objects to solidify relationships and Luba art was copied by surrounding peoples hoping to emulate their prestige, objects such as this headrest must hold additional hidden stories. If they could speak, what would they tell us of the dynamics of power manipulation and royal politics around the edges of the Luba state?

The style of the figure, with its arms extended at right angles to the upper platform thus framing the head, reminds us of similar eastern Luba configurations. Other details such as the flattened and elongated fingers (the Buli master also used this) are more Hemba. The reason why the eyes were inlaid with metal is a mystery for it is not a common practice in the area.

69. Headrest with

latched box

Shona or Tsonga;

Zimbabwe or

Mozambique

Wood, leather string

19 x 14.5 x 9.5 cm.;

box cover 9 x 1.5 cm.

FMCH 86.1720

This very unusual headrest can probably be localized in terms of style characteristics to being from an area in southeastern Zimbabwe or southern Mozambique. The configuration of the upper platform with triangular motifs on the upturned ends, and the flat board-like base put this in the area where southeastern Shona and Tsonga people share a common style. In this area rectangular or circular tabs are usually carved under both ends of the upper platform but they may have been omitted here to incorporate the four corner columns (one has cracked off).

   Door locks are not usually made in this area as, for example, is the pattern in West Africa among groups such as the Dogon, so this is an unusual example in terms of the latching mechanism. Containers incorporated into headrests are often seen in northern Zaire and southern Sudan among such groups as the Bwaka and Azande (Maes 1929:pl. VIII; Sieber 1980:120). Among southeastern Africa groups box headrests are rare but not unknown. One is illustrated from the Brenthurst collection (Becker 1992:fig. 27) and another which is on display in the Zimbabwe National Gallery in Harare (acc. no. 1972.41) has a smaller box form incorporated into the central supporting column. Each of the three examples seem to be from the Shona/Tsonga area of southeastern Zimbabwe or southern Mozambique but each is unique in style. Perhaps the reason is that this is also the area where there is the most variation in the central column design. How these container headrests were used in southeastern Africa has not been documented but it would make sense to place any valuable small objects (such as money after the turn of the century) right under your head while you slept.

70. Headrest

Shona?; Zimbabwe

Serpentine

11.2 x 19.9 x 4.5 cm.

FMCH 91.65

This headrest certainly looks like wooden examples carved by the Shona people of Zimbabwe but the questions of who made it, when it was made and whether it was ever used are unresolved. Stone carving is known to have been done at the ancient sites of Great Zimbabwe (twelfth-thirteenth century A.D.) and Khami (A.D. 1450-1650). Seated birds are the most famous stone carvings from Great Zimbabwe (Huffman 1985) but bowls and plinthes are also known from Great Zimbabwe and Khami (Garlake 1973, 1978; Robinson 1959). While there is some evidence that headrests were made and used at ancient Zimbabwean sites (see Chapter 2), these were of wood with sheet metal attached and there is no evidence that stone headrests were ever made.

A new tradition of stone carving was encouraged by Frank McEwan (1968, 1972) with local artists at the National Gallery in Harare in the 1960s. This contemporary art (Arnold 1981) has become world-famous as "Shona" sculpture, but in fact there are Malawians, Ndebele and Shona artists producing the mostly figurative scupltures (Zilberg 1988). The National Gallery in Harare also has a gallery of traditional African art including numerous examples of Shona headrests. One could speculate that contemporary stone carvers saw one of these and decided to duplicate the form in stone. The ancient sculptors in Zimbabwe used "soapstone" or talc schist for their carvings and many of the contemporary sculptors follow the same pattern. Here a greenish variety, serpentine, was used.

71. Headrest

Tsonga?, Chopi?;

Mozambique

Wood

15 x 12.5 x 7.5 cm.

FMCH 86.2439

From the flat base and rectangular tabs apppended at either end of the gently curved upper platform, this headrest fits within the parameters of the stylistic area of the southeastern Shona and Tsonga. The decorative details around the edge of the base, however, are uncommon because usually this area is undecorated. The headrest is also unusual because it is one of only a small number with movable upper platforms. The interlocking arches are carved free of one another and the upper platform sits on, but is not attached to, one of the arches. Another example with a moveable platform, from the Musée de l'Homme, has been so frequently illustrated and mis-attributed that it bears examination. On that one two sets of interlocking rings are carved free of each other and the upper platform rests on, but again is not attached to, a central round column.

That headrest has been illustrated by Delange (1974:280) and Balandier and Maquet (1974:168), with the attribution "Shona, Zambia." It is also illustrated by Falgayrettes (1989:39) with the attribution "Shona, Zimbabwe." The Zambian designation is probably a misinterpretation of the term "Zambese" which is listed in the museum's inventory as being the area where much of the donor's collection was from. "Zambezia" for many years was the popular name given to the region around the Zambezi river. The Musée de l'Homme records, however, clearly say that the collector, A. Lombard, was a consular agent for France in Mozambique pre-1890. An inventory, "Objets de Collection de Msr. A. Lombard," lists "6 Carre-têtes en bois (Inhambane)," which I interpret as six head-recliners from Inhambane, a Tsonga or Chopi area of Mozambique.

There has not been enough research into just exactly what Chopi headrests style is, so the Musée de l'Homme and Joss headrests could be attributed as either Chopi or Tsonga. It should be remembered however that the Chopi area has witnessed a migration of Shona speakers into the area around the fifteenth century and an eighteenth-century migration of Tsonga people, all of which has resulted in a mixture of influences being preserved in Chopi culture (Smith 1973). Whether this has also caused a blending of headrest styles is unknown.

This figurative headrest (cat. 72) was originally attributed to the Yaka, probably because of its anthropomorphic or zoomorphic caryatid. The gently sloping base and the slightly curved rectangular upper platform with smaller rectangular tabs appended below the platform at either end, however, clearly place it within the stylistic parameters of the Tsonga and southeastern Shona areas of Zimbabwe and Mozambique. See for example cat. 73 from the Joss collection which has an almost identical form except for the two supporting columns instead of the caryatid figure.

Figurative sculpture is quite rare among the Shona but reasonably well-known among the Tsonga (see Nettleton 1988, 1991; Klopper 1991). The situation regarding figurative headrests, however, is not very clear. Quadruped zoomorphic headrests are known for both the Shona (eastern and southeastern) and the Tsonga from a stylistic area that encompasses both ethnic groups (see Chapter 2). The situation with anthropomorphic headrests seems to follow a similar pattern, although they seem much more rare. I have documented a few anthropomorphic headrests among the Shona (Dewey 1991:186-8, figs. 142-8). The two that are the most three-dimensional conform more to the Tsonga flat base style area than to other Shona areas. One was collected in the Mt. Selinda area before 1912 (Royal Scottish Museum, Edinburgh, acc. no. 1912.172) and the other was collected by Frobenius in the Charter District in 1928 (Museum für Völkerkunde acc. no. 2490 31-V, 438).

In her article on Tsonga headrests for the Brenthurst collection catalogue Rayda Becker illustrates several anthropomorphic headrests with good provenance information. Two from the Jacques collection "were made on order for him by a Shangaan carver and were based on designs from the Congo (Zaire)" (Becker 1991:68, figs. 56-7 citing Jacques c. 1941). Two more "genuine" Tsonga examples, however, are also given. One was collected c. 1918 in Groot Spelonken, a Tsonga-speaking area in northern Transvaal (Becker 1991:68, 196, fig. L51). Another classified as "Barotse" or "Rozwi," in the African Museum, Johannesburg, is illustrated in Wanless (1985:229, fig. 25; 235). It, like the other examples, has the flat board-like base typical of the southeastern Shona/Tsonga style area.

The most important example illustrated by Becker, however, is "one headrest in the Brenthurst Collection (fig. 55) with a radically truncated figure. The head is large and supported by two rectangular posts which could be legs. The arms, attached to the side of the head, stretch upward and outward acting both as additional supports for the crossbar and as extended lugs" (1991:68). This example does not have the eyes, fingers, or feet delineated, as they are on the Joss piece, but apart from these details they are very close in style. It is unknown whether these figurative headrests were used in a different way than non-figurative ones.

72. Headrest

Tsonga? Shona?;

Mozambique/

Zimbabwe

Wood, beads?

14 x 14.6 cm.

FMCH 86.1722

73. Headrest

Tsonga? Shona?;

Mozambique/

Zimbabwe

Wood

15.7 x 22.8 x 9.2 cm.

FMCH 91.597

Headrests like this have often been labeled as Zulu in the past. Nettleton (1988) has clearly demonstrated for figurative sculpture that this was primarily because of Westerners' better knowledge of and respect for the Zulu as powerful military adversaries but minimal knowledge of neighboring groups. Consequently everything from the general area became known as Zulu. The same has been true of headrests. Klopper (1991) has shown that even in the "traditional" core area for the Zulu the notion of Zulu ethnicity is problematic. While groups may now share a common language there is no proof they always did, and "Zulu" is better understood as a political construct of many disparate groups incorporated into Shaka's military state. Even attempts to link styles to kinship groups or clans is difficult because of "the fact that Shaka and his successors manipulated geneological links in a deliberate attempt to extend the power base of the ruling elite" (Klopper 1991:84 citing Hamilton 1985:213-16). The most recent preferred term, "northern Nguni," if it is thought of as an ethnic rather than linguistic term for those groups living along the eastern coast of southern Africa, also has problems (see Klopper 1991:82) but seems the best alternative.

There seem to be no well-provenanced headrests like the Joss example cat. 74, but there are several similar examples illustrated. In Grossert's article on the Zulu in *The Art of Africa* (Batiss et al. 1958) two headrests of the same form (a circle between the platform and base) connected by a wooden chain is labeled "Nguni, South Africa" (Ibid., 127). The chain-type motif is now considered more characteristic of the Tsonga, and a similar pair of headrests connected by a chain in the Brenthurst collection is labeled as Tsonga (Becker 1991:67, fig. 49). Two other single headrests from the Brenthurst collection are of exactly the same form as the Joss example. One without the triangular chip carvings on the surface is labeled "North Ngoni" (Becker 1991:66, fig. 45). The other example has almost the exact same pattern of triangular chip carvings around the edges of the circle and the base, with the addition of glass beads embedded on the sides of the tabs and the base. It is labeled "Tsonga/North Nguni" (Becker 1991:66, fig. 46).

The only provenanced example is illustrated by Wanless (1985:296, fig. 52; 299). Although the central support is two curved arches rather than a true circle, it has the same incised triangle motifs. It was collected by Alexandre Jacques circa 1930. Becker claims most "of the pieces (in the Jacques collection) were found in the Pilgrim's Rest (Bushbuckridge) area in the eastern Transvaal and were documented as Shangaan (Tsonga)" (1991:59). Wanless, however, notes that Jacques was stationed at a number of missions in eastern and northeastern Transvaal and also acquired a number of his headrests from another missionary in Mozambique (1985:293). Nettleton notes that the Tsonga and "Shangaan element of the Tsonga" moved into the Transvaal area in the nineteenth century and many settled in the Bushbuckridge area (1990:154, n. 22).

74. Headrest

North Nguni?, Tsonga?;

Mozambique?

Wood

17 x 25.7 x 9 cm.

FMCH 91.66

75. Headrest

double

N. Nguni?; South

Africa, Mozambique

Wood

33.5 x 15.5 x 7 cm.

FMCH 86.2411

The Tsonga and southeastern Shona often combine headrests with useful objects such as snuff containers, staffs, bowls and cups (see for example Figure 25 (chap. 2), also Johannesburg Art Gallery 1991:figs. 28, 61-2, 65; Wanless 1988:figs. 182-3; 1990:fig. 254). The usual pattern seen is for the headrest to have a staff extending to one side through the middle support structures. Wanless reports that this type of headrest was reported to be "used for traveling, carried over the shoulder with a bundle tied at the end" (1987b:320, fig. 161). In the National History Museum of Maputo, Mozambique, there are a number of headrest staffs of this type on display. Several also have bowls added on and one has a cup carved onto an extension of the staff. Cat. 76, however, is the only example known that incorporates a cup form directly into the support columns. There are a few "double" headrests from southern Africa that can be used either turned on the side or the base in the same manner as this headrest (Dewey 1991:figs. 137-8). Their function or meaning is unknown. Whether there are any special uses or meanings implied by this headrest-cup combination is also unknown but it certainly warrants further study.

Cat. 77 is an important example of a Tsonga headrest primarily because of the label attached underneath. It reads "Kaffir Pillow used by the 'Umkosikas' (Queen). Queens Kraal on the border (N.) of Swziland. A.P.W. to H.J.F." The term "Kaffir," now regarded as a highly derogatory epithet, is not an ethnic designation as many European museums believed at the turn of the century. It was instead the label often applied to all black populations by whites in the typically racist manner of the times. The information that it belonged to a "queen" and was from northern Swaziland could be important, but needs additional supporting evidence. Wanless also has documented some headrests of a similar type from Swaziland (1987b:315-16, figs. 154-5) that fit like this one into the Tsonga stylistic parameters. They all perhaps were made by the southern Tsonga or a subgroup, the Ronga. Tsonga headrests seem to be the most varied of southern Africa in

terms of structure of the support sculpture (see Becker 1991; Wanless 1986-1990) but are poorly documented in terms of provenance. With more information such as that on the Joss piece perhaps regional stylistic variations for the Tsonga can be discerned.

Becker (1991:72) says that both Tsonga and Chopi women used headrests. What is unclear is whether there was any difference in style. Becker also gives this information on usage (Becker 1991:74-5):

> As the headrest became embedded with body fat and personal materials (a number of headrests, for example, are adorned), it became more personalized, became so much a part of the owner that on his death the headrest was, in many instances, buried together with him and other personal items (L. Jacques 1949:340) ... Yet other circumstances prevailed as well, in some instances the headrest was preserved and kept as *mhamba*.

> H. A. Junod, the Swiss missionary who documented the life of the Tsonga and Ronga in the first decades of this century, defines *mhamba* as "any object or act or even person which is used to establish a bond between the gods and their worshippers" (1927 2:420). In other words a *mhamba* is a kind of communicating vehicle through which the ancestor may be contacted. It can function as a presence. In physical form a *mhamba* could exist in any kind of object, such as snuff boxes and beads and not only headrests. Junod cites a case which explains the use of a headrest as *mhamba*:

> "The Thongas [sic] have no sacredotal caste but the right of officiating in religious ceremonies is strictly confined to the eldest brother ... If, after the death of his parents, their son should happen to dream of them, he must offer worship to the deceased by pouring some ground tobacco on to his wooden pillow, this being the commencement of his religious functions" (1927 2:411).

(left)

76. Headrest

Tsonga;

Mozambique/N. Swazi-

land/South Africa

Wood, beads

14.9 x 13.9 x 8.8 cm

FMCH 91.295

(right)

77. Headrest

Tsonga;

Mozambique/N. Swazi-

land/South Africa

Wood, beads

14 x 14.7 x 6 cm

FMCH 92.355

78. Headrest, *izigqiki*

Zulu; South Africa

Wood

47 x 13.6 x 10 cm.

FMCH 86.2460

The Zulu- and Swazi-speaking language groups have distinctive headrest styles which are easily distinguishable from their neighbors to the north such as the Shona or Tsonga. While these latter groups typically make headrests with a base, central support and upper platform, the Zulu and Swazi headrests usually are made without a base and have a series of legs (two to eight) supporting a longer horizontal upper platform. While there are many substyles, Zulu headrests, as a general rule, either have horizontal ridges or square motifs carved onto the legs, while the Swazi ones mostly have vertical ridges. The raised squared motif on the sides of the four legs and truncated projections in the center of the Joss example are known as *amusumpa* or 'warts'. It is a motif also seen on Zulu beer pots, milk pails, meat trays and cast brass prestige bracelets (see, for examples, Conner and Pelrine 1983).

Sandra Klopper has found that this motif is most often found now on the objects produced in central Zululand, or the area of the Valley of the Kings (1991:85). Rather than being associated with particular ethnic or kinship groups, she argues "that in practice this pattern probably functioned above all as a symbol of royal patronage and power"(1991:86). Given the dynamics of Zulu politics, such as incorporations of other groups, gifts of prestige items to political allies of the Zulu, and possible copying by others to invoke associations with the Zulu, it is futile to try to assign too precise a provenance without reliable collection information (Ibid).

A number of Zulu headrests either are literal representations of cattle (e.g. Sieber 1980:22; Johannesburg Art Gallery 1991:pl. 17) or like this example allude to cattle.

Most headrests of this type have two legs with a third, truncated leg in the center, obviously phallic in implication. In view of the crucial importance of cattle to the political economy of the Zulu kingdom, and to communications between the living and their ancestors, the prominence evidently afforded these animals is certainly understandable. There is even evidence to suggest that the *amasumpa* (warts) pattern found on headrests,... may also allude to large herds of cattle (interviews) (Klopper 1989:36; also see Berglund 1976 and Nettleton 1990 on cattle symbolism).

Michael Conner (personal communication, July 1992) points out that the Zulu also decorated their cattle with *amasumpa*-like patterns. This was done by lifting and tying the skin into nodules and he notes that Fynn (c. 1824) described cattle "with pendulous projections, four or six inches long, which covered a considerable portion of the animal" (Fynn 1950:75).

Although male wood carvers make the headrests, and their cattle symbolism associates them with Zulu male activities, both men and women use the headrests. Klopper relates that

traditionally, the Zulu woman commissioned two headrests before her marriage, one for herself and one for her future husband. Although they could be identical in design, a woman might choose to acknowledge her husband's status by giving him a more elaborately treated headrest than her own. Headrests are now seldom used or commissioned, but are kept as ancestral relics. Alternatively, they may be buried with their owners (Klopper 1986).

Cattle are also immensely important in the economic, political and cosmological systems of the Swazi (see Marwick 1940; Kuper 1963). Their headrests seem to allude to cattle even more consistently than their southern neighbors the Zulu (see Wanless 1988). As Nettleton has pointed out:

> Among the Swazi headrests there is a fairly consistent pattern of two legs supporting the horizontal cross-bar, with a lug pendant from the centre of the underside of this crossbar. The legs appear to be almost invariably fluted with vertical grooves, and in some examples, tails and leg-like forms are added at the short end of the headrest (1990:152).

The Joss examples illustrate nicely some of the stylistic variety that exists. Cat. 79 has an unusual loop, instead of a lug, hanging below from the middle. Cat. 80 has three pairs of legs, a stylistic type which, although not as common as the two-paired variety, is seen quite often in collections. Cat. 81 seems close in style to other Swazi examples but for the absence of fluting and the elaborate four-part projections slanting up from between the legs at either end of the headrest. Whether they are meant to represent tails, heads, horns or something else, is unknown.

There is no specific research known to have been done on Swazi headrest symbolism and usage. Therefore it is usually assumed that they must have followed a pattern similar to their southern neighbors, the Zulu, with whom they share many cultural patterns. There has, however, been some additional research done on the headrests of other related Nguni-speaking groups such as the Ngoni. During the period of intense war that engulfed much of southern Africa in the early 1800s, this group, originally from the Swaziland Transvaal area, left led by Zwangendaba. They moved northward through Mozambique and Zimbabwe to eventually settle in eastern Zambia, Malawi and southern Tanzania. Headrests that are very similar to the Swazi ones, with tail or head projections, are found among both the Tanzania Ngoni (see Krieger 1990:figs. 514-19) and the Malawi Ngoni.

Michael Conner, who has studied the Jere and Maseko Ngoni of Malawi, reports that several headrest styles are known that relate to where a man or his ancestors lived before being assimilated into the Ngoni. He notes that

> headrests, *chigoqo*, were one of the many valuable personal objects which were normally broken and buried with their owner. Dreams were believed to be an important vehicle of communication with one's ancestors. Dreams were frequently acted upon. Perhaps to facilitate this valuable communication, headrest forms were conservative and usually replicated from father to son.... [Of three "Swazi" style Ngoni headrests illustrated] the "abstract" shapes carved onto these three headrests depict the head, horns, hump, genitals and tail of a bull. Headrests were frequently carved with the same head-like shape at both ends (1991:145).

In addition he reports that in polygamous families the headrests were moved from house to house of each of the wives and that "modern feather pillows are still regarded as intimate objects which are carried from location to location, and often buried with the deceased, just as wooden headrests had been" (personal communication, July 1992).

79. Headrest, *sicamela?*

Swazi; Swaziland

Wood

48 x 10 x 15 cm.

FMCH 88.993

80. Headrest, *sicamela?*

Swazi; Swaziland

Wood

40 x 9 x 12.6 cm.

FMCH 89.784

81. Headrest, *sicamela?*

Swazi?; South Africa,

Swaziland

Wood

48.3 cm.

FMCH 92.8

82. Headrest

Ovumbundu?; Angola

Wood

11.3 x 10.5 x 6.2 cm.

FMCH 87.1510

83. Child's stool, *dwa*

Akan; Ghana

Wood

13.7 x 26.3 x 12.5 cm.

FMCH 91.58

The low height of this example suggests that it could have been used as a headrest, but the form is clearly in the shape of an Akan stool made for a child (Doran Ross, personal communication, July 1992; Sharon Patton, personal communication August 1992). Akan stools are relatively well known because of their use as chieftaincy regalia. Cole and Ross have noted that the "Akan stool *(dwa)* is the most important and symbolically complex of all Ghanaian art forms" (1977:134). There is an intimate link that Akan people ascribe to a person and their stool. They are used for everyday activities but are also used ritually to signify various important points in a person's life (ibid).

The close association between an individual and his stool persists even after death, for a man's soul is believed then to inhabit his stool. When one vacates a stool, it should be tilted on its side to prevent another spirit, particularly a bad spirit, from occupying it. The stools of chiefs are identified not only with the man but with his office as well (Fraser 1972:142).

Upon the death of important individuals such as chiefs, priests and queen mothers, their stools are blackened and stored in a special room. These spiritually-charged objects, arranged to reproduce the geneaologies of families and kingdoms, are then regularly propiated to venerate the ancestors. The Asante took this symbolism to its peak of efficacy and created at the end of the seventeenth century a single stool, the *sika dwa* ('golden stool') to represent the spirit of the whole Asante nation. This elaboration of stools "as personal, genealogical and state symbols with strong spiritual and ancestral associations seems to be unique to Akan peoples" (Cole and Ross 1977:145).

Sharon Patton has indicated that this type of child's stool would never be blackened and placed in an "ancestral stool house." The complexity of the design suggests to her that it was probably made for a child of high status and she notes that the design, although not an exact copy, was modeled after the *sika dwa*, the Asante Golden Stool. While it has the traditional Asante/Akan rectangular seat and base it does not have the usual four columns around the central columns. Instead the rounded central column (its checkerboard motif is called *dame-dame* 'draughts') has two slightly angled columnar side supports like the Golden Stool. Patton reports that this *sika dwa*-type support on a stool is rare and that she has only seen one other example like it on an adult stool in the Ghanaian National Museum in Accra. It was said to have been from Agona Kwabre, Asante region (personal communication, August 1982).

While headrests were almost universally declared, by scholars I asked, to be unheard-of among the Akan I did hear of one unusual instance of their use. Mrs. Pauline Adansi of Agona Asafo related to me (June 1992) how she had visited a specialist near Winneba in the early 1980s concerning her brother's mental illness. This *opanyin odunsin* ('distinguished healer') had recommended the needed treatment and indicated his charges while "in a trance" with his head resting on a carved headrest in the shape of an animal. The implication is that the headrest accoutrement was essential for him to acquire the knowledge and authority for the diagnosis.

84. Headrest

Baule; Ivory Coast

Wood

9.2 x 17.3 x 8.4 cm.

FMCH 91.56

The Baule of the Ivory Coast seem to be among the very few West African people who have, until recently, produced and used wooden headrests. Philip Ravenhill (personal communication, July 1992) indicates that he saw a number of them in the art market in Bouaké in the early 1970s but subsequently they disappeared. He also has seen them on Baule ancestral altars, which are normally composed of various types of blackened stools. Just as is the case among other Akan speakers, the very identity of their owners is felt to be manifest in the Baule stools and therefore the ancestors themselves can be venerated through the stools on the altars. Ravenhill feels the same type of usage with Baule headrests indicates a similar type of association.

Ravenhill reports that cat. 85, with its double columns, is very similar to another example in the Abidjan museum. The pattern of usage on this headrest, which is clearly abraded on the side, seems to indicate that it was regularly tipped on its side. Perhaps this was done to prevent bad spirits from entering it when not in use, as is the practice with Akan stools. Cat. 84 has a chip-carved zig-zig on the central column. Ravenhill reports that this a common trait seen on carvings from the central and Boundoukou regions of Ivory Coast.

Unfortunately there seems to be little other information on the use of Baule headrests. Ravenhill speculates that he "would imagine that they were used for sleeping and thus dreaming of the *blolo*" (personal communcation, July 1992). *Blolo bian* and *blolo bla* are otherworld lovers (male and female respectively) that are believed by the Baule to be able to manifest their feelings on their real-world counterparts. When these spirits are jealous or angry they may cause their worldly partners problems in their wordly pursuits such as school, business or more often sexual matters. Divination will reveal that in order to alleviate these problems it is necessary to have a statue carved to which offerings can be made (Vogel 1973) and devote one night a week to the spirit lover. During this night, which is spent alone away from your spouse, it is expected that knowledge of the spirit lover will be gained through dreams and that the dreams will be sexual in nature (Ravenhill 1980:2).

●

(right)

85. Headrest

Baule; Ivory Coast

Wood

7.6 x 20.3 cm.

FMCH 91.572

●

(below)

86. Headrest

Senufo; Ivory Coast

Wood

52.9 x 6.1 x 14.5 cm.

FMCH 92.27

87. Headrest

Fulani; Futa Jallon,

Guinea

Wood

21 x 18 x 10.5 cm.

FMCH 86.2446

88. Headrest/stool

Lobi; Burkina Faso,

Ghana, Ivory Coast

Wood

20.2 x 42.4 x 11.1 cm.

FMCH 91.63

89. Headrest/stool

Dagari; Burkina Faso,

Ghana

Wood

6.9 x 43.5 x 12.8 cm.

FMCH 91.70

All of these headrest/stools have three legs, indicating that they were used by men. Among many groups in Burkina Faso, Mali, northern Ghana and Ivory Coast the number three is associated with men and four with women. Stools often reflect this symbolism with the number of legs they contain. Cat. 88 is a Lobi example. Cole and Ross report that these "are traditionally commissioned by men upon reaching manhood,... (and that at) initiation ceremonies they are hit on the ground by initiates to honor and announce the arrival of elders" (1977:145). Traditionally carried by hooking the legs over the left shoulder (Roy 1979:29; Kyeryerematen 1964:10), it has also been reported that it could be used as a weapon (Labouret 1931:188). While most often refered to in publications as stools, men also rest their heads on them, illustrating again that African furniture is often multifunctional. The Lobi headrest/stools have such a close association with their owners that Christopher Roy reports they are frequently placed on shrines after the death of their owners and become symbols of those ancestors (Roy 1987:62).

The larger knob protruding from the one end of the Lobi example suggests a head such as are often seen on Lobi headrest/stools (Meyer 1981:121-22, 141). The fact that the single leg is not hoof- or phallic-shaped perhaps indicates that it was made by the northern Lobi whose style is closer to their Nuna and Bwa neighbors (see Roy 1987:60-64). The more emphatic phallic shape of the Dagari headrest/stools' single legs, such as cat. nos. 89 and 90, has often caused them to be confused with Lobi. The gently curving double legs, however, are quite different from the perpendicular ones on Lobi examples (Christopher Roy, personal communication, June 1992). Information about the Dagari and how they use these headrest/stools, unfortunately, is almost non-existent, but from the extensive wear and the care taken in repairing cat. 90 with metal "staples," it seems likely that they were treasured as family heirlooms.

90. Headrest/stool

Dagari; Burkina Faso,

Ghana

Wood, metal repairs

86.4 cm.

FMCH 91.303

91. Double stool or

headrest

Nuna; Burkina Faso

Wood

9 x 89.5 cm.

FMCH 89.371

This double stool or headrest is similar in form to a larger one illustrated by Christopher Roy in the *Art of the Upper Volta Rivers* (1987:65) which has been identified as being from the Nuna people of southern Burkina Faso. That one has eight rather than four legs and incised surface decorations delineating the features on the animal's head. Chris Roy nevertheless feels the Joss example is of the same tradition (personal communication, June 1992).

The Nuna are one of the so-called "Gurunsi" peoples (a pejorative name used by their neighbors, the Mossi). They are a farming group that live in the sparsely populated area between the Red and Black Volta rivers. Much of Nuna religion revolves around nature spirits who can intercede to aid the community or harm their enemies. The quite well-known plank and animal masks are carved by the Nuna to represent these bush spirits. While the masks are publically used among the Nuna, this stool or headrest probably is part of divination equipment which is kept hidden in peoples' homes. Men known as *vuru* are believed to have special skills to harness the most dangerous of the nature spirits in order to solve clients' problems and predict the future (Roy 1987:204-49). While there is no hard evidence, Chris Roy believes the headrests could have been used by these diviners to dream of and consult with these powerful nature spirits (personal communication, June 1992).

92. Headrest/stool

Bobo; Burkina Faso

Wood

12.7 cm.

FMCH 91.304

Cylindrical stool forms are found in many areas of Africa and as Roy Sieber has succinctly noted, it not only "reveals its origin as a section of tree trunk ... (but also) is another instance of a critical minimum of functional stool-ness" (1980:152). Such minimal forms are extremely hard to localize in terms of regional style for they are rarely seen in museums, even in ethnographic collections, and hardly ever noticed by ethnographers or art historians. Ernie Wolfe III notes in correspondence to Jerry Joss that it is a

man's headrest/stool combination, (of the) Bobo people, southwestern Burkina Faso. This small yet symetrical, almost spool-like form is very similar except for its size to the larger examples commonly found among the Gurunsi, Gormache, Bobo and Bozo groups. The striations on the top suggest that it might have been used as a chopping block ... Because of its size, it would seem likely that the use of this object (was) more commonly as a headrest rather than a stool (May, 1991).

93. Headrest

Tellem; Mali

Wood

16 x 41 cm.

FMCH 89.381

94. Headrest

Tellem; Mali

Wood

12.7 cm.

FMCH 91.301

95. Headrest

Tellem; Mali

Wood

16.5 cm.

FMCH 91.302

These three headrests conform exactly to Tellem types excavated by Rogier Bedaux from caves in the Bandiagara cliffs above Dogon villages of Mali (Bedaux 1974; 1988). Bedaux notes that headrests were found to occur primarily in eleventh and twelfth century contexts. A few, such as cat. 95 with more pronounced curvature of the upper platform (compare to Bedaux 1974:fig. 51), can be dated to the thirteenth century. Similar headrests are illustrated in Ezra 1988, Imperato 1978, Sieber 1980 and Falgayrettes 1989.

The Tellem buried their dead in communal graves in caves sealed off by mud bricks. Objects presumed to be gifts for the dead were interred with them and seem to relate to the daily activities of the deceased. The headrests show signs of usage so they do not seem to have been manufactured exclusively for the burials (Bedeux 1988:42). No Tellem occupation sites have been excavated, however, so as Kate Ezra has pointed out, "it's impossible to say how these headrests were used during their owners' lifetimes" (personal communication, July 1992).

Tellem headrests, such as those in the Joss collection, were always associated with male skeletons. They were only found in eight of the thirteen caves excavated and in these there was a ratio of one headrest for every ten skeletons. Bedaux consequently hypothesizes that they must have been reserved for men of high status. These wooden headrests were generally carved with one, two or three support columns. Only one excavated by Bedaux had the handle-like extension seen on cat. 93 (see also Ezra 1988:102). Some Tellem females were buried with rectangular-shaped wooden objects. Bedaux has identified them as women's headrests but Sieber has suggested that they may instead be headboards used during a woman's life for carrying things (Ezra 1988:103). In the fourteenth century the wooden headrests were no longer used and instead "iron votive headrests" (Bedaux 1988:40) appeared for a short while before headrest usage totally ceased.

96. Headrest/stool

Dogon?; Mali

Wood

34.5 x 11.5 x 4.5 cm.

FMCH 86.2412

These two headrests present a perplexing puzzle. They and a few other similar examples have somtimes been attributed to the Dogon but there are questions whether the Dogon even use headrests. Bedaux categorically states, "headrests are encountered only in the older Tellem period. They are very rare in West Africa today and do not occur in Dogon contexts" (1988:43). Imperato also states that the "Dogon of today do not use headrests either for sleeping nor as grave gifts in burial caves" (1978:27).

Bedaux illustrates one headrest that is somewhat similar to the Joss examples (1974:fig. 16 and pl. 4). It was recovered from a Tellem cave (eleventh-twelfth century A.D.) and has three rectangular columns supporting the curved upper platform from which an appendage or handle extends at one end. It perhaps could be interpreted as an animal. The whole surface of that headrest is covered with a dot-within-a-circle motif. Bedaux notes that two headrests from other collections, unexcavated and with no provenance information are comparable (Davison 1966:163; the same headrest in Sotheby's 1987: no. 187, ex-Harold Rome collection; and another headrest in Tervuren's Musée Royal). He wonders if they are also Tellem but from a different regional tradition (1974:15). The surface decoration on these is composed of lines and chevrons. Another example of almost the exact form and surface decoration, from the Richman collection of Atlanta's High Museum of Art, is attributed to the Dogon (Mullen Kraemer 1986:27). Imperato illustrates two similar examples (1978:66, figs. 82-3), but attributes them to the Tellem.

Kate Ezra has informed me that the Metropolitan Museum of Art also has three comparable examples. "They don't really correspond to any of the types excavated by Bedaux, and the animal heads are very much like heads found on other types of Dogon objects, e.g. small trough-like containers and benches ... we've catalogued [these examples] as Dogon, notwithstanding Bedaux's statement ... that the Dogon don't use neckrests" (personal communication, July 1992).

One headrest, now in the Musée de l'Homme (illustrated in Falgayrettes 1989:47), has been documented as having been collected among the Dogon. Louis Desplagnes found it in front of the tomb of a chief and called it the stool of a Hogon priest (1907:pl. 53, no. 113). It is very different in form from the headrests discussed thus far, but Bedaux nevertheless feels it must be a Tellem headrest, reused and reinterpreted by the Dogon (1974:22). Falgayrettes (citing Dieterlen 1982:68-9) describes the use of a figurative headrest by a Hogon priest (1989:102-3), which has unfortunately never been illustrated. Sieber, noting that headrests may have a religious nature, quotes Igor de Garine's remarks (in Balandier and Maquet 1974:178) that "the heads of some individuals in high authority (for example the Hogon, who is the high priest of the Dogon of Mali) must not touch the ground" (1980:107). Until headrests like these in the Joss collection are dated, and more definitive field work is done among the Dogon, the question will remain whether the Dogon really do make and use headrests or reuse Tellem ones.

97. Headrest/stool

Dogon?; Mali

Wood

31 x 11.6 x 10 cm.

FMCH 86.2416

II

DECLARATIONS OF STATUS AND CONDUITS TO THE SPIRITS:

A CASE STUDY OF SHONA HEADRESTS

WILLIAM J. DEWEY

Headrests are probably the most commonly recognized examples of Shona sculpture because of all Shona objects, headrests are the most often illustrated in surveys of African art (see for example Leuzinger 1972:360; Willett 1971:20; Sieber 1980:117; Elisofon and Fagg 1958:248-9). Beyond this general acceptance of headrests as an example of the broad variety of African sculptural forms, however, dreadfully little has been written on the parameters of style, usage and symbolism of this intimate but exquisite art form.

HISTORY OF THE USE OF HEADRESTS

While there is no conclusive evidence to demonstrate how long the Shona type of headrest has been utilized in the area, archaeological, historical and oral evidence combine to make a strong case for a long history of usage. In a burial, for example, at the archaeological site of Mapungubwe (dated to the twelfth century A.D.) the remains of what was apparently a headrest were recovered. "Where the skull had lain were found pieces of curiously shaped gold plate, the convolutions of which suggest that they had adorned the wooden headrest of the corpse" (Fouche 1937:2, pl. A).[1]

Unfortunately, because of the fragmentary nature of the remains we shall never know exactly what the style of the

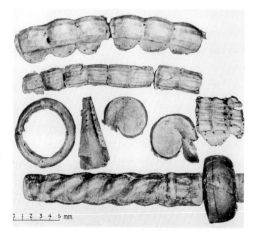

FIG. 4.
Gold sheathing, some of which is believed to come from a headrest recovered from a burial at the archaeological site of Mapungubwe, dated to the 12th century A.D.

headrest was like. Figure 4 shows those segments of sheathing that are believed to have come from the headrest. The two fragments from rows one and two appear to have been attached to a curved upper platform such as those typical of later headrests. The parallel ridges (which may just have been the carver's adze marks on the supporting wooden structure underneath) and the bead-like segmentation on these curved pieces are, however, unlike the more modern examples, which are either squared off or smoothly curve down from the top. If the circular "convolutions" from the third row of figure 4 were part of the headrest, perhaps they ornamented the sides of the central support as is the pattern of many more recent examples (e.g., fig. 9 or 20).

At other later archaeological sites in Zimbabwe, gold-covered headrests were apparently also found. Unfortunately a company known as the "Rhodesia Ancient Ruins Ltd," formed in 1895 (Schofield 1935; Garlake 1973:70-71), systematically ransacked more than fifty ruins looking for gold (fig. 5). The only proof of the existence of headrests is in the writings and letters of some of the members of this group where they mentioned finding headrests ornamented with gold wire or beaten sheets of gold covering them. One document, for example, stated that "corpses have been found buried with what seem to be wooden pillows covered with beaten gold and nailed on with pure gold tacks" (National Archives of Zimbabwe, file R.H.10). Hall and Neal (Neal was one of the original members of the Ancient Ruins Company) also state that "many of the wooden pillows and other articles buried with the ancients were covered with plates of gold fastened on with solid, wedge shaped gold nails and tacks. The wood is decayed but the gold plates and nails remain" (1902:95). In describing the burial customs of the "ancients" they state that

> His head either rested on a pillow of water-grooved stone or on a wooden pillow very similar to those seen in Egyptian museums and in ancient paintings of Egyptian tombs, resembling in shape and pattern the best sort of pillows used by the Kaffirs of today. The wooden pillows were frequently covered with beaten gold fastened on by solid gold tacks weighing 3 dwts each, or were beautifully worked on both sides in gold wire with patterns of the oldest Zimbabwe chevron decoration (1902:103-4).

Of the ransacked ruins, the sites of Chumnungwa, Mtelegwa, Mundie and Dhlo Dhlo (the last, now known as Danangombe, dates from 1680-1840 [Beach 1984]) apparently contained particularly rich finds of gold, but at which of these the "wooden pillows" covered with sheet gold were found is unknown. At the site of Great Zimbabwe, with the main occupation and building dates ranging between the thirteenth and fifteenth centuries A.D. (Huffman 1991), small sheets of gold, copper and bronze, perforated around the edges and apparently riveted with tacks to the now-decomposed underlying objects, have also been found (Garlake 1973:115). What type of object was being so adorned with metal here (and at many other related archaeological sites where these thin sheets of metal are ubiquitous) is unknown, but

there is a very strong possibility that some were headrests. The size of the metal sheeting preserved in museums or illustrated in publications[2] is for the most part quite small when compared to those from Mapungubwe. Unfortunately, without further evidence no speculations about the form, shape or decorations (other than that quoted from Hall and Neal [1902:4], describing gold wire "patterns of the oldest Zimbabwe chevron decoration") on these early Zimbabwe headrests can be made.

It is not surprising that the people buried at these sites, who appear to have held high status, would have been buried "sleeping" on their headrests. Many Shona sources told me that this was how important men used

FIG. 5.
Members of the company known as the "Rhodesia Ancient Ruins Ltd.", (circa 1895), with some of the gold they plundered from more than fifty ruins in Zimbabwe.

to be buried (see also Aschwanden 1987:259; Mahachi 1987).[3] More recently, wooden headrests have occasionally been found in caves[4] (fig. 6) and it should be noted that caves were commonly used as graves by the Shona people. Sekuru Bwanya, the spirit medium seen in figure 7, claims, for example, that the ancestral spirit that possesses him actually used the headrest seen resting beside him (fig. 8) when it was alive. When the possessing spirit first manifested itself, the spirit told people to go and collect its things in the cave where he had been buried.[5]

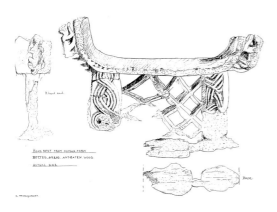

FIG. 6.
Headrest found in a walled-in cave burial, central Shona area, Castle Kopje, Zimbabwe. Drawing by C. Thornycraft. Headrest is now housed in the Children's Library in Marondera, Zimbabwe.

Another use of the headrests was noted by Thomas Baines, who traveled in the Shona area in 1870 and wrote that "to keep the well oiled [hair] locks from being soiled by dust, every man carries with him a neck pillow, like a little stool, which suffers not the head to come within eight or ten inches of the ground" (Baines 1877:27). J.T. Bent, who was in the Shona areas in 1891, noted that the Shona sleep "with their necks resting on a wooden pillow, curiously carved; [for] they are accustomed to decorate their hair so fantastically with tufts ornamentally arranged and tied up with beads that they are afraid of destroying the effect, and hence these pillows" (Bent 1892:36). While men no longer fix their hair in the ways that have just been described, or in the manner which is seen, for example, in Baines' 1870 drawing of a man (fig. 14), it used to be common prac-

tice.[6] Andre Fernandes, who visited the area in 1560, observed that "some [of the Shona] wear ten horns, others more, others less" (Beach 1980:156). Using the headrests to protect elaborate coiffures has therefore probably had a long history in the area.

The headrests were and still are kept in the rafters of their owners' huts. Bent noted, "These blackened rafters of the roof the Makalangas (Shonas) use as cupboards, sticking therein their pipes, their weapons, their medicine phials, their tools, and their pillows, and we soon found that this was the place to look for all manner of curios" (Bent 1896:87). Lucy Jaques-Rosset has commented about headrests of the Tsonga (southeastern neighbors of the Shona) that "these head-rests are used almost exclusively by the old Natives who, when dawn has come, place them on a string, with great care, in a special place of their roof, where the smoke, mixed with the fat of their hair, gives this household implement a magnificent mellowed patina" (Battiss et al. 1958:79). The same could equally well have been said of Shona headrests.

Sources explained to me that a user could either sleep on his back with the headrest under the back of his neck or he could sleep in the manner illustrated in figure 9, a photograph taken by Frobenius in the "Wanoe" (Nohwe) Shona area in 1928, which shows a man sleeping on his side with the headrest under his chin and one ear. Many headrests in museums still have cords attached to them. As can be seen in the turn-of-the-century photograph reproduced in figure 10, Shona men carried the headrests around the neck (as in this example) or at the waist[7] when they were travelling, in the same way a Westerner would carry a bedroll.

Almost without exception, sources in every Shona area claimed that headrests were only used by adult males. Several sources told me that in the olden days a man with several wives would place his headrest by the hut of the wife he was going to sleep with that night. This use was rather poignantly confirmed to me one cold winter morning while I was sitting by a fire in a hut talking to a carver about the various uses of headrests. His grandmother had been quietly sitting beside us listening until this use of the headrests was described. She chuckled, and as she had obviously had some experience in this, said, "Yes, that was true, if you saw the headrest you would know that you were going to have a visitor that night."[8]

In contemporary society the utilitarian aspect of headrest use has nearly ceased and it is very difficult to find any headrests, much less someone who still uses them. Instead, the religious usage of headrests has apparently come to the forefront. Chief Musarurwa of Nharira, for example, explained that the headrest in his posses-

sion had belonged to his grandfather (figs. 11-12). He described how he would bring out the headrest when praying to his ancestors and would begin by saying "Grandfather, here is your headrest ..."[9]

Personal items such as this, if not buried with a person (Magava 1973:154), are distributed to their relatives at an inheritance ceremony (usually known as *nhaka*) after their death. The traditional rules of inheritance are that the position of head of the whole family group (and ownership of family cattle and wives' reproductive value) is first passed on laterally (brother to brother in a single generation) and then lineally (father to son). Personal items are supposed to be distributed equitably by the inheriting head of the household among all of the relatives (Bourdillon 1987:29, 214-16; Holleman 1952:234-40; see also Dewey 1991:24-5). It is not clear from the literature who exactly should receive a man's headrest. From my own limited experience with inherited headrests (only three were actually seen and a few more that my sources no longer possessed were remembered) it appears that they could only be inherited by a male relative. Perhaps inheritance of the headrest also signified the inheritance of the position of head of the family. All examples were from the owner's father or grandfather. Whether in former times, when the headrests had a greater utilitarian function, the

FIG. 8.
Detail of Sekuru Bwanya's headrest.

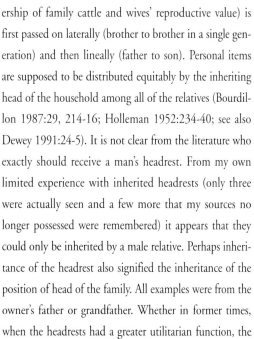

FIG. 7. (left)
Shona spirit medium Sekuru Bwanya with items kept as ritual paraphernalia. Note headrest, said to have been found in cave burial of possessing spirit/former owner. Shamva, central Shona area, Zimbabwe, 1984.

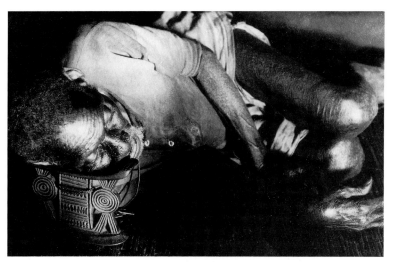

FIG. 9.
A Nohwe Shona man
(central Shona area,
Zimbabwe), sleeping on
his side, using a headrest.
Frobenius expedition
photograph, 1928.

FIG. 10.
Shona men often
carried their headrests
suspended from their
necks when traveling.
Turn-of-the-century
photograph.

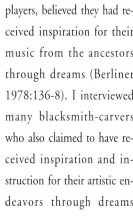

about the ancestors (Dewey 1986; 1991:33-47).

The other category of people who are now still using headrests are spirit mediums such as the one shown in figure 7. For some, such as this spirit medium, Sekuru Bwanya, who had retrieved his headrest (fig. 8) from a cave, it is obviously one of the authenticating symbols or accoutrements of his trade. Other spirit mediums use the headrests in the same way as Chief Nyoka, to facilitate having dreams about the ancestors.[11] Headrests are rarely made presently, but several of the artists who still make them told me that they had been requested to do so by spirit mediums. Though they were not always sure of the intended purpose, they surmised that the headrests were meant to facilitate having dreams of the ancestors.[12]

HEADREST STYLES AND DISTRIBUTION

Previous research has not clarified the parameters of Shona headrest styles and their regional distribution patterns. Turn-of-the-century collectors, as evidenced by many catalogue and accession entries around the world, frequently labeled anything from southern Africa as "Kaffern" (or some variation of that spelling) or "Zulu." This revealed their ignorance of the complex ethnic diversity in the area and also the general prejudice of the time toward lumping any artistic or cultural activity with the best-known and what was considered the "most civilized" group in the area, the Zulu. More recently, any

headrest could be given (if it was not buried) to any male relative (part of the general distribution of personal items) or only to the head of the household is unclear.

Another use of the headrests that continues to be important was explained to me by Chief Nyoka, who said that he had been having problems in judging cases which came before him, and so had a headrest commissioned (fig. 13). By sleeping on it he had dreams that would help him decide the cases.[10] Whether it is done on a headrest or not, dreaming is a very important way of acquiring knowledge for the Shona (Kriel 1971; Lan 1983). Paul Berliner, for example, documented that many musicians, particularly the *mbira* (thumb piano) players, believed they had received inspiration for their music from the ancestors through dreams (Berliner 1978:136-8). I interviewed many blacksmith-carvers who also claimed to have received inspiration and instruction for their artistic endeavors through dreams

headrest from southeastern Africa, if not clearly Zulu, has often been indiscriminately labeled "Shona," as the Shona have now become one of the better-known ethnic groups of the area.

Beyond more general attribution difficulties, there have also been problems understanding the origin of those styles legitimately documented as made by the Shona. Assumptions are often made that there were a large number of styles available in the Shona artist's repertoire, or that the artist typically displayed a great amount of artistic freedom.[13] Alternatively, assumptions are made that the various styles reflected changes (e.g., classic, baroque or degenerated phases) over time. In fact, the available data does not allow for very much historical reconstruction of style change, but does clearly illustrate the existence of a number of regional style areas. This does not mean that there was no variation within style areas, for there obviously was, and some artists were clearly more skilled than others, but the majority of

artists, as is the general pattern throughout Africa, seem to stay within the general framework of the style from their own area.

Hints that there were regional styles came as early as 1892 with Bent's illustration of two different styles of headrest in *The Ruined Cities of Mashonaland* (1892:35, 45). He noted that in "Chibi's country and with the neighboring dependent tribes" a particular pattern of scarification was admired so much that it was put "on their pillows" (1896:47). He later illustrated a variety of scarification patterns of women from different areas (Bent 1892:fig. 164) and thus the question arises, do headrests likewise have regional variations?[14]

FIG. 11. (left) J. Madzivire, Acting chief Musarurwa, of Nharira, with his inherited neckrest, 1984.

FIG. 12. Detail of Chief Musarurwa's headrest, an example of the "central tabbed" style.

The only speculations about style variation since then, according to recorded sources, are seen in Ellert (1984:18-19; see note 14), Berlyn, and Nettleton. Berlyn in a very general article on Shona material culture, says of the headrests,

> Design and height of the upright varies according to the carver's whim, to the availability of the right piece of *mutiti* wood, and, to a lesser extent, to the *rudzi* of the people (clan or tribe). The people of the southern areas use a lower rest than that

FIG. 13.
Chief Nyoka holding his headrest. Manyene, central Shona area, 1984. He commissioned this headrest so that, by sleeping on it, he would have dreams that would help him decide cases.

found in the northern parts of Mashona-land (1968:70).

Nettleton, who does an elaborate stylistic analysis of Shona headrests, comes to the conclusion that

The degree of variation within the headrest form appears to represent differing degrees of status-value, the more elaborate being more valuable, and the appearance of certain motifs only within the more elaborate examples, such as the concentric-circle motif in type A, would suggest a corresponding differentiation in symbolic content. Thus it might be postulated that the headrest types recorded here, types A to H, reflect status relationships rather than area- or family-related differences (1984:126).

She does acknowledge Berlyn's idea about clan or tribe differences (1984:122-3), but links the idea to symbolism rather than style:

If these *hakata* [divination dice] characters are linked to the *mhondoro* [regional guardian spirit] and *mudzimu* [family spir-

it] of the spirit world *(pasi)* as postulated, the use of the designs associated with them in the context of the headrests explains the link between the elaboration of the head-rest and the *rudzi* (patrilineage and founders of the lineage)[15] of the user, pointed to by Berlyn (1968:70). The differences in design between the headrests of types A.1-3 are less radical than the differences in design between headrests of type A as a whole and the other types of Shona headrest. Yet this cannot be explained through a difference in the area of origin of the headrests from the documentation available (1984:157).

The lack of documentation is further acknowledged when she states that she was not

able to correlate the differences of design in the headrests with different districts among the Shona, but this may be owing to the dearth of accurate documentation

FIG. 14.
Shona man with elaborate hairstyle which could be protected by the "stick-type" headrest seen to his right. Thomas Baines' drawing, 1870. British Museum (Natural History), London.

rather than to a lack of such differentiation in the past (1984:125).

Working from some of the same examples that Nettleton used, and other examples from different museums and some field examples, I took a different tack when organizing my corpus of headrest examples. Whereas she organized her examples by "formal types" (1984:123), I organized my examples primarily by geographic region, and then examined style groupings as they related to region. In collecting data I paid particular attention to the attributions of origin in museum records, so the bulk of my illustrations are of those pieces with the best provenance (owners and collectors who are known to have been in particular locations) and the best data on origin.[16] In my dissertation (Dewey 1991) numerous examples are given from various sources[17] as I felt it was better to present as much of the data as possible to prove my points rather than leave the state of Shona stylistic studies susceptible to even more speculation; in this abridged version I will merely outline the areas and give a few examples.

The nature of the evidence upon which I am making my geographic and stylistic conclusions needs some discussion. Museum records for African objects (and for most ethnographic collections) are notorious for giving very little, or no information about who collected an object, or when and where it was collected. If later attributions are given, only rarely will there be any record of who did the attribution and why. Therefore when I was examining museum records, if a specific area or dialect group, or better still, a town, village or chieftaincy was recorded, rather than just "Shona," I assumed that the reason this information was included was that the object had been collected there.

Problems of movement of objects (headrests are of course very mobile) could not be adequately addressed for lack of data, both in the literature and from sources, but I assumed that if several similar examples were said to be from an area they must be typical of the predominant style of the area. It is possible that there were itinerant carvers, or that headrests could have been traded over long distances, but I was never told this by sources and when asked where headrests came from I was usually told that it was experts in the area (occasionally names were remembered) who made them.

In a couple of cases investigations of collectors' identity and where they had travelled, when not included in the museum records, provided enough information to make a hypothesis about where objects had been collected (for example, W.H. Brown and R. Baden-Powell who collected figs. 20 and 23). Further investigation on other collectors would probably be useful. Evidence of in-situ examples that were personally observed or that were in archival photographs was also used, but there were few examples of

FIG. 15.
Eastern style area headrest. Museum für Völkerkunde, Berlin. 13 x 17.3 x 6.8 cm.

this to rely on. The style of headrests made by contemporary carvers was used only when appropriate.[18]

While there is some basis for ascribing specific ethnic attributions to particular styles of stools and headrests (for example, Gwembe Tonga stools or Zulu headrests are very different from Shona headrests), the evidence on Shona headrests points more to style areas that overlap each other and do not coincide with "ethnic boundaries." It should be noted again that the notion of a "Shona" ethnic group is a modern concept (see Ranger 1989; Dewey 1991:8-10). These peoples identified themselves earlier primarily by dialect, regional names, or chieftaincy names. The very concept of ethnic identity is receiving renewed attention in many disciplines. Ethnic identity is not necessarily a fixed concept and it is not conceived of in the same way by all peoples. African art historians are also re-examining ethnic labeling of artistic styles and investigating more closely what happens in the areas where two different styles abut each other (see for example McNaughton 1987). I will first review the evidence and styles from the following Shona areas: eastern, north-eastern, north-central, central, south-west and south-east. I will finally look at some zoomorphically figured headrests.

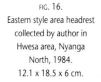

FIG. 16.
Eastern style area headrest collected by author in Hwesa area, Nyanga North, 1984.
12.1 x 18.5 x 6 cm.

Carved wooden headrests[19] were apparently used throughout all of the Shona areas, but it is difficult to distinguish many formal and stylistic features common to all of them because of extensive variety. The basic format of a curved upper platform, a flat bottom platform and some manner of supporting post between the two is common to most Shona headrests and also to many other African groups.

An upper platform that is rectangular both in plan and section is the most consistent feature of all the Shona examples and is quite distinct from, say, Zulu or Swazi upper platforms, which are thicker and often triangular in section (see Conner and Pelrine 1983:37; Wanless 1988:93; Sieber 1980:121-2), or East African types such as Somali headrests, where the upper platforms are usually elliptical in shape (see Sieber 1980:114; Loughran, Johnson and Samatar 1986:54-5) The upper platforms of Pokot, Turkana and Karamajong examples, although also rectangular, usually curve down across the long axis (see Sieber 1980:111-12; Wolfe 1979:14, 18) while the Shona platforms curve up at the ends of this axis. Appendages from the upper platforms of the Shona examples (carved flaps or rings appearing at the sides and/or underneath the platform), or the absence of them, are one of the key elements to differentiate the various Shona substyles.

The central support between the upper platform and the base is generally thin and more narrow than the other two elements, but beyond that it is the most varied of all the elements, with styles ranging from almost square lintels (for example fig. 18) to combinations of circular, triangular and rectilinear shapes (as in fig. 20) to fully three-dimensional figurative supports (fig. 27). The various shapes and decorative details on this central support are the most important distinguishing characteristics of the regional substyles.

The base is usually elliptical or figure-eight shaped, although some of the figured ones have no base. The volumetric shape of the base (whether conical, flat or rounded, with squared-off or tapering edges), is also an important element for differentiating regional styles.

Headrests from the eastern area are usually like those seen in figures 15 and 16. Figure 15 is labeled in Berlin Museum für Völkerkunde records as "Manika und Maswina."[20] Maswina was an old name for Shona (see Rasmussen 1979:316). Manyika (variations, Manica, Manyica or Manyika) can be defined as a linguistic cluster east of the central Zezuru and north of the Ndau-speaking people, which is located mainly in the present-day districts of Makoni, Mutasa, Mutare and Nyanga but also extends into Mozambique[21] (Rasmussen 1979:170). It also was the name of an important kingdom in existence in the area from the sixteenth century onwards (Bhila 1982). While the location indicated for figure 15 is not very precise, the fact that "Manika" is mentioned is probably significant, since in the records for other Berlin examples it is not (they are usually labeled Makalanga or Maswina). Figure 16[22] is from a northern Nyanga area where the Hwesa under Chief Katerere live. This is just outside the Manyika area and in fact technically it is not a Shona-speaking area. It is important to note, however, that the area was conquered by the Manyika in the late eighteenth and early nineteenth centuries, and the language of the area is a hybrid cross between Shona and

Sena (Beach 1980:186). This will be the first of several examples of the futility of trying to neatly fit particular styles with particular ethnic groups.

The style in this area usually adheres to the following parameters.[23] The upper platform has no appendages and is consistently decorated on the upturned ends of the platform with a chip-carved series of parallel lines, diamonds or a zig-zag line. The top surface of the platform invariably has at least two sets of triangles carved into it. The triangles are invariably composed of smaller triangles within a larger one with the apexes pointing toward each other. The bases are usually figure-eight shaped in plan, and gently taper inward toward the central support. The bases have downward-pointing V-shaped protrusions carved onto them bisecting each side of the base. The central support consistently is composed of two pairs of upward- and downward-pointing V-shapes separated by two circular shapes. The Vs have a series of two to three lines parallel to the Vs carved in them and the circles have two to four concentric circles carved within them. The centers of the circles have various geometric designs in them, dots, horizontal lines, diagonal crosses or a pair of diamonds. The triangular spaces between the branches of the Vs and the central circular motifs are cut more deeply than the surrounding areas, or are cut right through. Sometimes the circular motifs abut each other and in the others they are separated by either a horizontal or vertical band filled with zig-zag lines, diagonal crosses or diamonds. These decorative bands between the circular and V-shaped motifs are much smaller than those seen in the headrests of the central style region.

The geographic core area for this eastern style seems to be the area where the Manyika linguistic group live, in east central Zimbabwe and extending over the border into Mozambique. How far south the style goes is unknown. There is very little Ndau material in museums and in my brief visit to the Ndau area I saw no headrests. The eastern style extends into the central part of Zimbabwe, but a slightly different style is more common there. To the north the style can be seen extending into the Budya area[24] and a few similar examples occur even across the border into Zambia,[25] but other styles also exist in this northeastern area.

The next style area, from the northeastern region, is illustrated by figures 17 and 18.[26] Figure 17 was collected by Leo Frobenius from the "Batonga of Portuguese East Africa,"[27] a non-Shona-speaking group usually referred to as Barwe-Tonga. Figure 18 from the Queen Victoria Museum in Harare is recorded as coming from the "Budjga" people, from "Mutoko kraal, Mutoko."

The style of base in this northeastern area is the same as that seen in the eastern area. The upper platform is also basically the same, with the possible exception that opposed triangle motifs do not appear here as consistently. The central rectilinear supporting pillars, however, make this style area quite distinct from the eastern one. These pillars are sometimes separated by small horizontal rods (e.g. fig. 17, where the rod is partially obscured by the shadow). No circular motifs appear ornamenting the surface of these pillars, but otherwise the same motifs used to ornament the central elements of the eastern area headrests—parallel lines, zig-zags, diagonal crosses and diamonds—also ornament the supporting elements of

FIG. 17.
Northeastern style headrest
collected by Leo Frobenius
in Barwe-Tonga area,
Mozambique, 1928.
Museum für Völkerkunde,
Frankfurt.
11.5 x 13.2 x 5 cm.

the northeastern area headrests. Two headrests from the Joss collection, cat. nos. 98 and 99, clearly fit into the style parameters of this area. While there is no provenance information for one, the other (cat. 98) is said to have been collected from a "Kalanga chief in the Mteka region." The Kalanga label does not necessarily mean the ethnic group of that name in the west of present-day Zimbabwe and northeastern Botswana, for at the turn of the century Shona speakers were sometimes referred to as "Karanga" or "Kalanga." The "Mteka" region could be a misspelling of Mutoko, a Budya, Shona area where similar headrests have been found.

The geographic center for this style area appears to be among the Barwe-Tonga and Budya peoples of northeastern Zimbabwe. How far into Mozambique the style extended is unknown. It does not seem to have extended very far to the west of the Budya or Tavara but, occasionally is seen to the south in the eastern and central style areas.

The next style area, from the north-central area of Zimbabwe, is represented by figure 19.[28] This example was collected by Richard Douglas in the Mazoe district.[29] Like the northeastern style, the most important distinguishing characteristics in the north-central style are found in the decoration on the central support. The base is essentially the same as in the two previous styles with the exception that three-lobed examples are more common here. The upper platform never appears to have the opposed triangle motif on its upper surface, but the ends usually have the typical zig-zag, parallel line or diamond motif on them. The central support portion is composed of opposed triangle shapes separated by circular motifs in a fashion similar to the eastern style, but the surface decoration is quite different and the negative space between the shapes is always cut right through. These primary shapes are sometimes separated by small horizontal rods, as is seen in this example and as has been

noted is the fashion in the northeast style area. This north-central area is also the area where, in addition to the more typical pattern of two pillars, three central pillars[30] and multiple circular motifs (usually in multiples of two, on top of each other) occur quite regularly. The surface decoration in the central area is, however, the most important characteristic for distinguishing this style. The two most typical patterns are horizontal lines dividing areas of closely spaced parallel vertical lines or attenuated diamonds, and closely spaced parallel angled lines with one side of the angle parallel to one side of the V-shape and the other horizontal. This tendency towards dense surface decoration is also seen in the center of the circular motifs. Here is seen the same type of parallel line, in addition to closely packed rows of zig-zags, diamonds and dots.

The main geographic area for this style seems to be among the Korekore of north-central Zimbabwe, extending to the south into the northern Zezuru Shawasha area, to the east to the Budya of the Mutoko area and to the northeast into the Barwe-Tonga area.[31] How far the style extends to the west is unknown. No collections are known to have been documented from that far western area, nor was it visited during my fieldwork. One exam-

FIG. 18.
Northeastern style headrest collected in Budya area, Mutoko, 1963.
Queen Victoria Museum, Harare.
14 x 8.5 x 6.3 cm.

ple from the Joss collection, cat. 100, seems to be have some characteristics that are typical of that area. In particular, note the surface treatment of the central area with densely packed horizontal elements (straight lines and zig-zags). The shape of the central support, however, is more typical of the next style area to be discussed, so perhaps a "borderland" example with influence from both areas is represented here.

The next central style area includes figure 20, which was acquired by William Harvey "Curio" Brown in Chief Musha-yamombe's area[32] within the Zezuru dialect area, and figure 21, which was labeled as being from "Rusape." Three field examples that can be added to this set of examples include figures 7 and 8 from Shamva, another northern Zezuru area; figure 9, a photograph taken during the Frobenius expedition of 1928 in the "Wanoe" (Nohwe) area, a northeastern Zezuru area; and figures 11 and 12, the headrest of a Rosvi chief from Nharira, Charter district. Within this central area three style variants co-exist. The first is exemplified by figures 9 and 20. This style is very similar to the eastern style in almost all respects. The main differences are that the central rectangular element (horizontal or vertical) in the middle support is usually wider than that seen in the eastern area. The opposed triangle pattern typically

seen on the top surface of the upper platform of eastern examples is rare in this area in all three style variants, and the central support occasionally has three (rather than the more common two) opposed triangles separated by a circular motif, such as is more common in the north-central area. Cat. 101 from the Joss collection, with its three central circular motifs, is perhaps from this area.

Horizontal type surface decoration, again more common in the north-central area, only occasionally appears in this central area. There is a tendency for the V-shapes of the central supports to become more U-shaped and the lines of the surface decorations are more widely spaced and deeply cut (see fig. 12) than in the other style areas. The parallel lines in the V or U areas of the central supports are sometimes replaced by rows of raised dots or diamonds[33] (figs. 7 and 8 show a related style from this area).

Closely related to this style is the variant typified by figures 21, 7 and 8.[34] All details of this style variant are like the previous one with the exception that the circle motifs on the central support become, on at least one side of the headrest and sometimes on both, a horizontally elongated oval motif.

The third style variant of the area, which I will call

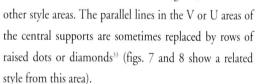

FIG. 19.
North-central headrest, collected by Richard Douglas in Mazoe area, 1906. American Museum of Natural History, New York.
14.5 x 16.3 x 6.7 cm.

the "central tabbed" style, is exemplified by figures 11 and 12.[35] This style variant tends to have a more widely spaced variety of surface decoration carved on the central support and either has the two opposed Vs or Us separated by a circular motif or three opposed V or U shapes, as is seen in this example. The most important distinguishing characteristic for this style variant is the presence of rectangular tabs or flaps placed at either end, underneath the upper platform, and always placed perpendicular to the main plane of the headrest's central support. The usual surface motifs seen on these tabs are zig-zag lines, parallel lines and concentric squares.

The geographic limits of the first of these style variants is problematic. The style seems to center in the Zezuru area, but is occasionally seen further north, for example in the Mutoko area. To the east there seems to be a gradual shift from central to eastern styles with significant overlap of the two styles. How far the style extends to the west is unknown as there are few documented collections from those areas. To the south this style begins to mix with the "tabbed" style among the southern Zezuru, but how far south it extends is unknown. The second style variant, with the elliptical central motif, has the same geographic distribution as the one just described. The third "central tabbed" style variant is present only in the southern portion of this area. It would be tempting to associate this style with an ethnic group but the data will not allow this. Frobenius labels the example he collected in Marondera district as Zezuru.[36] The ones from Charter district, however, he does not give ethnic labels to and could be Rosvi[37] (like figs. 11 and 12), Njanja (Zezuru) or Hera (Zezuru or Karanga). As with

the other styles it seems better to think of it as a regional style rather than an ethnic one.

The next style area, from the southwest, is represented by figures 22 and 23. Figure 22 was collected by Bent in Chief Chibi's area where the Mhari (subgroup of the Karanga) live. Figure 23, which was collected by Robert Baden-Powell, is identified in the Pitt Rivers Museum records as being "Matabele." In his book, *The Matabele Campaign* (1896), Baden-Powell describes, however, how in the battle against Chief Wedza[38] he and his men came upon Wedza's abandoned village and "each man carries an empty nose-bag [presumably a horse feeding bag], and as soon as these are filled (with corn), and some errant chickens killed with sticks, and curios taken from the huts, we burn the kraal" (1897:392-3). I strongly suspect therefore that the headrest was acquired here from Wedza's Shona,[39] rather than among the Ndebele.[40]

This style is clearly very different from those styles to the north. The collection data for my examples, however, is so meager that any conclusions must be regarded as being tentative. The bases of this group, although usually figure-eight in plan, are for the most part higher and more conical than examples to the north. One of the most important distinguishing characteristics between southwestern styles and southeastern styles seems to be that the bases of those to the east are like those of the Tsonga, board-like and flat, while those to the west are more conical. The upper platform of the southwestern type is either undecorated on the top or has zig-zag, diamond or parallel lines on the upturned ends (fig. 23) as is typical for the other Shona style areas. The upper platforms almost always (fig. 22 is an exception) have

FIG. 20.
Central style headrest
collected by William H.
Brown, probably in Chief
Mushayamombe's area,
1893. National Museum
of Natural History,
Smithsonian Institution,
Washington, D.C.
Height, 11.5 cm.

appendages on their lower surfaces. Some are of the same rectangular variety as seen in the "central tabbed" style area and others are of the semi-circular ring variety (such as fig. 23).[41] The central support is composed of a series of cylindrical columns (occasionally rectangular in section) which are divided by, or are on top of, a larger shape (sometimes rectangular, sometimes ellipsoidal). The sides of these latter shapes are often ornamented with zig-zags, diamonds or interlace.

The geographic extent of this style is very hard to pinpoint because so little is known of Kalanga, Basuto or Venda[42] headrests. Nettleton, however, notes that in "Botswana a particular shape of headrest using as a caryatid a semicircle standing on its ends with two to three columns supported on its arc seems to have been current in the late nineteenth century" (1991:153).[43] Those seem very similar

FIG. 21.
Central style headrest
collected in Rusape area
before 1927.
Cambridge University,
Museum of Archaeology
and Ethnology.
No dimensions available.

there is little Zimbabwean collection data for examples from this area and much confusion as to what the ethnic labels mean. Figure 24 was collected from Jekero village, Zaka district, in 1984. The carver, Muraho Thully, a seventy-seven-year-old man who claimed to have always lived there, is, I believe, either of Karanga or Duma descent. Figure 25[44] is said to be from "Chimanimani," an Ndau, Shona area. An example from the Joss collection, cat. 105, is quite obviously done in the same style. Numerous similar examples (headrests in the same style with attached staves) are housed in the Museu de Historia Natural in Maputo. None of them have any documentation but I suspect they are Tsonga or Ndau. Other well-provenanced headrests are said to be "Shangaan"[45] from the Chipinge area of eastern Zimbabwe.

The upper platforms in this style usually have the typical zig-zag, diamonds or parallel lines ornamenting the upper ends. The upper platforms almost always have appendages hanging from their lower surfaces. These can be either rectangular, semicircular, or ring-like and placed parallel to either of the main two axes of the headrest.

The base is usually elliptical or figure-eight shaped. A variation of the figure-eight shaped base that has two Vs inserted between the two lobes, as is seen in figure 25, seems restricted to this style area. The bases are usually quite flat and squared-off, but not always. The bases with more tapering sides may be restricted to the overlap areas with the style areas to the north, northwest and west, or to the Mozambique coastal areas such as the Chopi area.

The central supports display a number of different patterns. Rectilinear pillars (single or double) with horizontal fluting is a common one. Squared-off or rounded

to the southwestern Shona style so I would put them in the same style area. It appears to be a style which extends to the south and west beyond Zimbabwe's borders.

In the Joss collection, cat. 104 seems to be exactly like the Botswana ones described by Nettleton which I would place in this regional style of southwestern Zimbabwe, eastern Botswana. Cat. 103 is quite similar to the Baden-Powell example except for the rectangular tabs off the upper platform, two as opposed to three upper supporting columns and the horizontal striations on the rectangular dividing block. Cat. 102 also seems to fit in this style area even though the conical lobes of the base are separated rather than forming the usual figure-eight shape.

The final style area to be considered, from the southeast, is represented by figures 24 and 25. Once again diagonal X-shapes are seen, as are columns on dividing supports such as is seen on the Joss collection example, cat. 106. Headrests from the Tsonga of southern Mozambique and northeastern South Africa seem to have an almost infinite variety of designs on the central support (Wanless 1985-1990; Becker 1992). How much of this tendency also occurred among the southeastern Shona groups is hard to tell. Fully three-dimensional figures also occasionally appear. Carved wooden chains, such as that seen connecting the two headrests in figure 24[46] are also a stylistic feature particular to this area of Zimbabwe[47] but also extending to the southeast right down to the Zulu area. Cat. nos. 107 and 108 of the Joss collection (both Tsonga examples from Mozambique or South Africa), for example, are carved in this manner. Both are carved of a single piece of wood with the wooden chain connecting the two headrests.

It is clear that the style of this southeastern area is very close to that of the Tsonga,[48] if not the same. The style seems to encompass the Ndau areas as well as the southeastern Zezuru and eastern Karanga among Shona speakers, and then extends from the far southeastern (Hlengwe, Tsonga) areas of Zimbabwe into the Tsonga and Chopi areas of Mozambique and south into the Transvaal area of South Africa. Again the futility of trying to restrict style areas to particular ethnic groups is quite apparent with these examples. More work is needed to distinguish substyles within this area. An attempt to correlate these substyles with historical events (kingdoms, migrations, etc.) would also be most interesting to explore.

Several headrests from the Joss collection, cat. nos. 109-112, seem to fit somewhere on the margins between the central and southeastern style areas. Perhaps they are from the eastern Karanga areas but I have no documented or field collected examples to support this and can only surmise this based on their style. The rectangular tabs appended to the upper platforms place them as being southern Shona. Their bases with sloping sides and downward-pointing V-shapes bisecting each side seem to take them out of the areas of the either the southeastern style area with its flat, board-like base or the southwest with its more conical bases. The central supports with their X-shaped forms also show characteristics of both central "tabbed" style and southeastern style. It is hoped that further archival and field studies will help localize these styles more precisely.

The last set of headrest examples to be considered are those with zoomorphic representations.[49] Only two Zimbabwe examples have good collection information. One was collected by Frobenius from the Charter district (Dewey 1991:fig. 151) and as with the other examples he collected there, it could be Rosvi, Njanja or Hera. Figure 26 from the Queen Victoria Museum in Harare is recorded as coming from "Zimunya T.T.L [Tribal Trust Land, now called Communal Areas], Umtali, Manicaland."[50] Zimunya is just to the south of the modern city of Mutare and although it is usually thought of as a Manyika-speaking area, it is close to the Mozambique border and the Ndau are neighbors to the south.

Figure 27 is one of the few examples without appendages from their upper platforms, and clearly adheres in its other characteristics to either the central or eastern style areas. The positioning of the torso of the "animal" between the inverted V-shapes of the central support is the only known example like it. It seems to be on the edge of the main area of zoomorphic headrest production, and to have combined some of the stylistic features of that area with those of stylistic area they are closest to.

Figure 26 and cat. nos. 114 and 115[51] are representative of the main area of zoomorphic headrest production which corresponds almost exactly with the southeastern

FIG. 22.
Southwestern style
headrest collected by J.T.
Bent in Chief Chibi's Mhari
area, 1891. Museum of
Mankind, London.
17 x 19.3 x 5.7 cm.

style area already described. It encompasses southeastern Shona groups of Zimbabwe (and probably southern Shona and Ndau groups of Mozambique) and Tsonga groups of Zimbabwe, Mozambique and the Transvaal area of South Africa.[52] All of these headrests have quadruped caryatid figures whose feet flare out at the bottom, no base, rectangular pillars or rounded columns between the animal and the upper platform, and rectangular or half-ring appendages[53] underneath the upper platforms. Cat. 116, but for its base with the flat board-like characteristics of other non-zoomorphic headrests of this area,[54] exhibits the same style. The shapes of the animals' heads, horns (or ears) and eyes, and the degree of overall surface decoration are quite variable but because

southeastern Africa is not an area with a strong figure-carving tradition, I conclude that these examples hold together as a cohesive style area.

This proposed schema for a mapping of Shona headrest styles obviously must be viewed as a preliminary attempt. More work is needed to determine what the parameters of style are in all of the areas that surround the Shona-speaking peoples. More work is also needed within the Shona areas. Headrests are fast disappearing from the entire area, but a concerted attempt must be made to document headrests that are still retained as family heirlooms and find out as much as possible about the histories of each individual headrest and what their owners may know about the artists who created them. Additional research is also needed to try to discover more about the origins of the hundreds of examples in European and American museums and private collections.

SYMBOLISM

Given the foregoing description of Shona headrest styles and their geographic distribution, it is now appropriate to look at the symbolism which may be embodied in them. Interpretations offered by other scholars will be examined first and then the Shona explanations that I was able to elicit during my fieldwork will be reviewed. Any conclusions that I have been able to draw will also be presented.

J.T. Bent was the first to offer an explanation of the meaning of the headrests. "These pillows are many of them pretty objects, and decorated with curious patterns, the favorite one being the female breast, and resting on legs which had evidently been evolved out of human form" (1896:36). His only other comment comes in a discussion on cicatrization when he compares a particular pattern to "the furrows on a ploughed field" and claims it was such a favorite in

> Chibi's country and with the neighboring
> dependant tribes for female decoration,
> and they admire it so much that they put
> it also on their drums, on their granaries,
> and on their pillows and, as I have said, on
> their forges. The "breast and furrow" pat-
> tern, one might technically term it, and I
> fancy it has to do with an occult idea of
> fertility (1896:47-8).

His conclusions are apparently based on a very small sample of objects. Only two headrests illustrate his book and only ten that he collected are in the Museum of Mankind collections in London. Of these, one is from Botswana, another two are very unusual in comparison to a larger corpus or perhaps are from a "borderland" area, and two are from Chibi's area in the southwest, leaving only four[55] that on the basis of style are from the central or eastern style areas. The "breast and furrow" idea he seems to have gotten in the southwest area where he saw scarification patterns (1896:304), granaries (1896:46), drums (1896:78) and smelting furnaces (1896:308) that displayed the same pattern, and then applied the idea to headrests that turn out to be from the central area. Bent's expertise was as an archaeologist in the Middle East and although his is one of the better accounts of Shona life at that time, he was only there a few months and should hardly be considered an expert. It is doubtful if he ever asked any Shonas what was being represented on the vari-

ous artifacts and why. In the case of the headrests (as will be discussed) it is doubtful the circular motifs on headrests are even meant to represent breasts.

Hugh Marshall Hole, an early administrator and amateur historian, repeats many of Bent's ideas.

> Their implements for example, frequently
> bore evidence of a form of sex-worship.

FIG. 23.
Southwestern style
area headrest collected by
Robert Baden-Powell,
probably among Chief
Wedza's Dumbuseya, in
1896-97. Pitt Rivers
Museum, Oxford.
13 x 15.3 x 7.7 cm.

> The earthenware furnaces in which they
> smelted iron were rudely modeled to imi-
> tate a woman's trunk and legs, the upper
> part being decorated with moldings of the
> two breasts and navel, and indented marks
> corresponded to the pattern with which
> women tattooed their stomachs — differ-
> ing for each tribal division. Similar designs,
> sometimes more, sometimes less conven-
> tionalized, were carved on their wooden
> war drums, on the headrests which served
> as pillows and on other articles of common
> use, and it was a custom in some districts
> to reproduce the breasts, navel and tattoo

FIG. 24.
Southeastern style
area headrest collected by
author in 1984 from carver,
Muraho Thully, Jekero
village, Zaka.
14 + 13.7 x 22.8 + 23
(overall with chain)
x 9 + 9.3 cm.

marks in the clay forming the interior of
dwelling huts (1928:48).

Hole obviously had many years of experience among the
Shona, but it is not clear what body parts he feels are reproduced on the headrests. It also seems evident that he
had read and been influenced by Bent.

The next interpretation seems to be from Berlyn (already mentioned in the style section), who only says that
the headrest designs vary "to a lesser extent" according to
the clan or tribe of the maker (1968:70). Ellert feels that
there is no significance in the designs of the headrests
and states, "it has been suggested that the two circular
patterns common to some examples represent the female
breasts but this could not be substantiated. This would
tend to suggest ownership by a woman whilst the other
type of *mutsago* [headrest] would have belonged to a
man" (1984:18). Ellert was on the right track in dis-
counting the breast idea, but evidently believes that various regional styles are made and used in the same area.

Another person who has done work on the symbolism of the Shona headrests is Anitra Nettleton, who

devoted a large portion of her dissertation (1984) to the
topic, and has recently published a summary of some of
her ideas (1990). Her style analysis has already been examined in the section on style, and although she came
up with some thought-provoking ideas on the symbolism
of Shona headrests, it is clear that her misinterpretation
of the nature of Shona headrest style distribution has
contributed to a misconception of headrest symbolism
as well.

One of the key components of Nettleton's interpretation is the linking of the meaning of the motifs seen on
Shona divination dice *(hakata)* with the meaning of the
motifs seen on the headrests. One of the main problems
with this is that the divination dice have not historically
been used by all Shona groups, as Nettleton implies.
Today there is a lot of mixing of traditions because of the
greater mobility of people (among other reasons) and I
found (in conducting interviews) that the divination dice
were almost universally recognized throughout the various Shona areas. Those in the northern and eastern areas
I talked to, however, invariably declared that they "tradi-

tionally" had used seed pods or bones for divination in their areas (see also Bourdillon 1987:153-4).

Even within the central and southern areas where the divination dice have long been used, there are questions as to whether there is one overriding set of motif interpretations that all groups adhered to (see also Bourdillon 1987:155-6). Likewise I wonder if the knowledge of the symbols and their meanings was restricted primarily to the diviners and not part of the broader general cosmological knowledge of the people.[56] There is also a question of whether there is a universal "decorative language in which certain messages or meanings are encoded" (Nettleton 1984:124-5) for the motifs on all Shona decorative work (the same motifs occur on pottery, baskets, house painting, knives, axes and snuff bottles in addition to headrests), or even a common one shared between divination dice and headrests. My sources almost never saw any connection between the decorations on the divination dice and any other type of object and even when asked a leading question like, "don't these designs look like those on the *hakata*," would acknowledge the similarity, but claim there was no implied common meaning. Nettleton's assertion of a common symbolic language for divination dice and headrests is therefore suspect.

Nettleton correctly made a connection between the surface decorations on the headrests and female cicatrization (scarification). As I will show later, the cicatrization designs also have regional distributions, so there can be no one set of designs that can be read as cicatrization on the headrests as Nettleton implies (1984:139). My sources, however, did regularly give the same name,

nyora, to both body and headrest scarification. Nettleton's identification of a zig-zag line seen on some headrests as a Shona women's waist girdle, *mutimwe*, is also questionable (1984:106-9, 177, 181). The kind of beads she describes in the holdings of the Queen Victoria Museum as being *mutimwe* sound more like *tsungare*, or the band of beadwork worn round a woman's head. The *mutimwe* beads I saw, or was told about, were composed of strands of single beads (see also Bent 1896:44). While the *mutimwe* beads are an important symbol used to signify transitional stages in a woman's life (Aquina 1968; Aschwanden 1982:80-90 passim), it is doubtful that they were represented with a set design motif on the headrests, as Nettleton proposes.

Nettleton's most problematic analysis is her insistence that the concentric circle motif equals breasts (1984: 132-6, 139). As part of her proof she notes that Bent (1892:268) and Franklin (1945:4, 6) both illustrate breasts that are represented on Shona smelting furnaces with the use of the same circle-dot motif as appear on the headrests. My copy of Franklin, however, shows three-dimensional breasts. I am also not convinced that in Bent's line drawing of a furnace (1896:308) or his drawings of drums and a granary which also are ornamented with the "breast and furrow" motif (1896:78, 46), the breasts were intended to be "read" as being two-dimensional. Her point that there is a difference in the Shona representation of breasts in clay and wood (three-dimensional and two-dimensional respectively) because they are different types of medium and worked by different sexes (women-clay, men-wood) is also not convincing because the furnaces of clay are made by men and some headrests, which have the flat circle motif on one side, also have three-dimensional breasts on the other.

If the headrest is to be interpreted as a torso, her point that the circles are found midway between the two platforms, which would be anatomically correct, is true. But she does not then explain the reasons for triple and multiple circle motifs or for some, admittedly unusual ones, where the circles appear as pendants to the upper platform. While she does say the motif could alternatively be meant to symbolize eyes or pools, she never mentions the only thing that my sources ever told me the circle motif represents, a circular conus shell ornament known as *ndoro*.

Nettleton's best idea links the "headless" nature of both headrests and smelting furnaces with the Shona belief that a woman's fertility is only on loan to the husband's family and notes that this has been verbally expressed in the saying *Mukwasha chake mutimbi, musoro, ndowavatezvara* ('as for the son-in-law, his is her body, but her head belongs to her father') (Nettleton 1984:141, quoting Hodza and Fortune 1979:324). It is an idea that deserves further research. Unfortunately, however, Nettleton's laudable goal of showing how the headrests "may be a symbol of sexual identity, moral or ethical values and cosmological concepts" (1984:52) is not realized. She provides little or no field data to support her linkage of Shona cosmology and the headrests.

Trying to elicit information about the meaning and symbolism of the headrests from Shona sources proved to be a difficult task for me as well. Part of this stems from the fact that in any society such knowledge is not always widely known. Compounding this in the case of the Shona is the fact that the headrests are rarely used in contemporary society and few that I interviewed had ever seen a headrest, much less owned one. However most people had at least heard of them and knew some basic information of how they were used and who used them. The most common answer given as to why headrests were decorated and what the decorations mean was: to beautify *(kunangaidza),* to decorate *(kunyerenyeta* or *kushongedza),* or to make it look attractive *(kunangaidza).* Such answers should not be viewed as an indication that the person did not know any deeper meaning, for it seems clear that not all decorative details were ever meant to have symbolic meaning. The act of embellishing or decorating may have a deeper significance beyond just being the carrier of specific symbolic messages.

While the breasts on headrests[57] were always identified as such by my sources, the concentric circle motifs were never identified in that way. They were, however, identified by several carvers and a chief as being a conus shell ornament known as *ndoro.* (The meaning of this ornament and its applicability to headrest symbolism will be discussed later.) It is not surprising that those who knew this information were experts who would have paid more attention to such matters, or that they all came from the central or eastern style areas where headrests have "traditionally" been carved with the concentric circle motif.

It is also significant that many people identified the incised surface decorations on the headrests (and axe blades and knife sheaths) as *nyora,* the same word as is used for human cicatrization.[58] One carver, Stephen Dekeya, even volunteered the information that a "husband would wake up with cicatrization on his face the following morning (having slept on a headrest with these incisions on the upper platform) and cause the women to laugh as they loved to see that."[59]

The only more elaborate explanations were provided by two carvers from the eastern style area, Joram Mariga and Brush Masusa. Mariga explained that

> Mutsago long ago was a woman. Can you see here that which is like a moon [the upper platform], it's a woman's hand carrying her husband's head. This and that [pointing to the concentric circle motifs on a headrest], are *ndoro* which were put on the forehead or tied around the neck. *Ndoro* are for great hunters. You see these scarifications they are for the hands and face of a woman. These *ndoro* are used to dream for meat by *hombarume* [title given to great hunters]. Can you see these, [pointing to the V shape on the base, then said in English] these are female organs.[60]

Brush Mususa explained that on his headrests (fig. 16), the central support area represented two hunters with the upper Vs representing their arms and the lower, downward pointing Vs representing their legs. The concentric circle motifs, he said, were *ndoros* to show that the men were hunters and were utilized to please the *shave* or ancestral spirits and insure that the hunt was successful. The V-shape on the base represented the groin area of the hunter's wife.[61]

I am not positive that the two explanations of Mariga and Mususa are independent[62] of each other, nor am I sure that they are not isolated, imaginative explanations, with little cosmological or historical basis, given to answer an inquisitive investigator. They do however, seem to fit into the pattern of other information offered by independent Shona sources, and so while I am not willing to accept them as the complete answer to the meaning of the headrests, they should not be discounted.

Several key concepts are relevant in interpreting the headrests' meaning. These include cicatrization *(nyora)* and the conus shell ornaments *(ndoro)*. It is necessary to

FIG. 25. Southeastern style area staff with headrest and snuff bottle, collected in Chimanimani area. Mutare Museum, Zimbabwe.

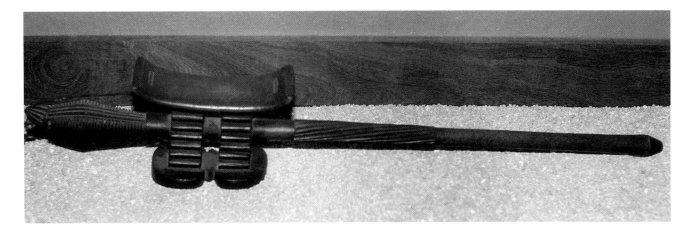

summarize what the importance of these are in Shona society before proposing any hypothesis on the symbolism of headrests.

CICATRIZATION MOTIFS

Cicatrization has virtually disappeared from practice in most Shona areas, but there are enough brief descriptions in written accounts, and some photographic and diagrammatic documentation to at least construct an outline of the former practices. Gelfand and Swart (1953), in the only published study of body scarification in Zimbabwe, correctly classify the types of *nyora* into those made for medical and magical purposes on men or women, and those, which are pertinent to this study, classified as "tribal beautification" patterns which are only made on women.

FIG. 26.
Eastern style area zoomorphic headrest collected in Zimunya area. Queen Victoria Museum, Harare.
17.5 x 16.4 x 8 cm.

The "tribal *nyora*," they point out, have both public and private aspects (the latter intended only to be viewed by a woman's husband), and were almost invariably put on women at puberty.[63] The reasons their subjects gave for having them done included group identification ("to keep up the nation ... it is our custom") and enhancement of beauty and sexual stimulation (1953:7). My sources echoed these ideas; Chiefs Katerere and Zimunya, for example, both explained that they were to show ethnic group affiliation, and Chief Chiswiti explained that they were to "beautify ... and make them (women) attractive to men." Chief Maranke said they were done "so they (women) could quickly arouse the opposite member's nature."[64]

Distribution of cicatrization motifs seem to follow regional rather than strictly ethnic patterns in a way very similar to headrest style distribution. Documentation for the motifs of various areas is examined in my dissertation (1991:203-206) and will not be repeated here. What is immediately clear is that the cicatrization motifs do not match the headrest motifs from each respective style area (as Nettleton implies) in more than a general way. The linkage of female body cicatrization and headrest surface decoration sources spoke of using the word, *nyora*, must therefore be thought of as a metaphoric link (both are "cut" and meant to "beautify") rather than a literal one (where the motifs correspond).

SHELL ORNAMENTS

Throughout the history of *ndoro* use in the Shona area it has been associated with political and religious leadership or thought of as a prestige adornment. Today the shell ornaments are very hard to find in anyone's possession, but copies fabricated in either plaster or plastic are still sold in markets and the disks are still important religious emblems.

Conus shell disks have been used throughout central and Southern Africa for many years. Jane Safer, in a general account of how shells function as emblems of status notes that conus shell disks are

> circulated widely as media of exchange in Angola, Zambia, Mozambique and Southern Zaire. Cut from Leopard Cone *(Conus leopardus)*, Betuline Cone *(c. betulinus)* and Prometheus Cone *(c. prometheus)*, they were commonly called *mpande* shells. In the mid-nineteenth century the British explorer and missionary, Dr. David Livingstone [1858], reported that two cone shell disks could purchase a slave, while five bought an elephant's ivory tusk. Anyone might own a cone shell disk, but in most tribes only individuals of high rank could wear them as ornaments, although the precise category of high ranking personage varies from group to group (1982:97-8).

Among the Shona there is archaeological, historical and contemporary data[65] relating to the usage of the cone shell ornaments, but there does not seem to be any one type of usage (denoting political, religious or economic status) that has predominated.

Joao dos Santos, a Portuguese who traveled among the Shona, recorded in 1609 that

> Monomotapa and the Mocarangas his vassals, wear a white shell on the forehead, hanging from the hair as an ornament, and Monomotapa wears another large shell on his breast. These shells they call *andoros [ndoro]* (Theal 1893-1903 7:1289).

At some point after this, the Portuguese began to mass-produce porcelain copies of the natural conus shell disks for trade into the area. It is not uncommon now to find quite old copies such as these in possession of Shona families (Loveridge 1982:188; Ellert 1982:120-1, 1984:115-22, 1985:4-5).

In 1895 Alice Balfour noted that "another much-prized ornament you occasionally see [among the Shona] is an ivory-colored disk, with a hole in the middle by which it is hung round the neck. The disk is about as large as the bottom of a tumbler, and with a deep spiral groove on one side, the other being quite smooth" (1895:215-216). Harold Von Sicard (1953) has noted that the shells functioned both as a symbol of authority and as items of value that could be traded. Ellert notes that there are legends according magical powers to one of these ornaments (1984:120) and that occasionally the shells are used by *n'angas* for divinations and cures and that people possessed by *shave* spirits often wear them (1984:122).

The photographic record from the turn of the century indicates that the shells were worn as ornaments by both men and women. The context of these photographs (whether they were posed or natural situations) is unclear, so little can be generalized from them other than to note that the shells appear to have been a common form of adornment during that period.

The majority of my sources in 1984 were able to identify the conus shell I carried as an example by the name *ndoro*, but explanations about the usage of the *ndoro* shell varied greatly among the various Shona groups and from individual to individual. All of them seemed to indicate an association with either political leadership or religious usage, or that the shells were used as body ornamentation by those who could afford them.

Symbolism Conclusions

The fact that the female pubic area and female type scarification *(nyora)* are so prominently and consistently portrayed on headrests from almost all the Shona areas, means it must have been, at least in part, conceived of as being symbolic of the female gender.[66] Not just any female, but one who has reached puberty, has had the cicatrix cut on her body, and thus can be a bride, sexually please her husband and bear children. This is reinforced by sources' information that it is mature men who slept with the headrest and used it to indicate who their sleeping partners would be. That Shona men in a patrilineal society would so regularly use a female symbol must be tied to the fact that they practice exogamy (must marry someone outside of their own clan), and are depend on women of other lineages to loan their fertility or childbearing ability to their own lineages in order to ensure continuity and growth. The headrests therefore visually acknowledge the importance of women and more specifically wives,[67] in what may seem to be a male dominated society.

The prominence given by the Shona to the *nyora*, scarification, on their women and their headrests, fits in well with Arnold Rubin's remarks that such embellishments throughout the world are seen by their makers as marks of "perfection" on the body, and function as signs that the recipient has become socialized, enculturated and "civilized" (Rubin 1988:14, drawing on ideas from Vogel and Cole). The fact that the cicatrization also has erotic functions does not negate these meanings. Allen Roberts, investigating Tabwa scarification patterns, has cogently shown that there can be a reconciliation of the two seemingly contradictory concepts, for "eroticism leads to conception, birth, parenthood, and the furtherance of lineage and society. Eroticism, however, like other passions, must not be allowed free or excessive expression, but must be refined and channeled by the society. Nature is perfected by culture" (Roberts in Rubin 1988:48).

The identification of the concentric circle motifs as the *ndoro* ornaments, rather than as breasts, provides for a more satisfactory explanation of their occurrence on the headrests for (unlike breasts) the *ndoro* can be worn in various numerical combinations and on various parts of the body. The reasons for inclusion of the *ndoro* ornaments on the headrests are, however, more oblique. The gender of who wore the *ndoros* is not as important as the implied status they denoted, whether political, religious or pecuniary in nature. Shona society of the past century does not seem to be characterized by important class distinctions (as compared to societies where divine ruler/priests were in power). Shona political and religious leaders, while possessing a few restricted pieces of paraphernalia, for the most part utilized the symbolic accoutrements (axes, knives, snuff bottles and headrests) of the general population. Thus while the real conus shell ornaments are associated with leadership, the representation of these emblems in wood (in the geographic areas where they appear) was apparently not so restricted because most men owned headrests. The inclusion of the *ndoro* motif on the headrests must have denoted that the status of the man as head of the household and family unit[68] was also of considerable importance.

The association of the *ndoros* with spirit mediums or *shave* spirits also fits in with the described use of dreaming on the headrests in order to acquire specialized knowledge (how cases should be judged, where animals could be found by hunters, what the ancestors wanted to communicate). The inclusion of these emblems would no doubt have enhanced, as it did for those who wore real *ndoros*, communication with the spirits.

The fact that men were buried with their headrests also strongly links the usage of the headrests to communication with the ancestors. For with both the living and the dead resting their heads on these potent vehicles for other-world information retrieval, clearly those on either side of death were actively trying to keep communication lines open. The headrests thus should be seen as multivalent symbols pertaining to Shona male/female social relations, ideas of status and the ability to communicate with the spirits, either ancestral *(vadzimu)* or skill related *(shave)*.

FIG. 27.
Eastern style area
zoomorphic headrest.
Founders Society,
Detroit Institute of Art.
12.7 x 14.6 cm.

NOTES

There are many scholars and museums all over the world who generously helped in my dissertation research efforts on Shona arts and who deserve thanks.

In the United States these include: Christine Gross of the Field Museum of Natural History, Chicago; The Detroit Institute of Art; Doran Ross of the Fowler Museum of Cultural History, UCLA; Kate Ezra of the Metropolitan Museum of Art, New York; Evelyn Feld and Enid Schildkrout of the American Museum of Natural History, New York; Barbara Stuckenrath and Mary Jo Arnoldi of the National Museum of Natural History, Smithsonian Institution, Washington, D.C.; Janet Stanley, Roz Walker, and Nancy Nooter of the National Museum of African Art, Smithsonian Institution, Washington, D.C.

In the United Kingdom, these include: Malcolm McLeod, John Mack, and Bob Eckett of the Museum of Mankind, London; The Natural History Museum of the British Museum, London; Keith Nicklin of the Horniman Museum and Library, London; John Donne, Jonathan Lowen, and Toby Jack of London; Hermione Waterfield of Christie's, London; Derek Howlett of the Powell-Cotton Museum, Birchington, Kent; David Phillipson of the University Museum of Archaeology and Ethnology, Cambridge; Brian Cranstone, John Todd, and Lynn Williamson of the Pitt-Rivers Museum, Oxford University; Yvonne Schumann of Merseyside County Museum, Liverpool; Dale Indiens of the Royal Scottish Museum, Edinburgh; Frank Willett (then) of the Hunterian Museum, Glasgow; and Tess Gower of the Glasgow City Museum and Art Gallery.

On the European continent these include: Angelika Tunis of the Museum für Völkerkunde, Berlin; Eike Haberland and Elke Samke of the Frobenius-Institut, Frankfurt; Johanna Agthe and Gerda Kroeber-Wolf of the Museum für Völkerkunde, Frankfurt; Klaus Volprecht of the Rautenstrauch Joest Museum für Völkerkunde, Cologne; Wulf Lohse of the Hamburgisches Museum für Völkerkunde; Hans Joachim Koloss (then) of the Linden Museum, Stuttgart; Maria Kecskési of the Staatliches Museum für Völkerkunde, Munich; Lorenz Homberger and Eberhard Fischer of the Reitburg Museum, Zurich; C.E.L. Beumers of the Museum voor Land- en Volkenkunde, Rotterdam; the Museu Etnologia in Lisbon; Armand Duchateau of the Museum für Völkerkunde, Vienna; Hugette Van Geluwe of the Royal Museum of Central Africa, Tervuren, Belgium; and Francine N'Diaye of the Musée de l'Homme, Paris.

In Southern Africa these include: Augusto Cabral of the Museu de Historia Natural, Maputo, Mozambique; Tom Huffman, Elizabeth Rankin, and Anitra Nettleton of the University of the Witwatersrand, Johannesburg; Ann Wanless of the Africana Museum, Johannesburg; Patricia Davison and E. M. Shaw of the South African Museum, Capetown; Dana Anderson of the Natal Museum, Pietermaritzburg.

In Zimbabwe these include: Angeline Kamba, Ken Manungo, and R.G.S. Douglas of the National Archives of Zimbabwe; Doreen Sibanda, Jarmila Hava, and Jill Wylie of the National Gallery of Zimbabwe; Peter Locke, Mr. Tokozani, Phinias Mapfute, and Michael Muzawazi of the Mutare Museum, Zimbabwe; Peter Genge of the National Museum, Bulawayo; W. M. Sithole of the Midlands Museum, Gweru; Dawson Munjeri and Mr. Magira of the Great Zimbabwe National Monument, Masvingo; Gordon Chavunduka, Marshall Murphree, Robert Blair, David Beach, and Peter Garlake (then) of the University of Zimbabwe.

My heartfelt thanks go to Dr. Francis P. Matipano, Executive Director of the National Musums and Monuments of Zimbabwe, who arranged for my affiliation with the museums system. At the Queen Victoria Museum of Harare, my institutional base, I was truly made to feel at home and so special thanks must go to all her staff. In particular I would like to single out the ethnology and archaeology departments for their assistance. Special thanks to Thomas and Stanley Musendo, Chuck Bollong, and Charlotte Tagart. George Mvenge and Godfrey Kativhu, who accompanied me on some fieldwork trips deserve special praise.

Finally I am thankful for the generosity and patience of the many people of Zimabawe who aided me in this research: District Officers and their staffs, local clinics, missions, police and school officials; many local chiefs, religious specialists, and male and female artists. Above all, I am grateful to my field assistant, Noel Mtetwa, whose death in 1984 was a real tragedy. Noel's quiet, good nature and easy rapport with those we visited, his boundless energy in interviewing, transcribing, and translating, and his uncomplaining perseverence through difficulties were all much appreciated. He was also a good friend.

Lastly, the moral, physical, and financial aid of the Dewey, Kent, and Mavurudza families ultimately made it all possible. I owe them many thanks. To my wife Barb and son William, I owe my greatest debt of thanks. Their unrelinquishing love and support have been a constant source of strength.

[1] For an account of how J. van Graan discovered these and other gold artifacts from Mapungubwe in 1932, see van der Merwe 1984.

[2] Caton Thompson feels that any gold plating the Ancient Ruins Company plundered from Great Zimbabwe came "presumably, only from more accessible levels of Periods III and IV" (1970:21). Period III is now dated to the twelfth and early thirteenth centuries A.D., Period IV to the thirteenth and fourteenth centuries (Hall 1987:110 citing Huffman and Vogel 1986). Garlake feels that although gold was relatively rare at Great Zimbabwe, "it does not seem that it was valued more highly than copper or bronze to judge by the pieces lost and the pellets left in the flux of crucibles" (1973:116). Andrew Oddy of the British Museum found upon conducting a technological investigation of gold from such sites as Mapungubwe, Great Zimbabwe and other Iron Age sites from Southern Africa, that the techniques employed to fashion the gold artifacts were essentially the same as those used for manufacturing copper and copper-based items (Oddy 1983, 1984, personal communication, 1988). For a photograph of some gold sheet ornamentation from Dhlo-Dhlo and M'telegwa Ruins found by the Ancient Ruins Company see Hall and Neal 1902:90 and Mazikana, Johnstone and Douglas 1982:pls. 71-2. For inventories, descriptions and illustrations of sheet gold and copper found at Great Zimbabwe see Hall and Neal 1902:140; Hall 1905:113, 115, 442, 444-8; Bent 1896:xiv; Randall-MacIver 1971:79 and pl.

XXX; Caton Thompson 1931:208, 211, and pl. XXI:2; Garlake 1973:115-16 and plate 67; Mazikana, Johnson and Douglas 1982: plate 31. For inventories, descriptions and illustrations of sheet gold and copper found at other sites see Hall and Neal 1902: 145-151, 232, 239, 250, 255, 266, 268, 293, 298, 303, 305, 313, 318, 323; Randall-MacIver 1971:45, 55 and pl. XX; Caton Thompson 1931:219.

[3] The Zulu also buried headrests with their owners (Conner and Pelrine 1983:36) as did the Tsonga or Thonga (Nettleton 1984:21 citing Jacques n.d.:4).

[4] Only one headrest that I am aware of has been found in a controlled archaeological dig, in a walled in cave burial at Castle Kopje, Wedza (see Tagart 1988). This badly eroded headrest, which is perhaps one hundred years old or older, is now in the Museum section of the Children's Library in Marondera, Zimbabwe (Charles Bollong, personal communication, 1987; see fig. 6, drawing by C. Thornycraft). It is interesting to note that headrests have also been found with cave burials in Dogon country in the Bandiagara cliffs of Mali. The Dogon, however, do not make or utilize headrests and it is rather the so-called Tellem people (who lived in the area before the fifteenth century A.D. and are apparently unrelated to the Dogon) who made them. These Tellem wooden headrests have been found primarily in eleventh- and twelfth-century contexts. Bedaux believes that there were wooden headrests for both males and females (1974, 1988). The female variety, however, seem comparatively low and Sieber has suggested that they may be headboards used for carrying things on the head, rather than headrests (Ezra 1988:102-3).

[5] Interview with Sekuru Bwanya, Shamva, 30 June 1984. Another spirit medium (E. T. Marerwa, interviewed in Glen Norah, Harare 13 June 1984) claimed that a Mhondoro spirit told him in a dream to go and collect a staff and snuff bottle that had belonged to the spirit, in a cave in a certain plain, so that the objects could continue to be used.

[6] For other illustrations and descriptions see Bent 1896:90, 262, 326.

[7] Catalogue entries for a Shona headrest in the Museum of

Mankind collection, London (acc. #1935 2-2, 21) state that it was "bought by donor from one of his porters who carried it slung from a belt." An old label attached to the headrest reads, "Pillow or neckrest used at night, by day it is attached to a thong tied round the waist. Mashonaland, East Africa 1892."

[8]Interview with Rodwell Maisiri and his grandmother, Nharira, 31 May 1984.

[9]Interview with J. Madzivire, acting Chief Musarurwa, Nharira, 31 May and 2 September 1984.

[10]Interview with Chief Nyoka, Manyene, 2 June 1984. The style of this headrest (Dewey 1991:fig. 10b) is quite unlike the more typical Shona headrests seen in the other illustrations. The reason for this is not that there has been a deliberate change in style but rather because there are so few models left for artists to view and so they now often carve rather simple headrests. This was certainly the case with the majority of the recently-carved headrests that I observed, which had been commissioned by patrons or were for sale in markets (e.g., Dewey 1991:figs. 131-3). Why there are so few models still available stems partly from the fact that the headrests are rarely used these days, but I was also repeatedly told that such family heirlooms were lost or destroyed during the recent war. Those few headrests that I saw that still retained the typical Shona styles had either been passed from generation to generation or had been carved by very elderly carvers. This did not seem to be the case with axes and knives where the same typical Shona styles continue to be produced more faithfully.

[11]E. T. Marerwa, a spirit medium from Glen Norah, Harare, for example, explained that headrests were used to give *makope* or meaningful dreams (interview, 13 June 1984).

[12]For example, interviews with Simon Mawewe, Dotito, Mt. Darwin, 22 June 1984, and Peter Gamanya, Chikwaka 1 May and 2 July 1984. It is interesting to note that Peter Garlake has seen a headrest that was being kept in a rainmaking shrine in a Shona area (personal communication, June 1988). I have no other similar or corroborating evidence but as rainmaking is the domain of chiefs and high-level or regional spirit mediums this seems to fit with the use of headrests in appeals to the ancestors and by spirit mediums that I have observed.

[13]Patricia Wood, for example, remarks that "the headrests, too, are aesthetically pleasing, being finely carved and beautifully smoothed and polished over the years. No two are ever alike and the geometric patterns carved below the upper support are seldom, if ever repeated" (1978:6-7). Ellert says

> The designs of the various *mutsago* (headrest) do not appear to conform to any particular pattern and no significance can be detected in the absence of other evidence.... As indicated by the general conformity of style and pattern occurring amongst the vaKorekore, vaManyika and the vaNdau, a more reasonable theory is that as a good design, it was much copied. The variations are likely to have taken place at the whim of the artist susceptible to the foibles and inspirations common to all artists throughout the world (1984:18-19).

As Ellert does not identify any of the headrests he illustrates as being from the ethnic groups he mentioned (but does illustrate two as being "common in N.E. Zimbabwe" [1984:19]), it is hard to know whether he feels that each named ethnic group has its own particular style or that they all have the same style.

[14]The only indication for the provenance of the approximately nine headrests Bent collected is in the Museum of Mankind records. Unfortunately only four have any locations recorded (Dewey 1991:figs. 118-19, 145). The headrest seen in Dewey 1991:fig. 135 and others not illustrated have no location indicated.

[15]The dictionary definition of *rudzi* is 'race, breed, tribe, sort, species, clan' (for the Karanga, Manyika and Zezuru; for the Korekore *udzi* has the same meaning [Hannan 1981:570]). The more common word used pertaining to kinship is *dzinza*, which for the Karanga, Manyika and Zezuru means, 'line of descent, tribe, clan, stock, family name' (Hannan 1981:149).

[16]Nettleton, I believe, erred by placing too much confidence in the attributions assigned to the "Shona" headrests in the Museum

of Mankind collections. Even though many examples were collected around the turn of the century, without more specific attributions than the "Mashonaland" many of them carry, I do not believe they help define exactly what the Shona style variations are. The consequences of her stylistic method are further revealed in her statement that

> In some cases problems arise where the same type of headrest is documented among the Shona and one of their neighboring groups such as the Gwembe valley Tonga, the Tswana or the Tsonga of Mozambique. In these cases the headrests have been included in the Shona section, as for the most part they follow the typical Shona pattern (1984:125).

One is left wondering whether her "typical Shona" patterns are really Shona.

[17]In the case of the examples collected by Frobenius which are housed in the Museum für Völkerkunde in Frankfurt, I usually only illustrated in my dissertation one or two (he collected many) from a particular area that, given the weight of the evidence, seemed typical of the area.

[18]That is, when their style fit into the parameters of recognized Shona style types (which will be outlined). Some contemporary carvers, who perhaps have no prototypes to see, make quite unusual headrests (Dewey 1991:figs. 131-3).

To this, for my own purposes, I also added information from aesthetic comparison interviews I carried out (see Dewey 1991:65-88, "Shona Aesthetics" chapter, and figs. 174-7). This was only used as corroborating evidence rather than primary evidence, for this type of information is very subjective and would be almost impossible to prove. Sources would usually only identify a particular example as being like that which they remembered was used in their area and could not identify where other types came from.

[19]Very few tree branch headrests, such as those seen in Sieber 1980:109, were seen in museums or the field. The only documented example that I know to be definitely from the Shona is seen in Baines' 1870s drawing (see fig. 14, to the right of the seat-

ed man). A few contemporary sources claimed that women formerly had to sleep on calabashes, tree logs or smoothed plinths, but I never saw any of these.

[20]Another example from Berlin's Museum für Völkerkunde, acc.# IIID 2556, has the same collection information (Gift of A. Bedoug 1904, "Manika und Maswina") and is of the same style.

[21]There are several examples in a very similar style collected by Frobenius in Mozambique housed in the Museum für Völkerkunde, Frankfurt. Their records say "Tonga" but as the map of Frobenius' 1928 expedition to southern Africa, in the Frobenius Institute, Frankfurt, shows that he made two short excursions into Mozambique, one by the town of Mutare and one further to the north near Mutoko, I suspect that some of the headrests were collected on the former excursion, which is a Manyika rather than a Tonga area. Portuguese documentation of Mozambique art and ethnography is unfortunately almost non-existent. An illustration of a headrest in the same style is included in de Oliveira (1935:60) and labeled as being from "Zambezia." There are also a number of headrests in the same style in the Museu de Historia Natural in Maputo. No documentation to go with them could be found but I suspect that they are from the Manyika who live on the Mozambique side of the border.

[22]Another example from the Hwesa is in the Staatliches Museum für Völkerkunde, Munich, acc.# 32-2-2, purchased from Himmelheber collection, "Southern Rhodesia, Wawesa (Hwesa) Nyanga area." Although somewhat broken and rather poorly carved, it is essentially in the same style as the rest of the headrests in this eastern group.

[23]Several other examples with good provenance information and similar stylistic features are illustrated in Dewey 1991:figs. 87-94 (including figs. 15 and 16 here).

[24]Two of the six headrests (in the Museum für Völkerkunde, Frankfurt, acc.# 2456 31-V-404 and 2462 31-V-410) that Frobenius collected among the Budya of the Mutoko district are of this style.

[25]See, for example, a Soli example illustrated in Mubitana (1971:34) and Christol (1911:109, bottom left) of a "Zambeziens"

headrest (which could be from either side of the Zambezi River if the label does in fact mean the river area).

[26]Several other examples with good provenance information and similar stylistic features are illustrated in Dewey 1991:figs. 97-102 (including figs. 17 and 18 here).

[27]Two other Frankfurt Museum headrests were also collected by Frobenius among the "baTonga" of Mozambique. Nettleton (1984) made the mistake of assuming that this group of Tonga were the Gwembe Tonga, that live on either side of the Zambezi river, near Lake Kariba. Unfortunately there are many groups in southern Africa that have used or were given the name Tonga (see Lancaster 1974; Rasmussen 1979:325). That the Tonga under discussion are in fact the Barwe-Tonga is certain as the accession records in the Frankfurt Museum für Völkerkunde clearly say the examples were collected in Portuguese East Africa and the map of Frobenius' travels during this collecting trip (in the Frobenius Institute, Frankfurt) clearly puts him across the Rhodesia (Zimbabwe) border and labels the ethnic group there as "Tonga." Nettleton identifies another headrest in this style as having been collected in the Charter district by Frobenius (1984:fig. Sh 87). However, my records for this same figure, Frankfurt acc.# 2437 31-V-385, list it as being from Rusambo, an area to the north of Mutoko, probably in the Tavara ethnic area. The Tavara, who mostly live in Mozambique, are classified as a subgroup of the Korekore or as a separate ethnic group (Rasmussen 1979:318).

[28]Several other examples with good provenance information and/or similar stylistic features are illustrated in Dewey 1991:figs. 103-110 (including fig. 19 here).

[29]Douglas, a merchant among the Lozi of Zambia, undertook a collecting trip for the American Museum of Natural History among the Shona in 1906. In a letter to the museum he gave these details of his trip, "Here [Mazoe District] I found many kraals and Natives. I remained in this district only about one week; from there I went to Mt. Darwin and the Nyanga Districts but found very little material for my trouble ... In three weeks I had covered nearly 500 miles on a bicycle, travelling over very mountainous country with only Kaffir paths to follow."

[30]Simon Mawewe, a carver from Chief Dotito's area in the Mount Darwin district (Korekore area; 22 June 1984), claimed when asked to describe a headrest he had made, that his had three pillars and was ornamented with triangles on the tops and sides. As it was not seen, it is impossible to say exactly what it looked like (it may have been more like the northeastern style), but the important point is that even now this tradition of carving more than two pillars is continuing in the area.

[31]Of the six headrests Frobenius collected in Mozambique which are in the Frankfurt Museum für Völkerkunde, only one, acc.# 2486 31-V-434, is in this style.

[32]The Smithsonian's records for this headrest, for another in very similar style (acc.# 167448), and the headrest illustrated in Dewey 1991:fig. 137 all only say "Mashonaland, collector W. H. Brown." In Brown's book *On the South African Frontier*, however, he states that "On my way into Salisbury I spent some time at Machia-ngombe's [Mushayamombe's] villages, purchasing ethnological specimens" (1899:207). As his description of what he collected there (musical instruments, 1899:207, and medicines and medical instruments, 1899:215) closely matches what is in the Smithsonian collections, it is safe to assume that the headrests, although not specifically mentioned in the book, are probably also from this area.

[33]Richard Douglas collected one of this type in the Mazoe district in 1906 (American Museum of Natural History, New York, acc.# 90.0/1252).

[34]Frobenius collected an example in this style from Marondera district (Frankfurt acc.# 2450 31-V-398).

[35]Only one of seven examples collected by Frobenius in the "Marandellas" (Marondera) district is carved in this fashion, but eleven of the thirty-one examples he collected in Charter district have this style.

[36]One of the examples collected by W. H. Brown, presumably in Mushayamombe's area (Zezuru), also has tabs (Smithsonian National Museum of Natural History, acc.# 167448).

[37]A headrest carved by a contemporary Rosvi carver, also of Nharira, has very abbreviated tabs under the upper platform, but

an old example seen in Nharira in 1988 was identical in style to figures 8 and 9 but without the tabs.

[38]Chief Wedza is the title of a leader of the Dumbuseya Shona, who apparently were a recent group "coalesced from various Shona refugee groups after the Ngoni invasions of the 1830s" (Rasmussen 1979:79). This Wedza (there are several) is in the southwestern part of Zimbabwe, just to the west of Chibi's area. The confusion in labeling the object "Matabele" comes, I believe, from a generalization on someone's part that because Baden-Powell was involved in the "Matabele Campaign" any objects he collected must be "Matabele."

[39]A confirming bit of evidence is a Shona set of ivory divining dice (hakata) on display in the National Archives in Harare which are also recorded as having been collected by Baden-Powell in Wedza.

[40]None of the literature or museum collections consulted could give a good answer as to whether headrests were even used by the Ndebele. Confusing the issue further is the fact that "Ndebele" was originally more of a political concept (allegiance to the Ndebele king) than an ethnic one. One branch of the Ndebele arrived in present day Zimbabwe in the 1830s and began incorporating the Kalanga Shona people into their kingdom. While most of these local people adopted the Ndebele language, they remained as a separate "caste" known as the holi. What is Ndebele and what is Kalanga in the amalgamated Ndebele culture has never been adequately studied (Rasmussen 1979:135, 220-224). There are still Kalanga speakers in the far west and southwestern parts of Zimbabwe and in eastern Botswana, but this ethnic group is the most isolated and different group of Shona and some even consider it a non-Shona language. Ellert claims that headrests are common in the "Nata area of Bulilimangwe [a Kalanga area] where they are still widely used" (1984:18), but he does not illustrate them and I have no knowledge of what Kalanga headrests look like.

[41]An almost identical example, but with rectangular tabs, is in the Smithsonian's National Museum of African Art (acc.# 69-31-53), "Rhodesia Zimbabwe."

[42]Recent research by South African art historians is helping to resolve some of these questions but there is still much field and museum work to be done. Nettleton (1990:153) notes that "no reliably provenanced examples are found from the Venda or lowland Sotho areas" although Venda sources remember them being made in the past. Among the northern Sotho, Pedi headrests resemble the form of Swazi and Zulu examples, while Ntwane ones have upper and lower platforms divided by two or three rectangular columns (Nettleton and Hammond-Tooke 1989:18-19; Friedman 1986).

[43]A headrest illustrated in Ratzel (1897 2:432) and labeled as Bamangwato (Tswana) does fit in this stylistic group.

[44]An almost identical headrest on a staff, but without the snuff bottle on the end, is in the collections of the Royal Scottish Museum, Edinburgh (acc.# 1912.173) from Mr. John Ballantyne, who had been stationed at Mount Selinda. This is on the border with Mozambique just to the southeast of the town of Chipinge and is an Ndau area.

[45]Ndau people often identify themselves as Shangaan for reasons of prestige. Shangaan (variants Shangane, Changana) is derived from Shoshangane, who founded the Gaza kingdom in southeastern Zimbabwe and southern Mozambique in the early nineteenth century. "Since the mid-nineteenth century, however, the name Shangane has acquired a looser meaning. It is now frequently applied to Ndau, Hlengwe, and other peoples formerly associated with the Gaza. Most of the people now called 'Shangane' do not speak the Nguni language of the original Gaza. In contemporary usage the name is best regarded as a regional, rather than ethnic, identification" (Rasmussen 1979:293; see also Beach 1980:188).

[46]Another double headrest with chain, attributed to the Shona, is in the Merseyside County Museum, Liverpool (acc.# 49.41-5). G.L. Guy (1961:6) illustrates another double headrest in an article on the uses of wood in Zimbabwe. An unusual triple headrest connected by chains, also attributed to the Shona, is in the Museum of Mankind collections, London (acc.# 1939.Af 28, 2).

[47]The use and meaning of these double headrests is not totally clear. G. L. Guy says, "the well-off bride may have two pillows

joined together by a wooden chain, the whole being painstakingly carved by the bridegroom from a single block of wood" (1961:6). Ellert explains, "there is a colorful legend that the chains enabled one or other to warn his or her sleeping partner of the approach of danger by gently shaking the chain close to the sleeper's ear" (1984:20). When questioned about why the two headrests of figure 24 were connected by a chain, the carver, Muraho Thully, explained that it was to "show cooperation of the wife and husband because in the old days there was full (mutual) love." Among the Tsonga they are also described as being for married couples (see Battiss et al. 1958:79, 81).

[48]See Wanless 1985-1990; Becker 1992.

[49]A few Shona headrests that are very explicitly anthropomorphic are dealt with in Dewey 1991, but as they are relatively rare and from several stylistic areas, I will focus here on the more common zoomorphic examples.

[50]Another headrest almost identical to this one is housed in the Mutare Museum (acc.# RHD 11/E). It unfortunately has no collection information.

[51]Other zoomorphic headrests that fit into this include: Royal Museum of Central Africa, Tervuren (acc.# 550); Museum of Mankind, London (acc.# 1949 Af 46.844; 1956 Af 27.282); University of the Witwatersrand, Johannesburg (acc.# SBF/80.17; SBF 83.18.01); Becker 1992:pl. 29 and fig. 58; and Christol 1911:52 (animal headrest on right).

[52]Nettleton (1984:40, 181-2) argues that headrests in animal form are only attributable to the Shona if they have flat torsos and display surface decorations. Until more data has been collected this cannot be proved. I suggest that there is little difference between Tsonga and Shona animal headrests in my southeastern style area (or the more geometric non-figurative variety), and only in the "borderlands" do these headrests take on more "Shona-like" characteristics, as, for example, figure 27.

[53]Another animal headrest in the same style but with concentric circle disks on either end of the upper platform (as in Dewey 1991:fig. 141), is illustrated in a Sotheby's auction catalogue, November 1985, item #128.

[54]One illustrated in Monteiro (1891:73), presumably from "Delagoa Bay," Mozambique, also has a flat base.

[55]Museum of Mankind, London, acc.#s 1892.7-14.152; 1892.7-14.151; 1892.7-14.154; and 1892.7-14.156.

[56]Bourdillon notes that the family head may have a set of dice that can be used for consulting on minor matters, but that a professional will always be consulted on more serious matters (1987:156). From earlier accounts of travelers it is apparent that the dice were previously more commonly used. When I was conducting interviews, hardly any Shona could name the characters on the dice much less interpret the throws. They invariably said such knowledge is the domain of diviners. It is difficult to believe therefore that the symbols were ever the basis of a universal set of symbols for the Shona.

[57]I carried a black and white photograph of one from the Museum of Mankind, London acc. # 1949 Af 46.810 (Elisofon and Fagg 1958:249) with me on the interviews and would occasionally show it. An example of an actual headrest was shown during interviews in the Masvingo and Chipinge areas. The only explanation offered for such headrests was similar to that of Stephen Dekeya (Nharira, Charter district, 2 September 1984) who explained that it could be used by women who became possessed or by men who were possessed by a female spirit.

[58]The verb kunyora means to make marks on something and has come to mean, to write (Hannan 1981:493), an association that is apparently quite common in Bantu Africa (see for example Roberts 1988:41).

[59]Stephen Dekeya, Nharira, Charter District, 2 September 1984.

[60]Joram Mariga, Makoni, Rusape, 12 July 1984.

[61]Brush Mususa, Katerere area, Nyanga north, (questionnaire filled out in my absence, September 1984 with the help of Adrian Smyly from the nearby Elim Hospital).

[62]Mariga is an educated man, who as an extension supervisor of AGRITEX (Department of Agricultural, Technical and Extension Services) has promoted craft production in the rural areas of Manicaland for more than thirty years. He is also a member of the

National Art Gallery's Board of Trustees and a sculptor whose work has been exhibited internationally (see F. Wood 1984). The circumstances of his comments were that he was guiding me to visit some local artists in the Makoni area and while he refused to be interviewed himself, he interjected when no one we were interviewing knew anything about headrests. He also was the one that suggested that I find Brush Mususa in Nyanga North, as he was one of the few carvers, he knew, who still made headrests. I was unable to interview Mususa myself as he was away. He was, however, an elderly man, at least in his 70s, I was told, and as he lives in an extremely remote area I doubt that he has been influenced by the modern world to the extent that Mariga has. Both Mususa and Mariga's explanations are quite similar and I would not doubt that they have talked to each other about such matters.

[63]It is important to note that there has never been any formal initiation practiced by the Shona on girls or boys. Whereas cicatrization sometimes occurred in the context of initiation in other African societies, as far as can be determined this was never the case among the Shona.

[64]Interviews with: Chief Katerere, Katerere, Nyanga District, 13 July 1984. Chief Zimunya, Mutare District, 8 July 1984. Chief Chiswiti, Mt. Darwin District, 23 June 1984. Chief Maranke, Maranke, Mutare District, 7 July 1984.

[65]See Dewey 1991:206-212 for details.

[66]Attempts to anthropomorphize every component of the headrests seem counterproductive, for, as is the case in much of African art, the forms are representative not representational. It is interesting to note that in many parts of Africa, especially Bantu ones, ceremonial implements and even household sculpture such as the headrests, are often anthropomorphized and genderized. These utilitarian arts therefore probably have as much symbolic meaning as the more often studied figurative sculpture and masks and certainly deserve more serious study.

[67]Elizabeth Goodall's findings that anthropomorphized pots which are for use by men, have a similar meaning, adds weight to this argument. "Such pots were closely connected with the significance of married life. The young wife is regarded as the container of the maintenance of tribal continuance. The pot given by her to the man she marries is symbolic of her own body and therefore bears female signs" (1946:48).

[68]Why the headrest (fig. 6) found in the context of a Zimbabwe-type ruins (Castle Kopje see Tagart 1988) is stylistically so different from the other headrests of this central style area, may relate to the fact that it was from a time when class distinctions (as evidenced by the Great Zimbabwe tradition gold ornaments found in another burial there) were more important.

98. Headrest, *mutsago*

N. E. Shona, Barwe-

Tonga; Zimbabwe,

Mozambique

Wood, cord, and metal

34.2 x 16 x 9.5 cm.

FMCH 86.2413

99. Headrest, *mutsago*

N. E. Shona, Barwe-

Tonga; Zimbabwe,

Mozambique

Wood

13.3 x 13.3 x 5.2 cm.

FMCH 87.1511

100. Headrest, *mutsago*

Central and Northern

Shona; Zimbabwe

Wood

15 x 14 x 6 cm.

FMCH 86.2414

101. Headrest, *mutsago*

Central Shona;

Zimbabwe

Wood

20.4 x 15.8 x 7 cm.

FMCH 86.2415

102. Headrest, *mutsago*

S.W. Shona?;

Zimbabwe?

Wood

18.9 x 13.4 x 6.7 cm.

FMCH 86.2426

103. Headrest, *mutsago*

S.W. Shona?;

Zimbabwe?

Wood

13.9 x 16.9 x 7 cm.

FMCH 91.326

104. Headrest, *mutsago*

S.W. Shona; Zimbabwe,

Botswana

Wood

13.2 x 15 x 5.9 cm.

FMCH 92.82

105. Headrest-staff

Tsonga; S.E. Shona

Mozambique,

Zimbabwe

Wood

67.945 x 10.16 cm.

FMCH 88.302

106. Headrest

Tsonga; South Africa,

Mozambique

Wood

18.2 x 15.7 x 6.5 cm.

FMCH 86.2448

107. Headrest, double

S. E. Shona-Tsonga;

Zimbabwe,

Mozambique

Wood

14.7 x 89.9 x 7.3 cm.

FMCH 89.368

108. Headrest, *mutsago*

S. Shona?; Zimbabwe

Wood

15 x 14.9 x 6 cm.

FMCH 86.2442

109. Headrest

Tsonga? North

Nguni?;Mozambique,

South Africa

Wood

68 x 15.9 x 6 cm.

FMCH 86.2428

110. Headrest, *mutsago*

Shona-Tsonga?;

Mozambique,

Zimbabwe

Wood

17 x 14.9 x 8 cm.

FMCH 86.2450

111. Headrest, *mutsago*

S. Shona?; Zimbabwe

Wood

17.7 x 15 x 8 cm.

FMCH 87.614

112. Headrest, *mutsago*

S. Shona; Zimbabwe

Wood

13.97 x 15.875 x 8.5 cm.

FMCH 92.190

(above)

113. Headrest, *mutsago*

S. Shona; Zimbabwe

Wood

13 x 12 x 6.4 cm.

FMCH 88.963

(above, right)

114. Headrest

S. E. Shona-Tsonga;

Zimbabwe,

Mozambique

Wood

13.9 x 19 x 6.1 cm.

FMCH 86.2436

(right)

115. Headrest

S. E. Shona-Tsonga;

Zimbabwe,

Mozambique

Wood

17.3 x 13.3 x 6.6 cm.

FMCH 89.794

116. Headrest

S. E. Shona-Tsonga;

Zimbabwe,

Mozambique

Wood

17 x 27.1 x 8.8 cm.

FMCH 91.57

Asia

THE PILLOW IN EAST ASIA
TOSHIKO M. McCALLUM

From ancient periods to modern times East Asian people have made pillows from a wide variety of materials, commonly including stone, clay, grass, wood, rattan, bamboo, and cloth. Stone pillows have been excavated from burial sites in East Asian countries. Some fired-clay pillows and many ceramic pillows have also been found in archaeological sites. The ceramic pillow is one of the most noteworthy traditional sleeping accessories in East Asian cultures, and numerous varieties of headrests have been produced from this material over a span of thirteen centuries. Wood must have been a major material for pillows, since the Chinese character for pillow, 枕, has wood, 木, as an element. The Japanese words for 'wooden pillow' and 'grass pillow' appear in the oldest collection of Japanese poems, the *Man'yōshu*, which was compiled by 795. In fact the word for grass pillow in Japanese, *kusamakura*, has been used as the conventional epithet for 'travel' in traditional poems. Although actual evidence is lacking, we can assume that these perishable but easily obtainable materials must have been made into comfortable forms for resting the head since early in human history. Wooden pillows have never disappeared from East Asian countries, and have been made into many interesting forms. Rattan and bamboo pillows are still in people's lives in the present day. Cloth generally has been the most favored material for pillows for a comfortable night's sleep. Although not as popular as the materials mentioned above, animal products such as leather and horn are also employed. Even paper has been made into pillows. In Korea strong paper which contains large amounts of fiber has been twisted into rope, which is then tightly twined into cylindrical shapes and stuffed into the pillow. The objects dealt with in this essay are organized in terms of some of these materials.

STONE PILLOWS

Stone pillows are found in several mound sites of the Old Silla Kingdom (?-668) of Korea (Chōsen Sōtokufu 1916:pls. 1204, 1209, 1220). These pillows are simply polished on the surface, without decoration. The centers are drilled to form a sunken shape with a smooth surface in order to accommodate the head and neck. These Korean stone pillows are sometimes paired with a stone foot rest on the opposite side.

Some mound sites of the Kofun period (ca. 300-600) in Japan also contain pillows made from stone. One elaborate type of stone pillow from the mounds is shaped into a horse-shoe form, and the center of the top surface is carved down to a concavity and polished in order to accommodate the head and neck of the deceased. The surrounding area is decorated with incised straight and curved lines. This incised design is typical of the Kofun period, and it has been suggested that it contains some magical meaning. A fired-clay pillow of very similar shape and decoration to this type of stone pillow has been excavated, but the clay piece was painted red over its entire surface. Some stone pillows of this type have from six to twenty holes drilled along the near border of their surfaces. Apparently each hole held a pole-shaped stone ornament which had a symmetrical form of two *magatama* attached together (Yano 1985:23-24). The *magatama* is an ornament that appeared in the later part of the Jōmon period (ca. 10,500-300 B.C.), and frequently is discovered in sites of the Yayoi (ca. 300 B.C.-300 A.D.) and Kofun periods in Japan. It is also found in many sites in Korea. The ornament is usually shaped like a comma, with the upper part larger than the lower, and it may be made from jade, serpentine, glass, jasper and agate. It seems that the *magatama* functioned as a charm stone rather than being merely ornamental. Even today people carry a miniature *magatama* attached to a talisman. The decoration of two *magatama* attached symmetrically into the holes of the stone pillows may have had some symbolic meaning, perhaps related to human life and death. All of the pillows just mentioned were carved individually from one piece of stone, but many cases are also reported in Japan during the Kofun period where the headrest was carved as part of the stone coffin itself.

A much later period in Korea provides a zoomorphic stone pillow dated to the late Choson period (1392-1910). Two fantastic animals, probably lions, are carved between the upper oblong piece of stone for the head and the lower flat base. The lions are facing in opposite directions. This pillow was used for the deceased in a coffin (Tenri Daigaku and Tenrikyō Dōyūsha 1986:230, pl. 126). A Chinese stone pillow from the Northern Chou period (556-581), which also has an animal relief, is now kept in the collections of the Archaeological Research Institute of Kyoto University. These are particularly interesting stone pillows since, as we will see, the guardian animal motif is particularly prevalent among ceramic pillows.

During the last few decades there have been many splendid archaeological discoveries in China. One famous discovery of recent years is the underground crypt of Fa-men Temple near Hsi-an, discovered in 1987. The crypt contained pieces of the Buddha's *Sarira* (physical remains) as well as astonishingly rich and exquisite treasures offered by several T'ang emperors to the *Sarira*. There are gold and silver wares, glass wares, porcelains, silk fabrics

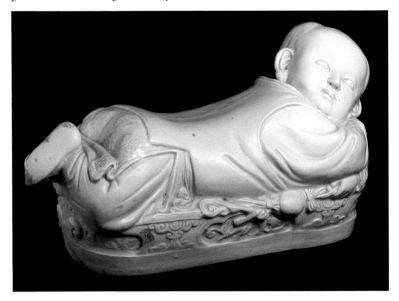

FIG. 28.
Chinese headrest in the form of a reclining baby.

and other precious articles which demonstrate the highest technological achievement of the T'ang dynasty. Among these treasures was found a finely polished solid crystal pillow. The upper surface of this pillow is slightly dented, and the upper part is larger than the base. This crystal pillow looks exactly like the stone pillows still used by Chinese country people today (Shao 1988:117).

Ceramic Pillows

The ceramic ware of East Asia constitutes a great tradition which exerted strong influence on the development

FIG. 29.
Koryo celadon
rectangular pillow with
an inlaid design of
peonies and a crane
with clouds.

of ceramic technology and use in other areas in the world. Ceramic pillows first appeared in the T'ang dynasty of China (618-907). From the T'ang dynasty onward, many of these pillows reflect the highest degree of this great ceramic tradition's technical and aesthetic achievement. Many pillows also give us intimate clues about people's social and spiritual life during the periods of their production through their formal expression and their decorative motifs. There are many excellent studies devoted to ceramic pillows (Ch'en 1954; Paine 1955; Osaka Shiritsu Tōyō Tōji Bijutsukan 1984). Among these, Mikami's article on ceramic pillows from the T'ang to the Yuan dynasties is especially useful and informative (Mikami 1984:10-15).

The earliest type of Chinese ceramic pillow probably dates to the eighth century, during the T'ang dynasty; it is shaped like a rather small box. Early Chinese ceramic pillows have two types of decoration. One type is a three-color lead-silicate glaze (although some examples of this type are actually two colors or even one color). The other type has a marbled grain which produces a wood-like pattern on the surface and also is glazed. These techniques show the highly developed ceramic tradition of the T'ang period. Since the earliest ceramic pillows are very small in size, they may not have been used as headrests; rather, it should be considered whether these objects fulfilled other functions, such as armrests. These high-quality pillows were probably produced in official kilns.

A large quantity of three-color lead-silicate glaze and marbled pillow shards have been excavated from the sites of official structures, aristocratic mansions, Buddhist temples and ritual grounds in Japan. Mikami argues that these pillows were brought to Japan during the middle and late eighth century. These shiny, colorful ceramic pillows must have dazzled the eyes of people who had previously only seen the unglazed wares which existed in Japan at that time.

One interesting example of a T'ang ceramic pillow of this period is the piece in the C. Adrian Rubel Collection (Paine 1955:pl. 1) which has an impressed design of a camel and people. This piece reflects the international nature of China during the T'ang dynasty, when traders travelling from the West via the Silk Road were a familiar sight on the streets of the capital city, Ch'ang-an (today's Hsi-an).

After the ninth century, larger rectangular pillows were produced in large numbers at the Ch'ang-sha T'ung-kuan kilns in southern China. The complicated technique of underglaze painting was developed in this area, and ceramics fired by this technique were exported to many areas in the world (Hsiao 1982:158-178). There are some fine examples of pillows decorated with this technique.

Another type of ceramic pillow also began to appear from the late T'ang dynasty, around the ninth century. These pillows are made in zoomorphic forms. The most popular animals were tigers and lions, who were believed to ward off the evil and dangerous spirits. Indeed, a large number of terracotta and ceramic figurines depicting imaginary animals have been found in tombs in ancient China, and some old tombs in Korea also have fantastic animals painted on their walls. These animals were considered to be guardian animals who protected the deceased from evil spirits. The state of sleep, in which people temporarily lose consciousness, is often thought to resemble death, when the loss of consciousness is permanent; hence people are thought to be especially vulnerable in sleep. In China fierce animals such as lions and tigers possess supernatural powers to ward off dangerous spirits. These animals have been used into the present as motifs on pillows and headrests throughout East Asia to provide protection during sleep.

The Chinese ceramic pillow tradition reached its peak during the Five Dynasties and the Sung, Chin and Yuan dynasties (907-1368). Compared to the previous periods, pillow production increased greatly. It seems that during these dynasties the custom of using ceramic pillows spread among much wider segments of the population and across larger areas.

Scholars have traditionally considered ceramic pillows to have been used solely as funeral offerings to the deceased, since so many of them have been discovered in burial grounds. However, other finds from this period suggest that the pillows were actually used in everyday life (Ch'en 1954: 1-3). Some pillows have the Chinese characters 'longevity and prosperity', or 'new bridegroom' written on the surface. Furthermore, ceramic pillows were excavated from a dwelling of Northern Sung dynasty date which had been buried under the soil by a great flood in 1108.

Rectangular pillows continued to be popular during this period, but other shapes developed as well. These include rectangular with a dented center, square, oblong, polygon, fan-shaped, oval, half moon, bean-shaped, leaf-shaped, and *ju-i t'ou*-shaped. (*Ju-i t'ou* is the head decoration of a ritual staff use by Buddhist monks at ceremonies and lectures. It is also an auspicious symbol.) Decorative techniques reached the highest point, and a great variety of methods was applied to produce the finest design for spontaneous folk-art type decorations (for decorative techniques see Itoh 1984:224-36).

Decorative motifs also include a wide variety of objects, such as flowers, birds, animals, geometric designs, playing children, women, scenes from dramas, landscapes, and calligraphy. Many of these motifs are auspicious symbols in the lives of the Chinese people (see cat. 120), and they seem to reflect very much the wishes of people and their celebration of life in this world. Mikami suggests that the decorative motifs of ceramic pillows show changes in popularity through the dynasties which correlate with motif changes in the general ceramic tradition of China during these historical periods.

During this time large numbers of zoomorphic ceramic pillows were also produced. Lions and especially tigers are the most popular forms. Like the animal-shaped pillows of the late T'ang dynasty, a type of pillow that has one or two of these apotropaic beasts carved between an upper piece (where the head rests) and a lower base existed during these periods. But the form of the animal itself also served as a headrest at this time. One example is the tiger-shaped pillow which was produced in abundance during the Chin dynasty. These tigers have been painted brownish yellow with black stripes on their bodies. Their backs, where one's head rests, are usually carved flat and have a white slip applied, with drawings of flowers or other motifs in iron brown. Child-shaped pillows which utilize a similar technique and design were also made during the same period. These tiger- and child-shaped pillows have folk-art-like characteristics which reflect the vivid, direct, humorous expression of the common people. In Chinese culture tigers have an enormous popularity. They have been used as motifs over and over in both fine and popular art. Apparently there are stuffed tiger pillows for children made from fabric which are still used in the northern part of China today.

All of the ceramic pillows mentioned thus far are stoneware. Mikami suggests that during Ming dynasty (1368-1644), when porcelain wares became the main ceramic material for daily use, the production of ceramic pillows rapidly decreased, probably due to the hard, uncomfortable touch of porcelain as a headrest.

Some very high quality porcelain pillows, however, also were produced during the Sung, Chin, and Yuan dynasties. There still exist splendid white porcelain pillows which were fired at the Ting kiln in northern China, a source for some of the most refined white porcelain ware during the Sung dynasty (tenth to thirteenth centuries) (Shanhai Jinmin Bijutsu Shuppansha 1981). One of the finest pieces in the Palace Museum in Beijing is shaped as an adorable child (fig. 28). The costume and hair style of this child are realistically carved, so it is also a good source for information on these aspects around this period. Pale blue and white *ch'ing-pai* glaze porcelain pillows are often excavated from sites of the Sung and Yuan dynasties. One example, Plate 1 in *Sō Gen seihakuji* (Shanhai Jinmin Bijutsu Shuppansha 1984) is shaped like a reclining lady with a stem of lotus leaves to serve as a headrest standing up from her back. Plate 73 in the same volume depicts a reclining child on a bed holding a lotus leaf.

The porcelain pillows made during these dynasties are very high quality, and frequently quite complicated in detail. Because of these characteristics they may not have been for everyday use; rather, they may have been produced as decorative objects, probably used rarely if ever during a person's lifetime, and finally buried to accompany their owners. Examples such as the headrest in plate 165 in *Sō Gen seihakuji* have such complicated detail—this one depicts a palatial structure containing ladies and a rabbit—that it is impossible to think of it as being a practical object.

Feng mentions that *ch'ing-pai* glaze ware, which is called pseudo-jade ware, is often discovered in graveyards, so these wares must have been buried with their deceased owners (Feng 1984:157-158). Considering the ancient Chinese practice of offering jade wares and pieces of jade with the deceased, the frequent discoveries of pillows of *ch'ing-pai* ware which is called pseudo-jade is very provocative. The popular motifs of *ch'ing-pai* pillows are children, women, lions and tigers. The deceased rest their heads peacefully on these pillows to go to the other world. The *ch'ing-pai* wares were exported to many areas in the world, and shards have been discovered even on the African continent (Feng 1984:179). In the case of *ch'ing-pai* pillows, one piece in the form of a reclining woman was found among the treasures of a sunken trade ship of the thirteenth or fourteenth century in the Shinan Coast of Korea (Mikami 1984:15).

During the Ch'ing dynasty (1616-1911) porcelain pillows continued to be produced, although they were not as popular as stoneware pillows during the Five Dynasties and the Sung, Chin and Yuan dynasties. Some

FIG. 30.
Harunobu print,
"Parting at Dawn"
(Kinu Ginu) showing
rectangular wooden
pillow.

have very decorative design in underglaze blue, or polychrome glaze, but some are simply glazed in one solid color (cat. nos. 119, 121-123). There were also zoomorphic pillows. One interesting example is a cat-shaped porcelain pillow in the collection of the Victoria and Albert Museum in London. Many similar porcelain pillows of cat shape are still found in antique stores in Beijing. Yano mentions cat-shaped pillows in the Ch'ing dynasty, although it is unclear what material the pillows are made from. He also suggests that a cat-shaped pillow may have served as a guardian against the evil spirits of night, much as the larger lions and tigers do (1985:113-15).

In Korea, where a distinctive ceramic tradition developed, celadon wares of the Koryo period (936-1392) are quite famous. There are very nice examples of Koryo celadon pillows. One piece has a form of two lions facing in opposite directions and holding a headrest slab on top of their backs. The form itself is exactly the same as the Chinese zoomorphic type. An especially beautiful type of Koryo celadon is inlaid ware. One example is a rectangular pillow with an inlaid design of peonies and a crane with clouds (fig. 29). The crane-and-clouds design symbolizes good fortune and long life, and is one of the most popular motifs in Korean iconography. In the Koryo period inlaid decoration was very popular in wooden and metal work, and this technique was adopted into the ceramic tradition as well during this period (Kawahara 1978:6). There are some fine examples of pillows of this technique in Korea.

The earliest type of T'ang dynasty ceramic pillows reached Japan, as mentioned above, but there is little evidence for the of use of ceramic pillows in Japan during the period from the tenth to the middle of the fourteenth centuries, when the ceramic pillow tradition reached its peak in China. However, ceramic pillows became quite popular during the Edo and Meiji periods (1603-1912) among those Japanese who admired the culture of China, such as members of the literati circles (cat. 123). Many types of stoneware and porcelain pillow were made, and particularly pillows from the Arita kiln in Kyushu were very popular. This kiln has been producing high-quality porcelain ware since the early seventeenth century, much of which has been exported to Europe as Imari or Arita ware. Some pillows have an incense burning device on the bottom of the inside (cat. 124). The ceramic pillow continued to be used in Japan through early Shōwa period (1926-1989), but there has been no commercial production of them after World War II.

BAMBOO AND RATTAN PILLOWS

Bamboo and rattan have long been an indispensable source of material culture in East Asia. Pillows made from bamboo and rattan are especially favored at nap time during the hot and humid summer. In China pieces of a whole stalk of bamboo, or one which is cut in half, are made into a neckrest (Kuo li chung yang t'u shu kuan 1980:pls. 43-45). In this case the smooth, cool surface of the bamboo provides comfortable support and stimulation to the neck. Pieces of bamboo strips are also constructed into pillows (cat. 125). This type always has open spaces between the strips, so air circulates and cools the resting neck and head. These bamboo pillows are particularly loved among the literati, who had strong admiration for bamboo and who anthropomorphized

FIG. 31.
Harunobu print from the late 1760s, from *"Eight Indoor Scenes: A Towel Stand" (Zashishi kakkoi: Tenugui kake no kihan),* showing a complicated wooden pillow with a little cloth pillow on top.

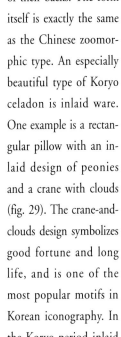

bamboo as possessing characteristics of nobility and cleanness (McCallum 1988:25).

One sleeping object is popularly called "Madam Bamboo" in East Asian countries. This is a cylinder made of bamboo strips in a plaited open-work form. Madam Bamboo is held while a person sleeps during the hot summer, so that air circulates through the bamboo open-work and cools the holder's body.

Rattan is highly flexible, and so the stalk can be bent and artistically constructed into a pillow with beautiful forms. Pillows which are plaited from narrow rattan strips have been made in great abundance, and they are still very popular in present-day East Asia (cat. 126). One of my childhood memories of summer is that one day, maybe in late June, a rattan pillow would be taken out from storage, and my father would take a nap in the coolest corner of the house.

Some pillows are constructed of both bamboo and rattan. Straight round stalks of bamboo are used for the body and legs, and more flexible rattan strips are employed to tie the bamboo pieces together. The rattan tie-and-knot work of this type of pillow can be complicated and elaborate.

Wooden Pillows

Several forms of wooden pillows were made in Korea, ordinarily used by men. There has been a traditional custom that an armrest was given to government officials to show appreciation for their service to the country at the time of retirement. Thus the armrest has been considered an important piece of furniture in upper-class Korean families. The form of the armrest has affected the devel-

opment of wooden headrests (Yi 1986:73) (cat. 130). Another type is a box-shaped wooden headrest with drawers. Still others are carved from a solid block of wood, or are worked by joined wood technique into a rectangular shape, and both these types have a hole at the middle for air to go through. Thus they are called 'wind pillows' in Korean. Some Korean wooden furniture has extensive inlaid work done in mother-of-pearl. Beautiful inlaid decorations are also applied to some wooden pillows, and the motifs include lucky symbols for long life and prosperity. Thin pieces of horn are applied to the wooden surfaces, as well. Some wooden pillows are shaped into animal forms, mainly in tiger shapes in Korea. These Korean wooden pillows are ordinarily used for a nap.

FIG. 32.
Kiyonaga print, from *Eight Elegant Drawing Room Scenes (Fūryū zashiki hakkei: Tenugui kake no kihan)*. This print of Kiyonaga was copied after the composition and theme of Harunobu's print (Fig. 31), about ten years later; this one shows the now-fashionable trapezoidal neckrest.

Concrete pictorial evidence of people using wooden pillows can be seen in Japanese picture scrolls. Picture scrolls, produced mainly from the Heian to the Muromachi period (794-1573), illustrate stories, lives of famous monks, and legends of temples and shrines in both written and pictorial form on rolls of paper or silk. The paintings include scenes from the everyday lives of the people of the time, and thus provide an excellent source for the study of

behavior, social customs, and material culture. The illustrations of some scrolls include private scenes such as bedrooms, and there we can find people using pillows. According to these paintings, people used two types of pillows during these periods.

The more popular type was made in a rectangular shape from wood, and was wrapped with fabric covers. The varieties of woods used include boxwood, zelkova, cedar, paulownia, mulberry wood, and nandin (Yano 1985:45). Sandalwood, which was imported and highly valued, was also made into pillows for the privileged classes. It emits elegant fragrances for the sleeper. A pair of sandalwood pillows is preserved at the Kyoto Imperial Palace (Tokyo Chūō Bijutsusha 1929 10:27, pl. 20). Each has a thin cloth cushion stuffed with cotton, attached to the upper surface where the head rests. Two pieces of cloth cover, which are sewn into fitted sizes for the specific pillow form, are put over the upper and lower parts of each pillow. The upper cover is made of chinese brocade, and the lower one is silk of yellow-green color. These covered wooden pillows are exactly like the pillows illustrated in picture scrolls, so most wooden pillows probably had two fitted covers to lay over them. These imperial wooden pillows may not have been put into practical use, for it seems that they

were kept in a fancy lacquered pillow box as a pair, and the box was used as a piece of decorative furniture in one living quarter of the palace, popularly called the Wisteria Quarter. These sandalwood examples show the highest quality of wooden pillows. The ordinary types must have been made from more common wood and would have a plainer type of cloth cover.

The other type of pillow occasionally depicted in picture scrolls has square wooden boards on the two sides of the pillow body. These two boards are secured by a wooden pole inserted at the centers of the boards. In other words, the two boards become the two outer surface of the pillow, and the central pole functions as its core support. Fabric is stretched over the four surfaces and a stuffing, such as grain husk, is put inside the fabric body. Thus this pillow is a combination of the cloth and wooden pillow. This type appears less often in picture scrolls than the wooden pillow, although it seems that it was used more often by Buddhist monks, who shave their hair, and also by older people, probably due to the softness of the cloth body.

Picture scrolls also show examples of pillows used by homeless and otherwise unfortunate people. A scene of *Ippen Hijiri-e* (1299) shows two people sleeping under the porch of a temple. One is using something like a rolled mat for a pillow, and the other puts his head on the top of an object like an upside-down wooden container. A sick man in *Kasuga Gongen genki-e* (1309) is reclining on a straw mat placed directly on the soil next to the main house. He is using a rounded mat as a pillow, just like the homeless person in *Ippen Hijiri-e*. It is explained that a sick person without family, or with no hope of recovery, was not allowed into the main house at this time (Shibusawa 1967:202).

Other pictorial sources which provide ethnographic evidence about the Japanese people in Edo period (1603-1867) are the illustrations in books and wood block prints called Ukiyoe. It has been generally agreed that the development of wooden pillows in the Edo period is related to the hair styles of that time. By studying both hair styles and pillow types in Ukiyoe art from the early to late Edo period, we can clearly follow the changes of pillow fashions influenced by hair styles of this period.

During the Edo period Japan had very limited relations with the outside world, except for trade with Holland, China, and Korea at Nagasaki in Kyushu, which was controlled by the government. Within such an isolated environment, new and distinctive cultural phenomena were able to develop in Japan. Highly complicated and elaborate hair styles became the norm, especially among women. Men wore their hair in a simpler topknot style. Moreover, the types of men's and women's hair styles were regulated strictly according to the social classes at this time. There were between 270 and 280 distinct hair styles created during the Edo period (Ōhara 1988:68).

The foundation of these elaborate hair styles for women was established during the early Edo period. However, early Edo hairstyles were still plainer than those of later periods, and women could manage their hair by themselves. The pillows depicted in illustrations and Ukiyoe works done by artists such as Hishikawa Moronobu, Torii Kiyonobu and Nishikawa Sukenobu, from the late seventeenth to early eighteenth centuries are predominantly stuffed cloth pillows of cylindrical shape. Probably because hair styles were still quite simple, people did not have to protect them while they slept.

During the middle Edo period women's hair styles became very complicated. Because of this, the number of hair stylists, who were mainly female, increased greatly. By using supporting gadgets and wax, hair forms spread widely on both sides of the face, and the hair at the back was held upward so that it did not touch the neck (Ōhara 1988:98-106).

Suzuki Harunobu (?-1770) left a large number of colorful and poetic Ukiyoe prints depicting peoples' lives. He was especially active, producing many splendid works, during the second half of the 1760s. This decade also correlated with rapid changes in hair styles. Reflecting these changes, many different types of pillows are found in Harunobu's work of this period. The prints of Harunobu, which show the usage of a variety of pillows, are very important sources to study the transitional period in the fashion of pillows in the Edo period. Cloth pillows of the same type as the previous period were depicted in some works. However, Harunobu also represented rectangular wooden pillows in his prints (fig. 30). Most wooden rectangular headrests depicted in Harunobu's works do not have attached cloth pillows on them, but rather are used independently. One work, however, done in late 1760's, shows a wooden pillow constructed in a complicated shape, with a little cloth pillow on the top (fig. 31). The wooden pillow assumed a trapezoid form shortly after Harunobu's time, a shape that became the norm for wooden pillows during the later Edo period, and a little cylindrical cloth pillow was always attached to it (cat. 131). In addition, pieces of folded paper were attached to the cloth pillow and changed when the old paper became soiled.

Many new fashions in wardrobe and hair style during the Edo period first originated in the pleasure quarters, such as Yoshiwara. In the case of pillows, it seems that the prints by Harunobu showing wooden rectangular pillows are generally scenes of courtesan's rooms, while the prints depicting cloth pillows are usually family scenes. However, this idea has to be studied further in order to make a more definite statement.

Torii Kiyonaga (1752-1815), who led the Ukiyoe world in the 1770s after the death of Harunobu, produced a very interesting work, probably in 1777. This print copied the exact theme of, and has a very similar composition to, one of Harunobu's works (fig. 31). But Kiyonaga used a trapezoidal wooden headrest with a little cloth pillow on it (fig. 32). Trapezoidal wooden pillows appear in many of Kiyonaga's prints. Rectangular wooden pillows, which were frequently depicted in Harunobu's prints, must have been designed to protect hair styles that were becoming increasingly complicated around his time. However, a trapezoidal wooden pillow was an improvement over a rectangular one, because it

could be put under one's neck in order to protect the ever-evolving hair styles. The upper section, which had a neck rest, was much smaller than bottom, and thus only the neck touched the pillow, while the other parts of the head were held away from it. In addition, the body of the pillow gradually expands toward the bottom, so it has a well-balanced, secure form. (For this reason, these wooden trapezoidal pillows are more appropriately called neckrests rather than headrests, and thus trapezoidal pillows will be referred to as 'wooden neckrests' from now on.) Wooden neckrests in Kiyonaga's prints usually have a flat bottom, but one of his works, *Sansei Ichikawa Yaozō to geisha*, illustrates a neckrest with a curved bottom. The curved bottom apparently allowed much easier movement in turning the head, and many neckrests of this type were produced (cat. 132).

Kitagawa Utamaro (1753-1806), who was the favorite in the golden age of Ukiyoe at the end of the eighteenth century, the beginning of the Late Edo period, left many works showing wooden neckrests (fig. 33). However, I have noticed that one print by Utamaro of a honeymoon couple's bedroom had cloth pillows of a type which could be seen in the works of Harunobu and earlier artists. Also, one print of a sleeping child by Utamaro has a cloth pillow. It seems that cloth pillows were still used in some households or by children. Actually, cloth pillows were called monk's pillows, since Buddhist monks who shaved off their hair did not have to worry about their hair style, so they used cloth pillows. Nevertheless, the hair styles of women kept changing during the late Edo period. Wooden neckrests became standard as the most suitable form to support the neck. Although men's hair styles were not as

FIG. 34.
Hokusai painting,
"New Year's Ritual."
Japanese people believe
that a good dream in the
first or second night of the
new year is a lucky omen
for the coming year.
In order to have a good
dream, people put an
auspicious painting under
their pillows.
This courtesan is putting
a picture of a treasure
ship under the
wooden headrest.

complicated as those of women they also used wooden neckrests. Around the time when Katsushika Hokusai (1760-1849) was very active, in the late Edo period, wooden neckrests were the norm except in a few segments of society (fig. 34).

Many varieties of wooden neckrests existed, from the very elaborate to the extremely plain. There are beautiful examples of gold-sprinkled lacquer decoration, lacquer with painting, or simple wooden surfaces. The degree of decoration and elaborateness clearly reflects social status during the Edo period, when a strict hierarchical order of society was established by the government. The finest lacquered neckrests, which were brought by the brides of lords at the time of their marriage, can still be seen in museums. But, at the other extreme, there are simple pieces of wood which farmers used as pillows in seasonal farm huts away from the main house. Moreover, large numbers of employees in big merchant households put their heads on a long pole of wood as a pillow at night, and every morning the end of the pole was beaten with a mallet to awaken them. This type of wooden pole pillow was also used in the young men's house where men lived during their bachelor years (Minzokugaku Kenkyūjo 1951:534). The custom of young men's houses has completely disappeared today.

Decorative motifs on lacquered neckrests include flowers (especially the chrysanthemum, which represents long life), scenery from famous poems or stories, or the crest of a family. One interesting decorative motif was an imaginary animal called *baku* which is believed to eat bad dreams. Its body is like a bear, its nose like an elephant, its eyes like a rhinoceros, its tail like an ox, and its legs are like a tiger. The image of *baku* was probably developed from an ancient Chinese mythological creature who was a guardian against evil spirits. Some neckrests have only the calligraphy of the character '*baku*', without a real image, thereby avoiding the rather fearsome character of the animal.

Various contrivances were also attached to wooden neckrests. Drawers were made inside of the neckrest, so people could store their belongings or valuables. Some of the drawers even have a lock, so they functioned as a safety deposit box. This type of neckrest was very convenient to take along during a long journey to keep valuables safely under the neck during the night at an inn. Many strangers usually shared a single room of an inn during the Edo period. Inevitably, however, thieves who specialized in stealing from neckrests also appeared. One extant example of this type of journey neckrest contained an abacus, a candle and candle stand, and a mirror.

Letter carriers during the Edo period, who traveled long distances, also carried a box-shaped leather pillow with a lock to keep important letters (Yano 1985:122-124). Fishermen took a wooden neckrest on board for fishing trips. They kept necessities such as fishing tools, tobacco and matches in the drawer.

Some neckrests have a device to allow incense to burn inside. The fragrance comes through the holes made on the body of the neckrest. This type was used in privileged households, or in the rooms of courtesans in the pleasure quarters, and they are usually elaborately decorated in lacquer. The kinds of incense burned included aloeswood and musk, and the smell of this incense was believed to act as an aphrodisiac.

Edward Morse, who went to Japan in 1877, just nine years after the Meiji period (1868-1912) started, was one of the foreign professors and advisors invited by the Japanese Government. He taught Biology at the institution that subsequently became Tokyo University. He was the first person to introduce the theory of evolution, and also contributed to the establishment of the subjects of archaeology and anthropology in Japan. The new Meiji government was eager to adopt Western technology and knowledge. In 1871, the government passed an ordinance allowing for the freedom to choose hair styles, and thus tried to promote more "civilized" Western hair styles. Morse mentioned that most young men whom he saw had Western style hair, but old people, farmers, and fishermen were still keeping the traditional hair styles. One student who worked with him was having a problem because his hair stood up straight, so it was difficult to comb neatly. This is because the front of the head was always shaved when men had the traditional topknot (Morse 1917:302-303). In any event, Western hair styles became a symbol of the "Civilization and Enlightenment" of the early Meiji period.

There were also many other changes in Japan around this period, but large areas of ordinary life still remained almost unchanged from the Edo period. One of the traditional customs and objects which caught Morse's curious mind was the wooden neckrest. Many accounts concerning it occur in his two books, *Japanese Homes and Their Surroundings* (1888), and *Japan Day by Day* (1917). Morse was a skillful illustrator and he produced all of the drawings in his two books. Among them there are a few illustrations of people using neckrests. One drawing shows a woman reclining, with her baby beside her, using a wooden neckrest in an ordinary farm house. He also drew the scene and wrote about one of the morning chores of a Japanese inn, when all the wooden neckrests were collected and the old papers on top of the little cloth pillow were changed to new ones. Morse experimented with using a neckrest himself, and wrote that he enjoyed using it for a nap of two hours, but he also thought that it might cause a cramp in the neck if used all night, unless one was accustomed to it. He also mentioned that this type of wooden pillow was developed because of women's and men's hair styles (Morse 1917:62-63). Wooden neckrests seemed to have been ubiquitous at the beginning part of the Meiji period.

It is interesting that traditional neckrests were still used by the majority of people, even if some people started having Western-style hair. Some illustrations of books from around this time actually represent men with Western hair styles using a wooden neckrest. Wooden neckrest lost their function of protecting men's topknots, but they continued to be used because that was the way things had always been done.

Movements to abolish women's traditional hair styles, which were said to be "wasteful, painful, rigid and unclean," in favor of Western hair styles, began around 1886. However, there was also severe criticism against women who drastically changed their hair styles (Ōhara 1988:172-177). Nevertheless, Western hair styles attracted young, progressive women. Although women's traditional hair styles existed for a long time, by the Taishō period (1912-1925) the easily-arranged Western hair style attracted more and more people. Following the change of hair styles more comfortable cloth pillows, which already existed in Japan, and also ones which were newly introduced from Western culture, gradually took over the popular position of the wooden neckrest of the previous periods.

CLOTH PILLOWS AND THEIR STUFFINGS

Cloth pillows have been popularly used in East Asian countries for a long time, since they are the most comfortable type of headrest for sleep. In Korea it was customary for a new bride to take a pair of cloth pillows embroidered by herself for honeymoon use. For this reason young women try to perfect their talents in embroidery (Tenri Daigaku and Tenrikyō Dōyūsha 1986:218). Embroidery motifs include auspicious symbols such as a pair of cranes or a crane and turtle for togetherness and longevity. But the most popular one is a nine-bird motif: a pair of birds, usually mandarin ducks, with seven chicks that symbolize a harmonious marriage blessed with many children. A pair of male and female mandarin ducks are believed to mate for life, and are idealized as a model for married couples in East Asian cultures. Although the most common bird of this motif is mandarin ducks, a pair of phoenixes with seven chicks, or a pair of chickens and their chicks also occur.

Shōsōin, an Japanese Imperial treasure house of the Nara period (710-794), has one large, white, twilled silk pillow that belonged to Emperor Shōmu (701-756). Two cloth pillows, one of purple silk with silk stuffing, the other white silk with millet stuffing, were found in the burial chamber of the Golden Pavilion at Chūsonji where the mummified corpses of three generations of Fujiwawa leaders (eleventh to twelfth centuries) were buried. Another pillow is also in the chamber, but only the wooden core is left, and the outside cloth parts have rotted away. The last example is the type of cloth and wood combined pillow which was described in the wooden pillow section.

Finally, I would like to describe the stuffing of cloth pillows. In Japan grain husks, such as rice or buckwheat, are the most common. Buckwheat husk is especially favored today, since it is believed that buckwheat husk helps to keep the head cool. Small grains such as millet or beans have been also used in pillows in the past, and such stuffing may have been eaten when famines occurred.

Some dried herbs are put into pillows in China, Korea and Japan, and are believed to clear the brain and eyes of the user. Used tea leaves are also dried under the sun and then stuffed in the pillows. Pillows with this stuffing have a pleasant odor. One of the most romantic stuffings of this type is chrysanthemum. Full blooming chrysanthemums are collected and dried completely in an airy, shady place, and then put into a pillow. Pillows stuffed with this flower have a very noble fragrance. Chrysanthemum is a symbol of longevity, so this pillow prolongs life as well as clears the brain and eyes, as do pillows stuffed with dry herbs. There are many poems and haikus about chrysanthemum pillows in Japan, and we find that many of these pillows were made by a woman for an important man in her life.

> Sewn with your favorite color,
> A chrysanthemum pillow,
> with an aqua tassel.
> —*Takahashi Awajijo (1890-1955)*

Conclusion

As we have seen, a great variety of pillows has been produced in East Asia throughout the ages. Many of these have been employed for naps. In an agrarian society, when the summer is hot and humid a nap is one indispensable part of the day. People choose a cool, breezy corner of the house or a shady place under a tree in which to doze. A pillow which provides cool touch to the head was used to increase comfort. For this purpose ceramic, bamboo, rattan and some types of wooden pillows worked very well. The places where people take a nap are usually more open, public spaces of the household than the ordinary bedroom for night sleep. For this reason, people made extra efforts to produce a variety of fine pillows, some of which we see in this catalogue. These pillows must have further enhanced the pleasant, relaxed moment of a naptime.

Nevertheless wooden pillows have also had a major function for nighttime use in Japan. Especially during the Edo period, we see a direct correlation between the development of unique and elaborate hair styles and the appearance of wooden neckrests.

We have frequently observed the presence of guardian animals on East Asian pillows. In those cases where we can assume that a pillow was made specifically for funerary use, the guardian animals must have been intended to protect the deceased from evil spirits. Naturally, the same motifs are also seen on pillows designed for everyday use. One imagines that in this case, the guardian animals were felt to protect the sleeping person during the potentially dangerous period of loss of consciousness that accompanies sleep.

The tremendous importance of dreams in pre-modern societies inevitably affected the iconography of the pillow. People wished to avoid bad dreams and nightmares, and hoped to have dreams that would indicate good luck. As was noted above, the *baku* devoured the negative dreams, while a variety of auspicious motifs can be associated with the desire for pleasant and positive dreams.

In any case, most of us spend approximately one third of our life resting our heads on a pillow of some type or other. East Asian people have included many wishes in a variety of pillows, including wishes for comfort, peace and lucky dreams while they slept.

Notes

I would like to acknowledge the generous assistance of Sarah Elman, Lillian Lau, Chonhee Rhim and Amy Tsiang in the writing of this essay. Also, I appreciate the cooperation of the East Asian Library at UCLA in facilitating my research.

117. Ceramic pillow

China

12th century

Stoneware

13.2 x 15.5 x 8.8 cm.

FMCH 91.598

The rectangular body is covered with white slip. Then green and yellow glazes are partly applied over the slip. The upper area has an incised design of undulating sea waves, and a crane standing on a rock. On the opposite side from the crane there seems also to be some incised figure, probably a turtle or a rising sun with clouds, but the area is worn so it is difficult to tell exactly what it is. A crane symbolizes long life; moreover, a crane standing on a rock beside the sea means that a person will gain an important official position (Nozaki 1928:478-9). Both sides are decorated with a relief of running deer with flowers and vines. A deer also symbolizes longevity. The sound and tone of the Chinese character for 'deer' is the same as the character for 'fief', so a deer is an auspicious sign for a successful career, riches, and honor in China. Each end panel has a relief of a standing human figure holding a long object. This figure must also have some symbolic meaning or function, perhaps as a guardian of some sort.

The rectangular pillow has a floral design in green, yellow, and colorless lead glazes. This type of three-color glaze was quite popular around this period in China. There is a very similar pillow in Chūgoku Tōchin (Osaka Shiritsu Tōyō Tōji Bijutsukan 1984:pl. 115).

118. Ceramic pillow

China;

12th-13th century

Stoneware

9 x 25.9 x 11.2 cm.

FMCH 92.15

119. Ceramic Pillow

China;

17th-19th century

Stoneware

11.2 x 23.2 x 10.4 cm.

FMCH 91.300

A brownish-grey glaze covers the whole body except the base. There are dark brown paintings of peonies and calligraphy on the front and back. The two ends have paintings of lotus flowers and butterflies, with circular open holes as the centers of the two large lotus flowers. These holes served also as the air holes for this ceramic pillow. All ceramic pillows have one or more air holes to allow air to escape from the inside while it is being fired, in order to prevent cracking. There is calligraphy painted with Chinese ink and brush on the base. This was probably done by the owners in a later period.

The porcelain pillow is decorated with several typical Chinese auspicious symbols, including a lion, bats, and plum blossoms. The lion is present to guard the sleeping person from evil spirits. In addition, the sound and tone of the Chinese character for 'lion' and those of the character indicating the very high status of government officials are similar, and thus a lion represents distinction in one's career. A lion is often depicted with a silk ball, as it is here, which is also a symbol of good luck. The two bats are shown holding two old open-work coins on the top of the pillow. The old coins represent wealth. The sound and tone of the Chinese character for 'bat' and that for 'fortune' are also the same, so a bat is considered to be an animal that will bring fortune. The plum blossom is highly prized by Chinese people since it opens with a noble fragrance in the earliest spring when it is still cold. Thus this pillow has a rich array of auspicious signs. There is a very similar pillow in the Folkware Collection of the National Central Library in Taiwan (Kuo li chung yang t'u shu kuan T'ai-wan fen kuan 1980:pl. 46.)

120. Ceramic pillow

China;

17th-19th century

Porcelain

12 x 13.6 x 6.1 cm.

FMCH 91.573

121. Ceramic pillow

China; 19th century

Stoneware

11 x 24.765 x 10.795 cm.

FMCH 91.574

The blue-glazed pillow has a floral design in a circular frame on one side. The other side has a hole in a double circular shape.

122. Ceramic pillow

China; 19th century

Stoneware

12.4 x 17.5 x 8 cm.

FMCH 91.575

A blue glaze covers the whole body. The glaze is thinner on the upper part, and becomes thicker towards the bottom.

123. Ceramic pillow

Japan;

19th-early 20th century

Porcelain

18.9 x 8.9 x 11.3 cm.

FMCH 86.2462

The pale green glazed pillow is decorated with simple Chinese-style motifs. This type of ceramic pillow was probably produced for people who admired Chinese style and liked to use objects with a Chinese flavor, such as members of the Japanese literati.

The blue-green glazed pillow has a rather large stopper on one side. An incense burner was probably put inside of the pillow, and fragrance came through the holes of both ends.

124. Ceramic pillow

Japan;

19th-early 20th century

Stoneware

21.5 x 11.2 x 12.3 cm.

FMCH 92.18

125. Headrest

China;

18th-early 20th century

Bamboo

16 x 22 x 15 cm.

FMCH 88.974

Two side slabs are carved into a U-shape and inserted into two thick slabs of the base. These four slabs act as the frame of the headrest. Other thinner slabs are inserted into the frame. The whole body was constructed by the insertion method. Between the inserted slabs, especially close to the frame, there are open spaces which allow cool air to circulate. The smooth, clean surface of the bamboo slabs is also cool to the touch of the user's head. Bamboo headrests are usually used for a summer nap.

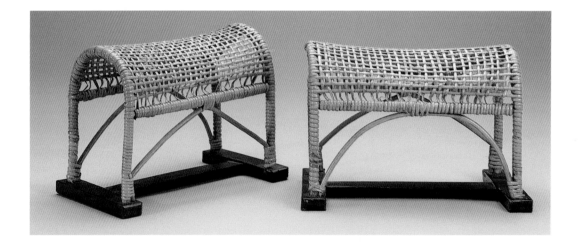

126. Headrest

Japan; 20th century

Wood, rattan,

and lacquer

15.2 x 22.1 x 11.6 cm.

FMCH 91.73

This type of open-plaited rattan headrest has been very popular and exists all over Japan. People still use it today for a nap in the summertime.

This long, square-ended pillow has a solid frame inside to protect the woven body. The body is finely twill-plaited all over, creating diamond-shaped designs on all four sides towards the outer edges and on the two ends.

127. Pillow

Japan?;

early 20th century?

Woven rattan and wood

13.5 x 55.5 x 13 cm.

FMCH 91.72

128. Pillow

Japan?; 20th century?

Rattan

30.5 x 17.7 x 17.5 cm.

FMCH 91.74

A bundle of rattan sticks supports the body and two circular rattan ends. Open-plaited, narrow rattan strips form a cylindrical body with a narrow center that flares out toward the ends. The form is reminiscent of a Japanese hand drum.

129. Headrest

China; 19th century

Wood and lacquer

19.2 x 41 x 13.8 cm.

FMCH 91.71

The two outer sides have relief work of peonies in vases. A peony symbolizes riches and honor in Chinese culture. The word for 'vase' and that for 'peace' have the same pronounciation in Chinese. Thus the vase motif is an auspicious symbol of riches, honor, and peace.

130. Neckrest

Korea;

19th-early 20th century

Carved wood

17 x 20 x 10.5 cm.

FMCH 88.1253

In Korea many types of headrest were made from wood. Men usually used them for naps. This type of neckrest developed from the shape of armrests, which were an important piece of furniture in Korean households. The ancient Korean custom of a king presenting an armrest to an official at the time of retirement to show appreciation for his service to the country continued into the Choson period (1392-1910).

131. Neckrest

Japan; 19th century

Pawlonia wood

and fabric

22.1 x 10.4 x 8.1 cm.

FMCH 86.2425

Thin pawlonia boards are constructed into a trapezoidal neckrest. This was the most popular shape for wooden neckrests from the nineteenth century to the beginning of the twentieth century in Japan. Moreover, the base is frequently curved, although many flat-based neckrests also existed. Apparently the curved base allowed the head to roll more easily from side to side than did the flat base. This period of Japanese history saw the appearance of wooden neckrests along with the development of elaborate hair-styles. People used neckrests to protect their hair-dos. A little cloth pillow was part of the top of the wooden neckrest, and a piece of paper was laid over the pillow to prevent it from being soiled. This particular neckrest was used by a man since the cloth pillow has a lion motif, which is often seen in Japanese sleeping accessories for men. The lion may have had the same iconographical meaning in Japan as that discussed for cat. 120, a Chinese porcelain pillow.

132. Neckrest

Japan; 19th century

Wood, lacquer, silk

19.5 x 18.8 x 11 cm

FMCH 86.2423

This neckrest belongs to the type called "Pick-shape neckrest," which was a popular shape for wooden neckrests during this period. The name derives from the fact that it looks like the shape of a pick used for a musical instrument such as a *samisen*. This piece is lacquered red and the cloth pillow is also red, indicating that it was used by a woman.

133. Headrest

Japan; late 19th-
early 20th century

Wood, fabric, and

buckwheat husks

17.1 x 8 x 14 cm.

FMCH 86.2437

The legs of this headrest are collapsible. When the legs are folded, the whole headrest becomes a compact oval shape for easy carrying. The top fabric section contains buckwheat husks, which are the most preferred stuffing for pillows in Japan today. Buckwheat husks are believed to cool the excess heat of people's heads, and thus produce comfortable sleep.

134. Headrest

Japan; modern

Wood

12 x 31.6 x 8 cm.

FMCH 91.328

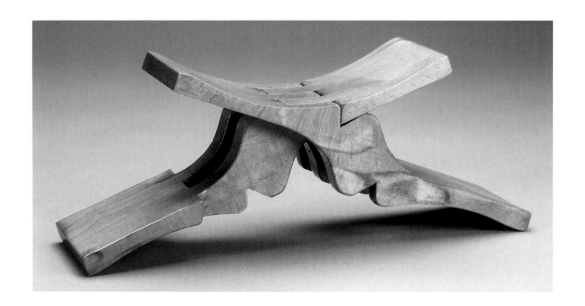

This type of travelling headrest exists in all East Asian countries.

This black lacquered box has a full assortment of Chinese auspicious symbols painted in gold. The Chinese characters for joy or happiness are held by bats. There are also formalized dragons, clouds, peonies, phoenixes, peaches, chrysanthemums, and other motifs. The gently dented upper part makes this box very suitable for a pillow. A black lacquered tray is set inside. The inside of the box is all covered in leather. There is a metal lock, and two metal hands on the two ends. Locked wooden neckrests existed in nineteenth- and early twentieth-century Japan. Valuables and important documents and letters were kept inside. If this box is actually a pillow, the owner must have kept very valuable and important things in it during his sleep.

135. Pillow?; box

China?

Wood, metal, lacquer,

and leather

41.2 x 16.7 x 16.6 cm.

FMCH 92.19

Oceania

HEADRESTS OF OCEANIA

JEROME FELDMAN

Throughout the Pacific region finely made utilitarian objects serve to enhance the lives of their owners. Frequently items such as bowls, pounders, spoons, bedposts, stools and headrests are not only beautifully crafted examples of indigenous esthetics, but also express complex and abstract societal values. The Western notion of a distinction between art and craft, as well as the categorization of regionally manufactured items as "material culture," have little meaning within a Pacific context. Even when Westerners appreciate such items for their artistic form, meaning is frequently overlooked. That element is an important factor in our understanding of how Pacific Islanders attribute significance to the objects they manufacture. Feldman (1986) in Micronesia and Peter Steager (1979) in Puluwat, for example, have explored the phenomenon of utilitarian objects and found that Micronesians recognize that certain utilitarian objects are great and revered art forms.

Elaborate headrests such as those in the Joss collection obviously transcend the function of simply elevating the head. Minimally, they serve as prestige items elevating one's position within a society of peers (who may have similar supports) and of those who have inferior supports or perhaps none at all. Throughout the Pacific the head is associated with spiritual power and the concentrated essence of a human being. From Indonesia through Polynesia it is considered rude to touch the head of a person to whom you are not intimately related. In some places, such as Tikopia, there are even certain circumstances under which a son cannot touch his father's hair (Firth 1963:183).

It is, therefore, not surprising to find that in many cultures, particularly in Melanesia, part of the veneration of ancestors includes the preservation of their skulls. In Cenderawasih Bay the ancestors' skulls are sometimes placed within statues *(korwar)*[1] where they can be consulted or called upon for protection. Sometimes these *korwar* skulls can be overmodeled in clay with stone or shell inlays in the eye sockets. Similar overmodeled skulls are found in the men's houses, *tambaran,* along the Sepik River of Papua New Guinea. In the Papuan Gulf they are sometimes suspended as necklaces by their descendants. In Vanuatu life-sized statues called *rambramb* are constructed out of twigs, bark cloth, clay and spider webs surmounted by brightly painted overmodeled skulls. These figures are stored in the rafters of one's house as a form of ancestral protection and veneration. Among the Maori of New Zealand the tattooed heads of ancestors are mummified to memorialize great warriors. Since these skulls are so highly valued by their descendants, the worst thing an enemy tribe can do is to capture such a head and defile it. Among the Asmat of Irian Jaya, an ancestor's head is frequently used as a headrest for his son, thus transferring spiritual power from one generation to another (Saulnier 1960:18) (fig. 35).

Heads of the living are also special and are greatly augmented by ornamentation. One's status is expressed by facial painting or tattoos, by elaborate coiffures (sometimes held together with mud and decorated with feathers of exotic birds), and by finely carved decorative combs. Combs are found in many areas of the Pacific;

the forms of those found in Samoa and Tonga are especially delicate and refined.

The headrest, therefore, is the support for the most important part of the human being. As such, it brings one's senses in close contact with whatever concepts inform the design of the support. Throughout much of Melanesia, headrests sport carvings in human and animal forms. Wherever these carvings have been investigated, tribal lore plays an important role.

In Cenderawasih Bay, among the Papuans of Waropen, beautiful headrests often have two figures at the base, reported by scholars to be male and female although no genitalia are visible. On top of the figures, a carved double-headed snake makes the object forbidden for women to handle. The taboo may be due to the fact that two snakes figure prominently in Waropen creation myths. One serpent, named Roponggai, was said to be the size of an ironwood tree and had a mouth larger than the central portion of a house. It stalked the back country devouring people in the region of the Woisimi River. The population consequently dispersed to the Numfoor region of the bay. Two people remained, however, and killed the snake. Roponggai then transformed himself into a canoe which was used by the pair to travel to Numfoor and report their victory

to the refugees (Held 1957: 285-6). Another mythological snake, Siroei, is likewise responsible for the dispersal of humankind. Siroei was created when a woman drank a snake egg, conceiving and giving birth to the giant devouring serpent. Men from the interior of the island killed Siroei, but he revived in the form of an iguana. When the men tried to cook the animal he attempted to reveal his identity, but to no avail, and he was eaten. The men died as a result and in revenge Siroei scattered humanity over the earth (Held 1957:308).

Waropen headrests *(runa)* also sometimes have the form of an iguana or crocodile (Held 1957:332). Not surprisingly, the cosmogonic devouring monster also took the form of these creatures. Like the snake, these creatures were killed, but with different results. The iguana's body was divided and the parts placed in various compartments of a house where they became the various families of the region. The dead crocodile's head became the central clan and its tail became another clan. Crocodiles are thought to be harmless and can be hunted with impunity, for only supernatural crocodiles may harm humans. Hence, a person who is injured or killed by a crocodile has encountered the supernatural reptile (Held 1957:310). In other parts of

FIG. 35.
Asmat man using an ancestor's skull as a neckrest. From T. Saulnier, 1960, *Le papous coupeurs de têtes, 167 jours dans la préhistoire*, Paris, p. 18.

FIG. 36.
Tonga *kali*. Pen and ink sketch by Johann Reinhold Forster, 1774, from his journal.

the bay sometimes bird forms can be seen (see Taylor 1991:262-3, fig, IX.16), although the bird's legacy to mankind is not explained in recorded myths.

When a couple marries, the wife lays her head upon a piece of bamboo or a block of wood while the husband uses the carved headrest or *runa*. According to one myth, at one time men conceived children through their ear

the snake bite the ends of the curving neck support. Abstract curvilinear design between the figures and the snake's body possibly shows the influence of Islamic decoration from the neighbors to the east in Maluku (eastern Indonesia).

Sexual mythology also plays a role concerning the headrests of the Azera people of northeastern New

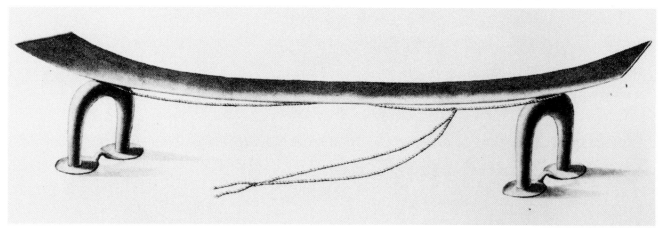

FIG. 37.
Tonga *kali*.
Pen and wash sketch
by John Cleveley
1774.

while it rested upon the *runa* (Held 1957:332). During the marriage ceremony the bride and groom are publicly laid on top of each other eight times. At the final time the man lies at the side of his bride and is given a *runa* to rest his head upon (Held 1957:109). This association of headrests with fertility may also have something to do with a story about how primeval women, the Aighei, played with the headrests of the men.

The Joss collection headrest is a superb example of the double-figured type (cat. 136). The pair are carved in the style of ancestor images, *korwar*, mentioned above. Although no gender is indicated they are probably male and female. The curving body of a double-headed snake perches directly above their heads. The open mouths of

Guinea. Carl Schmitz in his study of Azera headrests relates their human form to those of religious sculpture in the same area. Such sculptures represent the spirit or god Mungus. Mungus is a male god in the heavens, considered to be the "lord of the pigs" whose cannibalistic urges destroyed the world in primeval times. He was betrayed by an "earth mother" who gave birth to twins, one right-handed and one left-handed. The twins later killed the giant Mungus and freed the world for human culture to develop. The headrests, which show human figures lying face up, represent the body of the dead god upon which the twins rested after the battle. The headrests also duplicate the pose taken by successful warriors when they return from headhunting, the heads being offerings to

Mungus. Other headrests from this area represent pigs which the god consumed (Schmitz 1959:158-9).

Schmitz and other writers have related similar connections between headrest decoration and mythology in other areas of New Guinea. Papuan Gulf headrests resemble those of the Azera and Schmitz was quick to point out that the associated headhunting may point to a similar

fertility by creating twins from blood which flowed from her hands (Stöhr 1971:80).[2]

Lower Sepik headrests tend to be small and were most likely used for resting while one hunted rather than sleeping at night. There are two varieties, those made of a single piece of wood (as described above), and those made of wood, rattan and bamboo (Stöhr 1971:103) as

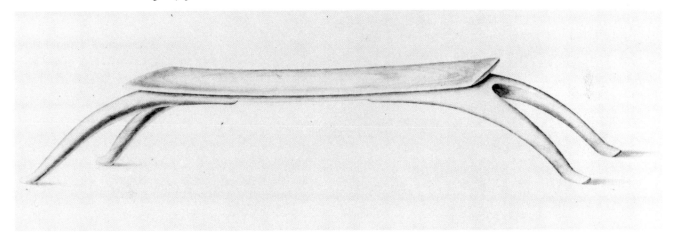

mythological source (1957:160). Whereas Azera headrests show figures lying on their back, Papuan Gulf examples lie face down (cat. 137). Both have odd twig-like shapes. This example is from the Fly River area but similar ones can also be found on the opposite side of the Gulf in the Kerewa area (Newton 1961:62-3, figs. 142-3).

It is very likely that the numerous head supports and headrests from the Sepik region likewise have mythological underpinnings. In the Lower Sepik, for example, small supports made of a single piece of wood often have female figures supporting the neck brace. Stöhr describes one in which two small figures emerge from the hands of the large female figure. He suggests that the support represents the story of the earth mother who expressed her

in the Joss collection (cat. 138). This object probably comes from the vicinity of Kararau village (Kelm 1956 1:479). On either end of the support there is a carving of a crocodile. This is a likely reference to a mythological cannibalistic giant who took a number of forms but especially became a crocodile when he created the Sepik river (Greub 1985:186; Kelm 1956 1:30).

The three headrests in the Joss collection from the Tami-Huon Gulf area of New Guinea are most likely from the Tami Islands or Tamigidu (cat. nos. 139-140). In other areas of this region only simple blocks of wood are produced. There are four types of headrest found in the Tami-Huon Gulf area. The first type (cat. 139) is supported by a single human figure whose posture

FIG. 38.
Tonga *kali*.
Pen and wash sketch
by John Cleveley
1774.

FIG. 39.
Portrait of Omai from Ra'iatea, Society Islands. Engraving by Bertolozzi 1775 after a painting by Nathaniel Dance Holland.

shows the strain of support. A second type has two rather abstract figures back to back. The third type is supported by an animal figure (e.g. a bird, as in cat. 140, or two snakes supporting a woman's head, cat. 143) and the fourth is balanced atop an abstract geometric form. Typically wood from the *afzelia biyuga* was used, although there are reports that formerly a wooden top was fitted to a rattan base (Bodrogi 1961:92-97).

The headrest plays a distinctive role in funerals. When a person dies, relatives would chew betel at the spot where the person spent most of his time. They would leave the headrest there and while hiding and request "if you are here, come and fetch your headrest and pouch." Later, relatives would retrieve the objects and bring them back to their village (Bodrogi 1961:91-2).

Although there is no certain interpretation of what beings are represented, the human face with triangles, *nausung*, above and below the eyes may represent Moro, one of two culture heroes. Moro was the "wise and gifted" hero whereas Aispel was a "foolish troublemaker" (Dark 1979:150).

Frequently headrests are non-representational. Most headrests from New Guinea are abstract, such as our example from Collingwood Bay (cat. 141) and the object from the middle Sepik which is likely a small stool (cat.

142). Micronesian headrests tend as well to be abstract. Examples from Kiribati resemble closely the minimalist esthetics of other Micronesian utilitarian arts (see Graebner 1927:7, fig. 7).

Fiji, Tonga and Samoa have been trading for centuries. Consequently they share much of their material culture. Their large, ocean-going canoes were nearly identical, and in the past Tonga produced small female figurines for use in Fiji. Headrests follow a similar pattern. It is very difficult to distinguish Tongan and Fijian examples, as nearly all variations were found in both locales. Most authors attribute the headrest of cat. 146 to Tonga, since that is where it was obtained. However there is a distinct name in Fijian *(hahapo)* as well as in Tongan *(fafapo)* for this type of headrest. Possibly it and cat. 147 were made in the Lau islands which are politically Fijian and culturally Tongan (Ewins 1982:66).

The generic term in Fiji and Tonga for a headrest is *kali*. In Fiji they were reserved for chiefs and were possibly intended to preserve the elaborate coiffures worn by those of high status. In Fiji, *kali ni bitu* are made of bamboo with wooden legs lashed onto the horizontal bar. Those with bars made of walrus tusk are called *kalitabua* (Clunie 1986:152-3: Ewins 1982:64-5). Two other headrests (cat. nos. 148-149) are generally believed to come from Fiji.

Another headrest is more often found in Tonga (cat. 150). The type, or one somewhat similar, appears in a sketch by Johann Reinhold Forster in Cook's voyage in 1774 (fig. 36). A similar four-legged version was drawn by John Cleveley on the same voyage (fig. 37). The type appears however in catalogues of Fijian material as well. The cylindrical cross pieces of cat. nos. 145 and 151 are variations resembling the Samoan *'ali* where the cross piece is made of bamboo.

Headrests in this region are highly abstract, and are made of hard, dark wood called *vesi* in Fiji. They are long and some may have been used for more than one individual. The designs are remarkable geometric abstractions. One type brought back by the Cook expedition was more organic with oddly-shaped outstretched legs (fig. 38) (Kaeppler 1978:229-30).

In Tonga headrests are seen as analogous to a mother's arm. An expression for a good child is *kali loa*, which means both a long headrest and a mother's arm. Good children have a reputation for sleeping on their mother's arms. This expression links a child's character to his, or her, closeness to the mother.[3]

Samoan headrests, *'ali*, are made of bamboo with wooden legs. They often appear to be more crudely made than Tongan and Fijian examples. An interesting custom relates that a person who uses the *'ali* must take great care as to how he orients his feet. While the head is a center of power, the feet are the opposite both physically and metaphorically. To accidentally aim one's feet at another person's head while sleeping would contaminate that person's *mana*. To avoid this, typically one should aim his feet towards the side pillars of the house. Another position is to cross the legs or cover them with a mat (Buck 1930:78-79).

Tahiti and the Cook Islands both produced items which could function as small stools or headrests. The nobleman Omai brought one with him when he traveled to England in 1773 aboard the *HMS Resolution*. He carried his "stool" with him as an emblem of his high rank (Barrow 1979:16, fig. 10) (fig. 39).

Throughout Oceania the head is regarded as the focal point of the body and hence its most valuable and vulnerable part. The headrest not only supports the head, it partakes of the custom and lore surrounding it. Mythological motifs and figures on headrests protect the head and serve as subliminal reminders of the mythical past as well as of one's own ancestral history. Hence headrests are loaded with meaning, have beautiful form and support the most important part of the body.

Notes

[1] *Korwar* refers both to the images of the ancestors and to the style in which they are carved.

[2] Myths of earth mothers who give birth to or otherwise create twins are found commonly in the creation myths of this area.

[3] I wish to thank Ms. Mele Taulanga, a recent graduate of Hawaii Loa College, for this information.

136. Headrest; *runa*

Cenderawasih Bay;

Irian Jaya, Indonesia

Carved, incised wood

17.145 x 16.6 x 16.2 cm.

FMCH 92.16

137. Headrest

Fly River;

Wabuda Island;

Papua New Guinea

Carved, incised wood

with pigment and fiber

58 x 22.5 x 17 cm.

FMCH 86.2458

138. Headrest

Lower Sepik River;

Papua New Guinea

Carved, wrapped wood,

vegetable fiber and

bamboo

33.5 x 14.5 x 9.1 cm.

FMCH 86.2422

139. Headrest

Huon Gulf;

Morobe Province;

Papua New Guinea

Carved, incised wood

with pigment and lime

11.6 x 13.8 x 5.5 cm.

FMCH 87.377

140. Headrest

Huon Gulf;

Papua New Guinea

Carved, painted wood

with pigment (lime?)

16.7 x 17.5 x 9 cm.

FMCH 86.2424

141. Headrest

Collingwood Bay;

Papua New Guinea

Carved wood

with pigment

13.4 x 10.7 x 7.5 cm.

FMCH 91.299

142. Stool, headrest?

Middle Sepik;

Papua New Guinea

Carved wood

13 x 46.5 x 16 cm.

FMCH 88.988

143. Headrest

Huon Gulf;

Papua New Guinea

Wood

16.5 x 14.5 x 4.5 cm.

FMCH 88.967

144. Headrest

Imbuando;

Lower Sepik;

Papua New Guinea

Carved, incised wood

with pigment

43.18 x 12.8 x 9 cm.

FMCH 92.20

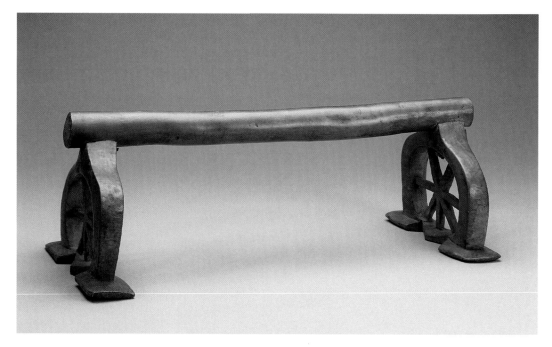

145. Headrest, *kali*

Tonga or Fiji

Carved, tied wood and

vegetable fiber

47.5 x 16 x 21.9 cm.

FMCH 86.2417

146. Headrest; *kali*

Tonga

Carved wood

15.7 x 30 x 9.8 cm.

FMCH 91.77

147. Headrest; *kali*

Tonga or Fiji

Carved, stained wood

12 x 40.5 x 9.1 cm.

FMCH 91.76

148. Headrest; *kali*

Fiji

Carved wood with

inlaid beads

21.3 x 44.9 x 8 cm.

FMCH 91.75

149. Headrest; *kali*

Fiji

Carved wood

36.5 x 18.5 x 9 cm.

FMCH 87.376

150. Headrest, *kali*

Tonga or Fiji

Carved, tied wood and

vegetable fiber

47 x 16 x 14.5 cm.

FMCH 86.2409

151. Headrest; *kali*

Tonga or Fiji

Carved, incised, braided

wood and plant fiber

41.5 x 13.2 x 13.5 cm.

FMCH 86.2455

● **AFRICA**

Agthe, Johanna
1983   *Luba Hemba.* Frankfurt: Museum
        für Völkerkunde.

Adamson, Joy
1967   *The Peoples of Kenya.* New York:
        Harcourt, Brace & World, Inc.

Allen, James de Vere
1976   "A Somali Headrest." *MILA* 5, 2:42-58.

Aquina, Sister Mary (A.K.H. Weinrich)
1968   "*Mutimwi*—A Note on the Waist Belt
        of the Karanga." *Native Affairs
        Department Annual* 11, 5:3-4.

Arnold, Marion I.
1981   *Zimbabwe Stone Sculpture.* Buluwayo:
        Books of Zimbabwe.

Aschwanden, Herbert
1982   *Symbols of Life.* Ursula Cooper, trans.
        Gweru: Mambo Press.

1987   *Symbols of Death.* Ursula Cooper, trans.
        Gweru: Mambo Press.

Baden-Powell, Robert S.S.
1897   *The Matabele Campaign of 1896: Being a
        Narrative of the Campaign in Supressing
        the Native Rising in Matabeleland and
        Mashonaland.* London: Methuen & Co.
        Reprint 1970. Westport, Connecticut:
        Negro University Press.

Baines, Thomas
1946   *The Northern Goldfields Diaries of
        Thomas Baines' Second Journey, 1871-72.*
        J. P. R. Wallis, ed. London: Chatto and
        Windus.

1877   *The Gold Regions of South Eastern Africa.*
        London: Edward Stanford.

Baker, Hollis S.
1966   *The Furniture of the Ancient World.*
        New York: Giniger Books.

Balander, J. and Jacques Maquet
1974   *The Dictionary of Black African
        Civilizations.* New York: Leon Amiel.

Balfour, Alice B.
1895   *Twelve Hundred Miles in a Wagon.*
        London: Edward Arnold.

Bastin, Marie-Louise
1969   "Arts of the Angolan Peoples. III
        Songo." *African Arts* 2, 3:50-57, 77-81.

Baxter, P.T.W. and Audrey Butt
1953   *The Azande and Related Peoples of the
        Anglo Egyptian Sudan and Belgian
        Congo.* London: International African
        Institute.

Battiss, Walter W., G.H. Franz, J.W. Grossert and
        H.P. Junod
1958   *The Art of Africa.* Pietermaritzburg:
        Shuter and Shooter.

Beach, David N.
1980   *The Shona and Zimbabwe 900-1850.*
        New York: Africana Publishing
        Company.

1984   *Zimbabwe before 1900.*
        Gweru: Mambo Press.

Becker, Peter
1975   *Trails and Tribes in Southern Africa.*
        London: Hart-Davis, MacGibbon.

Becker, Rayda
1992   "Headrests: Tsonga Types and
        Variations." In *Art and Ambiguity.
        Perspectives on the Brenthurst Collecton of
        Southern African Art*, 58-76.
        Johannesburg: Johannesburg Art
        Gallery.

Beckwith, Carol and Angela Fisher
1990   *African Ark*. New York: Harry N.
        Abrams Inc.

Bedaux, Roger M.A.
1974   "Tellem, reconnaissance archéologique
        d'une culture de l'ouest Africain au
        moyen âge: Les Appuie-Nuque." *Journal
        de la Société des Africanistes* 44: 7-42.

1988   "Tellem and Dogon Material Culture."
        African Arts 11, 4:38-45, 91.

Beech, Marvyn W.H.
1911   *The Suk: Their Language and Folklore*.
        The Claredon Press. Reprint 1969.
        New York: Negro Universities Press.

Ben-Amos, Paula
1989   "African Visual Arts from a Social
        Perspective." *African Studies Review* 32,
        2:1-53.

Bent, James Theodore
1892   *The Ruined Cities of Mashonaland*.
        London: Longmans, Green.

1896   *The Ruined Cities of Mashonaland*,
        3d ed. London: Longmans, Green.

Berglund, Axel-Ivar
1976   *Zulu Thought-Patterns and Symbolism*.
        Uppsala: Swedish Institution of
        Missionary Research. Reprint 1989.
        Bloomington: Indiana University Press.

Berliner, Paul F.
1978   *The Soul of Mbira*. Berkeley and Los
        Angeles: University of California Press.

Berlyn, Phillipa
1968   "Some Aspects of the Material Culture
        of the Shona People." *Native Affairs
        Department Annual* 9, 5:68-73.

Bhila, H.H.K.
1982   *Trade and Politics in a Shona Kingdom.
        The Manyika and their Portuguese and
        African Neighbours, 1575-1902*.
        London: Longman.

Biebuyck, Daniel
1985   *The Arts of Zaire. Vol. 1: Southwestern
        Zaire*. Berkeley and Los Angeles:
        University of California Press.

Bockhoff, Esther and Nancy I. Fleming
1986   *Tribal Traditions of Kenya*. Cleveland:
        The Cleveland Museum of Natural
        History.

Bourdillon, Michael F.C.
1982   *The Shona Peoples*. Harare:
        Mambo Press.

1987   *The Shona Peoples*, rev. ed. Harare:
        Mambo Press.

Bourgeois, Arthur P.
1984   *Art of the Yaka and Suku*. Meudon:
        Alain and Françoise Chaffin.

1982   "Yaka and Suku Leadership Headgear."
        African Arts 15, 3:30-5, 92.

Brown, Jean
1986   "The Pokot." In Esther Bockhoff and
        Nancy I. Fleming, eds., *Tribal Traditions
        of Kenya*, 27-32. Cleveland: The
        Cleveland Museum of Natural History.

Brown, William Harvey
1899   *On the South African Frontier: The
            Adventures and Observations of an
            American in Mashonaland and
            Matabeleland.* London: Sampson, Low,
            Marston. Reprint 1970. New York:
            Negro Universities Press.

Buffalo Museum of Science
1969   *Out of Africa.* Buffalo: Humboldt.

Burton, William F.P.
1960   "Notes and Watercolors of Luba
            Coiffures, 1915-1928/30, Congo
            Evangelistic Mission, Mwanza."
            Archives of the Section of Ethnography
            of the Musée Royal de l'Afrique
            Centrale, Tervuren, Belgium.

Caton-Thompson, Gertrude
1931   *The Zimbabwe Culture.* Oxford:
            Claredon Press.

1970   *The Zimbabwe Culture,* 2d ed. London:
            Frank Cass.

Cerulli, Ernesta
1956   *The Peoples of South-West Ethiopia and
            its Borderland.* London: International
            African Institute.

Cerulli, Enrico
1959   *Scritti vari editi ed inediti.* Rome:
            Amministrazione Fiduclaria Italia della
            Somalia.

Christol, Frederic
1911   *L'Art dans l'Afrique Australe.* Paris:
            Berger-Levrault.

Cole, Herbert M. and Doran H. Ross
1977   *The Arts of Ghana.* Museum of Cultural
            History, University of California.

Conner, Michael W. and Diane Pelrine
1983   *The Geometric Vision: Arts of the Zulu.*
            West Lafayette: Purdue University Galleries.

Cornet, Joseph
1972   *Artes de l'Afrique noire au pays du fleuve
            Zaire.* Brussels: Arcade.

Crowley, Daniel.
1958   "Aesthetic Judgment and Cultural
            Relativism." *The Journal of Aesthetics and
            Art Criticism* 17, 2:187-193.

Davison, Basil
1966   *African Kingdoms.* New York: Time-Life
            Books.

d'Azevedo, Warren
1958   "A Structural Approach to Aesthetics:
            Towards a Definition of Art in
            Anthropology." *American Anthropologist*
            60:702-14.

Delange, Jacqueline
1974   *The Art and Peoples of Black Africa.*
            Carol Jopling, trans. New York: E. P.
            Dutton and Co.

Delhaise, Charles
1908   "Ethnographie Congolaise: Chez les
            Warundi et les Wahorohoro." *Bulletin de
            la Societe Royale Belge de Geographie*
            32:429-50.

Desplagnes, Louis
1907   *Le Plateau Central Nigérien.* Paris:
            Émile Larose.

Dieterlen, Germaine
1982   *Le Titre d'honneur des Arou
            (Dogon-Mali).* Paris: Musée de
            l'Homme, Societe des Africanistes.

Dewey, William J.
1986   "Shona Male and Female Artistry"
            African Arts 19, 3:64-7, 84.

1991   "Pleasing the Ancestors: The Traditional
            Art of the Shona People of Zimbabwe."
            Ph.D. dissertation, Indiana University.

1991a   "Review of *Supports de Rêves*" *African
            Arts* 24, 1:92-4.

1991b   "Blacksmiths and Kings: Forging
            Symbolic Meaning in Luba Metal Arts."
            Paper presented at the Annual Meeting
            of the College Arts Association,
            Washington D.C.

Dewey, William J. and S. Terry Childs
Forthcoming "Forging Symbolic Meaning in Zaire
            and Zimbabwe." In Peter R. Schmidt,
            ed., *The Culture of African Iron Working*.
            Gainesville: The University of Florida
            Press.

Donovan, Alan
1988   "Turkana Functional Art." *African Arts*
            21, 3:44-7.

Douglas, Richard
1906   Unpublished letter to the American
            Museum of Natural History, New York.

Duponchael, Christian
1980   *Masterpieces of the Peoples Republic of the
            Congo*. New York: The African
            American Institute.

Edwards, I.E.S.
1976   "Catalogue: Annex." In Katherine S.
            Gilbert, Joan K. Holt, and Sara Hudson,
            eds., *Treasures of Tutankhamun*, 98-173.
            New York: Ballantine Books.

Edwards, William
1929   "From Birth to Death." *Native Affairs
            Department Annual* 7:16-42.

Elisofon, Eliot and William B. Fagg
1958   *The Sculpture of Africa*. London: Thames
            and Hudson.

Ellert, Henrik
1982   "The Ndoro of Zimbabwe." *The
            Zimbabwe Science News* 16, 5:120-21.

1984   *The Material Culture of Zimbabwe*.
            Harare: Longman.

1985   "The Ndoro has a Long and Interesting
            History." *Africa Calls from Zimbabwe*
            151:4-5.

Emley, E.D.
1927   "The Turkana of Kolosia District."
            *Journal of the Royal Anthropolgical
            Institute* 57:157-201.

Ezra, Kate
1988   *Art of the Dogon*. New York: The
            Metropolitan Museum of Art.

Falgayrettes, Christiane
1989   *Supports de Rêves*. Paris: Fondation
            Dapper pour les Arts Africains.

Fagg, William B. and Margaret Plass
1964   *African Sculpture: An Anthology*.
            London: StudioVista.

Fedders, Andrew and Cynthia Salvadori
1977   *Turkana Pastoral Craftsmen*. Nairobi:
            Transafrican Publications.

1979   *Peoples and Cultures of Kenya*. Nairobi:
            Transafrica Publications.

Forge, Anthony
1979   "The Problem of Meaning in Art." In S.
              M. Mead, ed., *Exploring the Visual Art of
              Oceania*, 278-87. Honolulu: University
              Press of Hawaii.

Fouché, Leo
1937   *Mapungubwe*. Cambridge: Cambridge
              University Press.

Fraser, Douglas
1972   "The Symbols of Ashanti Kingship." In
              Douglas Fraser and Herbert Cole, eds.,
              African Art and Leadership, 137-52.
              Madison: University of Wisconsin Press.

Friedman, H.
1986   "Ntwane Notes." In *Catalogue of the
              Standard Bank Foundation Collection of
              African Art*, n.p. Johannesburg:
              University of Witwatersrand.

Frobenious, Leo
1985   *Ethnographische Notizen aus den Jahren
              1905 and 1906. Vol. 1: Völker am Kwilu
              und am Unteren Kasai*. Stuttgart: Franz
              Steiner Verlag.

1987   *Ethnographische Notizen aus den Jahren
              1905 and 1906. Vol. 2: Kuba, Leele,
              Nord-Kete*. Stuttgart: Franz Steiner
              Verlag.

Fry, Peter
1976   *Spirits of Protest*. Cambridge: Cambridge
              University Press.

Fynn, Henry Francis
1950   *The Diary of Henry Francis Fynn*.
              Pietermaritzburg: Shuter and Shooter.

Gardner, Guy
1963   *Mapungubwe*. Vol. 2. Pretoria: J. L. Van
              Schaik, Ltd.

Garlake, Peter S.
1973   *Great Zimbabwe*. New York: Stein and
              Day.

Gelfand, Michael and Yvonne Swart
1953   "The Nyora." *Native Affairs Department
              Annual* 30:5-11.

Goodall, Elizabeth
1946   "Rhodesian Pots with Moulded
              Decorations." *Native Affairs Department
              Annual* 23:37-49.

Guy, G.L.
1961   "Domestic Uses of Wood." *Rhodesian
              Countryman* 1, 3:6-7.

Haberland, Eike
1963   *Volker Sud-Athiopiens. Band 2:
              Galla Sud-Athiopiens*. Stuttgart: W.
              Kohlhammer Verlag.

Hall, Martin
1987   *The Changing Past: Farmers, Kings and
              Traders in Southern Africa, 200-1860*.
              Cape Town: David Philip.

Hall, R.N.
1905   *Great Zimbabwe*. London: Methuen.

Hall, R.N. and W.G. Neal
1902   *The Ancient Ruins of Rhodesia*. London:
              Methuen and Co. Reprint 1969. New
              York: Negro Universities Press.

Hamutyinei, Mordikai A. and Albert B. Plangger
1974   *Tsumo-Shumo (Shona Proverbial Lore and
              Wisdom)*. Gwelo: Mambo Press.

Hamilton, C.
1985   "Ideology, Oral Tradition and the
              Struggle for Power in the Early Zulu
              Kingdom." M.A. dissertation,
              University of Witwatersrand.

Hannan, Micheal
1981   *Standard Shona Dictionary.* Salisbury:
            The Literature Bureau.

Hardin, Kris L.
1987   "The Aesthetics of Action: Production
            and Reproduction in a West African
            Town." Ph.D. dissertation, Indiana
            University.

Herbert, Eugenia E.
1984   *Red Gold of Africa: Copper in Precolonial
            History and Culture.* Madison:
            University of Wisconsin Press.

Hiernaux, J., E. de Longress, and J. De Buyst
1971   *Fouilles Archeologiques dans la Vallée du
            Haut-Lualaba. I. Sanga. 1958.* Sciences
            Humaines, 73. Tervuren: Annales Musée
            Royal de l'Afrique Centrale.

Hodder, Ian
1977   "The Distribution of Material Culture
            Items in the Baringo District, Western
            Kenya." *Man* 12:239-69.

1982   *Symbols in Action. Ethnoarchaeological
            Studies of Material Culture.* Cambridge:
            Cambridge University Press.

Hodza, Aron and George Fortune
1979   *Shona Praise Poetry.* Oxford: Claredon
            Press.

Hole, Hugh Marshall
1928   *Old Rhodesian Days.* London:
            Macmillan. Reprint 1968. London:
            Frank Cass & Co.

Holleman, J.F.
1952   *Shona Customary Law.* London: Oxford
            University Press.

Hottot, Robert
1956   "Teke Fetishes." *Journal of the Royal
            Anthropological Institute of Great Britian
            and Ireland* 86:25-36.

Huffman, Thomas N.
1985   "The Soapstone Birds from Great
            Zimbabwe." *African Arts* 18, 3:67-73,
            99-100.

1991   "The Chronology of Great Zimbabwe."
            South African Archaeological Bulletin
            46:61-70.

1992   "Burton and the Ceramic Prehistory of
            the Upemba Basin." In *The Collection of
            W. F. P. Burton,* 69-74. Johannesburg:
            University of the Witwatersrand Art
            Galleries.

Huffman T.N. and J.C. Vogel
1986   "The Chronology of Great Zimbabwe."
            Unpublished manuscript.

Huntingford, G.W.B.
1955   *The Galla of Ethiopia. The Kingdoms of
            Kafa and Janjero.* London: International
            African Institute.

Imperato, Pascal James
1978   *Dogon Cliff Dwellers: The Art of Mali's
            Mountain People.* New York: L. Kahan
            Gallery Inc.

Jacobsohn, Margaret and Peter and Beverly Pickford
1990   *Himba: Nomads of Namibia.* Cape
            Town: Struik.

Jack, Anthony
1991   *Relics of the Colonial Era.* London:
            Michael Graham-Stewart.

Jacques, A.A.
c.1941   "Tsonga Pillows." Unpublished lecture.

Jacques, L.
1949   "Art Indigène et Appuis-tête." *Bulletin de la Mission Suisse dans l'Afrique du Sud* 49, 633:333-40.

Jacques, Victor, and Emile Storms
1886   *L'Ethnographie de la Partie Orientale de l'Afrique Equatoriale.* Brussels: F. Hayez for the Academie Royale de Belgique.

Jensen, A.E.
1959   *Altvölker Süd-Äthiopiens.* Stuttgart: W. Kohlhammer Verlag.

Johannesburg Art Gallery
1991   *Art and Ambiquity. Perspectives on the Brenthurst Collection of Southern African Art.* Johannesburg Art Gallery/ Johannesburg City Council.

Jones, David Keith
1984   *Shepherds of the Desert.* London: Elm Tree Books.

Junod, Henri A.
1962   *The Life of a South African Tribe.* 2 vols. New York: University Books Inc. Reprint of 2d rev. ed., originally published 1927.

Junkers, Wilhelm
1889   *Rissen in Afrika 1875-1886.* Vienna: Eduard Holzel.

Kaemmer, John E.
1975   "The Dynamics of a Changing Music System in Rural Rhodesia." Ph.D. dissertation, Indiana University.

Kauffman, Robert
1969   "Some Aspects of Aesthetics in Shona Music of Rhodesia." *Ethnomusicology* 13, 3:507-11.

Kidane, Girma and Richard Wilding
1976   *The Ethiopian Cultural Heritage.* Addis Ababa: University of Addis Ababa.

Klopper, Sandra
1986   "Zulu Notes." In *Catalogue of the Standard Bank Foundation Collection of African Art,* n.p. Johannesburg: University of Witwatersrand, Art Galleries.

1989   "The Art of Traditionalists in Zululand-Natal." In David Hammond-Tooke and Anitra Nettleton, eds., *Catalogue: Ten Years of Collecting (1979-1989): Standard Bank Foundation Collection of African Art and Selected Works from the University Ethnological Museum Collection,* 32-8. Johannesburg: University of Witwatersrand, Art Galleries.

1991   "'Zulu' Headrests and Figurative Carvings: The Brenthurst Collection and the Art of South-East Africa." In *Art and Ambiquity. Perspectives on the Brenthurst Collection of Southern African Art,* 80-98. Johannesburg Art Gallery/Johannesburg City Council.

Koloss, Hans J.
1990   *Art of Central Africa. Masterpieces from the Berlin Museum für Völkerkunde.* New York: The Metropolitan Museum of Art.

Kriel, A.
1971   *An African Horizon.* University of
             Capetown School of African Studies
             Communication, 35. Capetown: School
             of African Studies.

Krieger, Kurt
1969   *Westafrikanische Plastik.* Vol. 3. Berlin:
             Museum für Völkerkunde.

1990   *Ostafrikanische Plaslik.* Berlin: Museum
             für Völkerkunde.

Kyerematen, A.A.Y.
1964   *Panoply of Ghana.* London: Longmans,
             Gwen and Co.

Labouret, Henri
1931   *Les tribus du rameau lobi.* Travaux et
             Memoires d'Institut d'Ethnologie 15.
             Paris: Institut d'Ethnologie.

Lan, David M.
1983   "Making History: Spirit Mediums and
             the Guerrilla War in the Dande area of
             Zimbabwe." Ph.D. dissertation, London
             School of Economics and Political
             Science.

1985   *Guns and Rain. Guerrillas and Spirit
             Mediums in Zimbabwe.* Berkeley and
             Los Angeles: University of California
             Press.

Lancaster, Chet S.
1974   "Ethnic Identity, History and 'Tribe' in
             the Middle Zambezi Valley." *American
             Ethnologist* 1, 4:707-30.

Lawrance, J.C.D.
1957   *The Iteso. Fifty Years of Change in a
             Nilo-Hamitic Tribe of Uganda.* London:
             Oxford University Press.

Lema, Guete
1978   *La Statuaire dans la Societe Teke.* Louvain:
             Université Catholique de Louvain.

Leuzinger, Elsy
1972   *The Art of Black Africa.* London: Studio
             Vista.

Lewis, I.M.
1955   *Peoples of the Horn of African.* London:
             International African Institute.

Livingstone, David
1858   *Missionary Travels and Researches in
             South Africa.* New York: Harper and Bros.

Loughran, Katheryne S., John L. Loughran,
     John W. Johnson, and Said S. Samatar
1986   *Somalia in Word and Image.* Washington
             D.C.: Foundation for Cross Cultural
             Understanding.

Loveridge, J.P.
1982   "The *Ndoro* of Zimbabwe are not made
             from Cowrie Shells." *The Zimbabwe
             Science News* 16, 8:188-9.

McEwan, Frank
1968   "Return to Origins: New Directions for
             African Arts." *African Arts* 1, 2:18-28, 88.

1972   "Shona Art Today." *African Arts* 5, 4:8-11.

McNaughton, Patrick
1987   "African Borderland Sculpture." *African
             Arts* 20, 4:76-7, 91.

Mack, John
1982   "Material Culture and Ethnic Identity in
             Southeastern Sudan." In John Mack and
             Peter Robertshaw, eds., *Culture History
             in the Southern Sudan. Archaeology,*

Linguistics and Ethnohistory, 111-30. Nairobi: British Institute in Eastern Africa.

1991   *Emil Tonday and the Art of the Congo 1900-1909.* Seattle: University of Washington Press.

Maes, J.
1929   *Les Appuis-Tête du Congo Belge.* Annales du Musée Royal du Congo Belge, Serie VI, Tome I, Fascicule 1. Tervuren: Musée Royale de l'Afrique Centrale.

Magava, E. B.
1973   "African Customs Connected with the Burial of the Dead in Rhodesia." In A. J. Dachs, ed., *Christianity South of the Zambezi.* Gwelo: Mambo Press.

Mahachi, G.
1987   "The Duma of South-Eastern Zimbabwe: A Preliminary Analysis of a Shona Burial Practice." *Zimbabwe Science News* 21, 11-12:141-4.

de Maret, Pierre
1985   *Fouilles Archéologiques dans la Vallée du Haut-Lualaba, Zaire. Sanga et Katongo, 1974.* 2 vols. Annales Musée Royal de l'Afrique Centrale, Sciences Humaines, no. 120. Tervuren: Musée Royal de l'Afrique Centrale.

de Maret, Pierre, Nicole Devy and Cathy Murdoch
1973   "The Luba Shankadi Style." *African Arts* 7, 1:8-15, 88.

Maurer, Evan and Allen F. Roberts
1985   *Tabwa. The Rising of a New Moon: A Century of Tabwa Art.* Ann Arbor: The University of Michigan Museum of Art.

Mazikana, P.C., I.J. Johnstone and R.G.S. Douglas
1982   *Zimbabwe Epic.* Harare: National Archives.

Meyer, Piet
1981   *Kunst und Religion der Lobi.* Zürich: Museum Rietberg.

Ministry of Internal Affairs, Rhodesia.
1974   *Tribe, Language, Relationship of Chiefs and Headman.* Salisbury, Rhodesia.

Monteiro, Rose
1891   *Delagoa Bay. Its Natives and Natural History.* London: George Philip and Son.

Mubitana, Kafungulwa
1971   "Stools and Headrests in Zambia." *Zambian Museum Journal* 2:7-38.

Mullen Kraemer, Christine
1986   *Art of Sub-Saharan African. The Fred and Rita Richman Collection.* Atlanta: High Museum of Art.

Muller, Hendrik P.N. and Joh. F. Snelleman
1892   *Industrie des Cafres Du Sud-Est L'Afrique.* Leyden: E.J. Brill.

National Archives of Zimbabwe
            File R. H. 10. "Ancient Ruins Company."

Nenquin, Jacques
1963   *Excavations at Sanga, 1957. The Prehistoric Necropolis.* Annales Musée Royal de l'Afrique Sciences Humaines, no. 45. Tervuren: Musée Royal de l'Afrique Centrale.

Nettleton, Anitra
1984   "The Traditional Figurative
            Woodcarving of the Shona and Venda."
            Ph.D. dissertation, University of
            Witwatersrand.

1988   "History and the Myth of Zulu
            Sculpture." *African Arts* 21, 3:48-51,
            86-7.

1990   "'Dream Machines': Southern African
            Headrests." *South African Journal of Art
            and Architectural History* 1, 4:147-54.

1991   "Tradition, Anthenticity and Tourist
            Sculpture in 19th and 20th Century
            South Africa." In *Art and Ambiquity.
            Perspectives on the Brenthurst Collection
            of Southern African Art*, 32-47.
            Johannesburg Art Gallery/
            Johannesburg City Council.

Nettleton, Anitra and David Hammond-Tooke
1989   *Catalogue: Ten Years of Collecting (1979-
            1989)*. Johannesburg: The University of
            Witwatersrand.

Neyt, Francois
1981   *Traditional Arts and History of Zaire*.
            Louvain: Histoire de L'Art et
            d'Archaeologie de l'Université de
            Louvain.

1982   *The Art of the Holo*. Munich: Galarie
            Fred Jahn.

Neyt, Francois and L. DeStrycher
1975   *Approche des Arts Hemba*. Villiers-le Bel:
            Arts d'Afrique Noire.

Nooter, Mary H.
1984   "Luba Arts and Leadership." M.A.
            thesis, Columbia University.

1991   "Luba Art and Government: Creating
            Power in a Central African Kingdom."
            Ph.D. dissertation, Columbia
            University.

Oddy, Andrew
1983   "On the Trail of Iron Age Gold."
            Transvaal Museum, Pretoria, Bulletin 19
            (Nov.):24-6.

1984   "Gold in the Southern African Iron Age:
            A Technological Investigation of the
            Mapungubwe and Other Finds." *Gold
            Bulletin* 17, 2:70-78.

de Oliveira, Nunes
1935   "Arte Gentilica em Mocambique."
            Mocambique 3:33-64.

Pankhurst, Richard and Leila Ingrams
1988   *Ethiopia Engraved. An Illustrated
            Catalogue of Engravings by Foreign
            Travelers from 1681 to 1900*. New York:
            Kegan Paul International.

Petrie, Flinders
1927   *Objects of Daily Use*. London: British
            School of Archaeology in Egypt.

Prins, A.H.J.
1965   "A Carved Headrest of the Cushitic
            Boni: An Attempted Interpretation."
            Man 221:189-91.

Puccioni, Nello
1936   *Antropologia e ethnografia della genti
            della Somalia*. Bologna: Nicola
            Zanichelli. English trans. 1960. New
            Haven: Human Relations Area Files.

Randall-MacIver, David
1906   *Mediaeval Rhodesia*. London: Macmillan
            and Co. Ltd.

1971   *Medieval Rhodesia.* Reprint ed. with new introductory note by Brian Fagan. London: Frank Cass & Co. Ltd.

Ranger, Terence O.
1989   "Missionary, Migrants and the Manyika: The Invention of Ethnicity in Zimbabwe." In Le Roy Vail, ed., *The Creation of Tribalism in Southern Africa,* 118-50. Los Angeles: University of California Press.

Rasmussen, R. Kent
1979   *Historical Dictionary of Zimbabwe/ Rhodesia.* Metuchen, N.J.: The Scarecrow Press.

Ratzel, Friedrich
1897   *The History of Mankind.* A.J. Butler, trans. from 2d German ed. London: Macmillan and Co. Ltd.

Ravenhill, Philip L.
1980   *Baule Statuary Art: Meaning and Modernization.* Working Papers in the Traditional Arts. Philadelphia: Institute for the Study of Human Issues.

1991   *The Art of the Personal Object.* Washington, D.C.: Smithsonian Institutions National Museum of African Art.

Reeves, Nicholas
1990   *The Complete Tutankhamun.* New York: Thames and Hudson.

Riefenstahl, Leni
1982   *Vanishing Africa.* Katherine Talbot, trans. New York: Harmony Books.

Roberts, Allen F.
1980   "Heroic Beasts, Beastly Heroes. Principles of Cosmology and Chiefship among the Lakeside BaTabwa of Zaire." Ph.D dissertation, University of Chicago.

1986   "Duality in Tabwa Art." *African Arts* 19, 4:26-35, 86-7.

1988   "Tabwa Tegumentary Inscription." In Arnold Rubin, ed., *Marks of Civilization,* 41-56. Los Angeles: Museum of Cultural History, University of California.

Robinson, Keith R.
1959   *Khami Ruins.* Cambridge: Cambridge University Press.

1962   "Conus Shell Ornaments in Africa." *Man* 62:170-72.

Rodrigues de Areia, M.L.
1978   "Le Panier Divinatoire des Tshokwe." *Arts d'Afrique Noire* 26:30-44.

Romano, James F.
1990   *Daily Life of the Ancient Egyptians.* Pittsburgh: The Carnegie Museum of Natural History.

Roy, Christopher D.
1979   *African Sculpture: The Stanley Collection.* Iowa City: The University of Iowa Museum of Art.

1987   *Art of the Upper Volta Rivers.* Meudon: Chaffin.

1992   *Art and Life in Africa. Selections from the Stanley Collections. Exhibitions of 1985 and 1992.* Iowa City: University of Iowa Museum of Art.

Rubin, Arnold
1988   *Marks of Civilization.* Los Angeles:
            Museum of Cultural History, University
            of California.

Safer, Jane F. and Francis Gill
1982   *Spirals from the Sea: An Anthropological
            Look at Shells.* New York: Clarkson
            Potter, Inc.

de Santos, Joao
1586   "Ethiopia Oriental." In G. M.
            Theal, ed., *Records of South Eastern
            Africa* (9 vols., 1898-1903), vol. 7. Cape
            Town: Government of the Cape Colony.

Schneider, Harold
1956   "The Interpretation of Pakot Visual
            Art." *Man* 56, 108:103-6.

Schofield, J.F.
1935   "Zimbabwe: The Ancient Ruins
            Company, Limited." *Man* (February):22.

Scott, Nora
1973   *The Daily Life of the Ancient Egyptians.*
            New York: The Metropolitan Museum
            of Art.

Schweinfurth, Georg
1874   *The Heart of African.* New York: Harper
            & Brothers.

1875   *Artes Africanae. Illustrations and
            Description of Productions of the
            Industrial Arts of Central African Tribes.*
            London: Sampson, Low, Marston, Low
            and Searle.

Sieber, Roy
1973   "Approaches to Non-Western Art." In
            Warren L. d'Azevedo, ed., *The

            Traditional Artist in African Societies,*
            425-34. Bloomington: Indiana
            University Press.

1980   *African Furniture and Household Objects.*
            Bloomington: Indiana University Press.

Sieber, Roy and Roslyn Adele Walker
1987   *African Art in the Cycle of Life.*
            Washington D.C.: Smithsonian
            Institution Press.

Simoni, A.
1940   *I Sidamo, fedeli sudditi dell'Impero.*
            Bologna: A. Cacciari.

Smith, Alan K.
1973   "The Peoples of Southern Mozambique:
            An Historical Survey." *Journal of African
            History* 14, 4:565-80.

Smith, Fred. T.
1978   "Gurensi Wall Painting." *African Arts*
            11, 4:36-41.

Sopor, R.C.
1985   *Socio-Cultural Profile of Turkana District.*
            Nairobi: Uzima Press.

Sotheby's
1987   *Tribal Art, Wednesday, May 20.* New
            York: Sotheby's.

Sweeny, James Johnson
1935   *African Negro Art.* New York: Museum
            of Modern Art.

Tagart, Charlotte
1988   "Recent Excavations at Castle Kopje."
            Prehistory Society of Zimbabwe Newsletter
            71 (July):3-6.

Theal, George McCall
1893-1903   *Records of South-Eastern Africa.* 9 vols.
             London: Printed for the Government
             of the Cape Colony.

Timmermans, P.
1962   "Les Sapo Sapo pres de Luluabourg."
             Africa-Tervuren 8:29-53.

Tracey, Hugh
1934   "The Bones." *Native Affairs Department
             Annual* 12:23-6.

Trowell, Margaret and K. P. Wachswann.
1953   *Tribal Crafts of Uganda.* London:
             Oxford University.

Tyrrel, Barbara
1968   *Tribal Peoples of South Africa.* Cape
             Town: Books of Africa.

van der Merwe, Chris
1984   "Mapungubwe." *Flying Springbok* 3,
             12:17-35.

Vogel, Susan
1973   "People of Wood: Baule Figure
             Sculpture." *Art Journal* 23, 1:23-6.

1986   *Aesthetics of African Art: The Carlo
             Monzino Collection.* New York: The
             Center for African Art.

von Sicard, Harald
1953   "Occam's Razor." *Native Affairs
             Department Annual* 30:53-56.

von Sydow, Eckart
1930   *Handbuch der afrikanischen Plastik. Vol. 1.
             Die westafrikanische Plastik.* Berlin:
             Dietrich Reimer.

Walker Art Center
1987   *Art of the Congo.* Los Angeles: Regents of
             the University of California.

Wanless, Ann
1985   "Headrests in the Africana Museum.
             Part 1." *Africana Notes and News* 26,
             6:218-37.

1985   "*Idem*, Part 2." *Africana Notes and News*
             26, 7:286-303.

1986   "*Idem*, Part 3." *Africana Notes and News*
             27, 2:55-72.

1987   "*Idem*, Part 4." *Africana Notes and News*
             27, 5:200-16.

1987   "*Idem*, Part 5." *Africana Notes and News*
             27, 8:305-20.

1988   "*Idem*, Part 6." *Africana Notes and News*
             28, 3:92-109.

1989   "*Idem*, Part 7." *Africana Notes and News*
             28, 7:257-93.

1990   "*Idem*, Part 8." *Africana Notes and News*
             29, 2:58-72.

1990   "*Idem*, Part 9." *Africana Notes and News*
             29, 4:131-47.

Willett, Frank
1971   *African Art.* New York: Praeger.

Wilson, J.G.
1973   "Check-list of the Artifacts and
             Domestic Works of the Karimojong."
             Uganda Journal 37:81-93.

Witwatersrand, University of the, Art Galleries
1992   *'Of course you would not want a
          canoe'...The Collection of W. F. P. Burton.*
          Johannesburg: University of
          Witwatersrand Art Galleries.

Wolf, J. (ed.)
1971   *Missionary to Tanganyika 1877-1888:
          The Writings of Edward Coode Hore,
          Master Mariner.* London: Frank Cass.

Wolfe, Ernie
1979   *An Introduction to the Arts of Kenya.*
          Washington D.C.: Smithsonian
          Institution, Museum of African Art.

Wood, Felicity
1984   *Ideas in Craft.* Harare: AGRITEX.

Wood, Patricia
1978   "Rhodesian Art. A General Survey."
          Arts Rhodesia 1:3-19.

Zeidler, Jeane and Mary Lou Hultgren
1988   "Things African Prove to be the Favorite
          Theme: The African Collection of
          Hampton University." In *ART/Artifact*,
          97-152. New York: The Center for
          African Art and Prestel Verlag.

Zilberg, Johnathan
1988   "Zimbabwean Stone Sculpture and
          Nyau Masquerades." Talk presented at
          the 31st Annual Meeting of the African
          Studies Association, Chicago, 28-31
          October.

● **ASIA**

Ch'en Wan-li
1954   *T'ao chen.* Pei-ching: Chao hua mei shu
        ch'u pan she.

Chōsen Sōtokufu (Government-general of Chōsen)
1916   *Chōsen koseki zufu.* Vol. 3 (Collection of
        illustrations of Korean historical
        remains). Tokyo: Chōsen Sōtokufu.

Feng Hsien-ming
1984   "Sō Gen seihakuji." In *Sō Gen seihakuji,*
        154-182. Chūgoku tōji zenshū 16.
        Kyoto: Bi no Bi.

Hsiao Hsiang
1982   "Chōsa dōkan yō." In *Chōsa dōkan yō,*
        158-178. Chūgoku tōji zenshū 8.
        Kyoto: Bi no Bi.

Itoh Ikutarō
1984   "Yō Eitoku korekushon no Chūgoku
        tōchin." In *Chūgoku tōchin: Yō Eitoku
        shūzō* (Chinese Ceramic pillows from
        Yeung Wing Tak collection), 225-234.
        Hong Kong: Yeung Wig Tak.

Kawahara Masahiko
1978   "Ataka korekushon no Tōyō tōji." In
        Tōyō tōjiten, Ataka korekushon, 3-8.
        Tokyo: Nihon keizai Shinbunsha.

Kuo li chung yang t'u shu kuan (China) T'ai-wan
        fen kuan
1980   *Kuo li chung yang t'u shu kuan T'ai-wan
        fen kuan chen ts'ang min su ch'i wu t'u lu*
        (The folkware collection of the National
        Central Library, Taiwan Branch).
        T'ai-pei: Kuo li chung yang t'u shu kuan
        T'ai wan fen kuan.

McCallum, Toshiko M.
1988   *Containing Beauty: Japanese Bamboo
        Flower Baskets.* Los Angeles: UCLA
        Museum of Cultural History.

Mikami Tsugio
1984   "Chūgoku no tōchin, Tō yori Gen e"
        ("Chinese ceramic pillows from T'ang to
        Yuan dynasty"). In *Chūgoku tōchin: Yō
        Eitoku shūzō* (Chinese ceramic pillows
        from Yeung Wing Tak collection), 10-
        23. Hong Kong: Yeung Wing Tak.

Minzokugaku Kenkyūjo (ed.)
1951   *Minzokugaku jiten.* Tokyo: Tokyodō
        Shuppan.

Morse, Edward S.
1886   *Japanese Homes and their Surroundings.*
        Boston: Ticknor and Co.

1917   *Japan Day by Day, 1877, 1878-79,
        1882-83.* Boston: Houghton Mifflin.

Nozaki Seikin
1928   *Kisshō zuan kaidai: Shina fūzoku
        no ichi kenkyū.* Tenshin: Chūgoku dōsan
        kōji.

Ōhara Rieko
1988   *Kurokami no bunkashi.* Tokyo: Tsukiji
        Shokan.

Osaka Shiritsu Tōyō Tōji Bijutsukan (ed.)
1984   *Chūgoku tōchin: Yō Eitoku shūzō*
        (Chinese ceramic pillows from Yeung
        Wing Tak collection). Hong Kong:
        Yeung Wing Tak.

Paine, Robert Treat Jr.
1955   "Chinese ceramic pillows from collections
          in Boston and vicinity." *Far Eastern
          Bulletin*, vol. 7, no. 3. Ann Arbor,
          Michigan.

Shao Meng-lung (ed.)
1989   *Fa-men ssu ti kung chen pao* (Precious
          cultural relics in the crypt of Famen
          Temple). Hsi-an: Sha-hsi jen min mei
          shu ch'u pan she.

Shanhai Jinmin Bijutsu Shuppansha (ed.)
1981   *Chūgoku tōji zenshū 9: Teiyō*. Kyoto:
          Bi no Bi.

1984   *Chūgoku tōji zenshū 16: Sō Gen
          seihakuji*. Kyoto: Bi no Bi.

Shibusawa Keizō
1967   *Emakimono ni yoru Nihon jōmin
          seikatsu ebiki*, vol. 4. Tokyo: Kadokawa
          Shoten.

Tenri Daigaku, Tenrikyō Dōyūsha (eds.)
1986   *Hitomono kokoro dai 1-ki dai 2-kan:
          Kankoku no minzoku*. Tenri-shi:
          Tenrikyō Dōyūsha.

Tokyo Chūō Bijutsusha
1929   *Nihon fuzokuga taisei* vol. 10. Tokyo:
          Tokyo Chūō Bijutsusha.

Yano Ken'ichi
1985   *Makura no bunkashi*. Tokyo: Kōdansha.

Yi Chong-sok
1986   *Hanguk ui mokkongye*. Seoul:
          Yorhwadang.

● OCEANIA

Barrow, Terence
1979   *The Art of Tahiti and the Neighboring Society, Austral, and Cook Islands.* London: Thames and Hudson.

Bodrogi, Tibor
1961   *Art in North-East New Guinea.* Eva Racz, trans. Budapest: Publishing House of the Hungarian Academy of Sciences.

Buck, P. H.
1930   "Samoan Material Culture," *Bernice P. Bishop Museum Bulletin* 75. Honolulu: Bishop Museum Press.

Clunie, Fergus
1986   *Yalo i Viti (Shades of Viti): A Fiji Museum Catalogue.* Suva: Fiji Museum.

Dark, P.
1979   "Art of the Peoples of Western New Britain and Their Neighbors." In S. M. Mead, ed., *Exploring the Visual Art of Oceania,* 130-58. Honolulu: University Press of Hawaii.

Ewins, Rod
1982   *Fijian Artefacts: The Tasmanian Museum and Art Gallery Collection.* Hobart: Tasmanian Museum and Art Gallery.

Falgayrettes, Christiane
1989   *Supports de Rêves.* Paris: Fondation Dapper pour les Arts Africains.

Feldman, Jerome and Rubinstein, Donald
1986   *The Art of Micronesia.* Honolulu: University of Hawaii Art Gallery.

Firth, Raymond
1963   *We, the Tikopia.* 2d abridged ed. Boston: Beacon Press.

Graebner, F.
1927   "Kopfbänke." *Ethnologica* 3:1-13.

Greub, Suzanne
1985   *Art of the Sepik River: Authority and Ornament, Papua New Guinea.* Basel: Tribal Art Center, Edition Greub.

Held, Gerrit Jan
1957   *The Papuas of Waropen.* Koninkijk Institut voor Taal-, Land-, en Volkenkunde (Netherlands) Translation Series, 2. The Hague: M. Nijhoff.

Joppien, Rudiger and Smith, Bernard
1985   *The Art of Captain Cook's Voyages* 2. New Haven: Yale University Press.

Kaeppler, Adrienne
1978   *Artificial Curiosities.* Bernice P. Bishop Museum Special Publication, 65. Honolulu: Bishop Museum Press.

Kelm, Heinz
1966-1968   *Kunst vom Sepik,* Vols. 1-3. Veroffentlichungen des Museum für Völkerkunde Berlin, n.f. 10-11, 15. Berlin: Museum für Völkerkunde.

Krieger, Maximilian
1899   "Entwicklungsgeschichte und geographische Verbreitung der Kopfbänke in Neu-Guinea." In *Neu-Guinea,* 473-91. Berlin: A. Schall.

Newton, Douglas
1961   *Art Styles of the Papuan Gulf.* New York:
            Museum of Primitive Art.

Steager, P. W.
1979   "Where does Art Begin in Puluwat." In
            S. M. Mead, ed., *Exploring the Visual Art
            of Oceania*, 342-53. Honolulu:
            University Press of Hawaii.

Saulnier, Tony
1960   *Le papous coupeurs de têtes, 167 jours
            dans la préhistoire.* Paris.

Schmitz, C. A.
1959   "Die Nackenstützen und
            Zeremonialstühle der Azera in
            Nordost-Neuguinea," *Baessler Archiv* n.f.
            7:149-163.

Snow, Philip and Waine, Stefanie
1979   *The People From the Horizon: An
            Illustrated History of the Europeans among
            the South Sea Islanders.* Oxford: Phaidon.

Stöhr, Waldemar
1971-1972   *Melanesien: Schwarze Inseln der
            Südsee.* Köln: J. P. Bachem.

Taylor, Paul Michael and Aragon, Lorraine V.
1991   *Beyond the Java Sea: Art of Indonesia's
            Outer Isles.* New York: Harry N.
            Abrams.

PHOTOGRAPHY CREDITS

FIG. 1.   Photograph by Herbert M. Cole.

FIG. 2.   Photograph by Angela Fisher.

FIG. 3.   Photograph by Angela Fisher.

FIG. 4.   Photograph by William J. Dewey. From Fouche 1937:plate A.

FIG. 5.   Courtesy of National Archives of Zimbabwe, Harare. From Garlake 1978:34.

FIG. 6.   Courtesy of Queen Victoria Museum, Harare.

FIG. 7.   Photograph by William J. Dewey.

FIG. 8.   Detail of photograph by William J. Dewey.

FIG. 9.   Frobenius Institut an der Johann Wolfgang Goethe-Universitat, Frankfurt. Photo neg.# 10864.

FIG. 10. National Archives of Zimbabwe, Harare.

FIG. 11. Photograph by William J. Dewey.

FIG. 12. Photograph by William J. Dewey.

FIG. 13. Photograph by William J. Dewey.

FIG. 14. British Museum (Natural History Division), London.

FIG. 15. Photograph by William J. Dewey. Courtesy of Museum für Völkerkunde, Berlin. Acc.# IIID 2555.

FIG. 16. Photograph by William J. Dewey.

FIG. 17. Photograph by Maria Obermaier. Courtesy of Museum für Völkerkunde, Frankfurt. Acc.# 2472 32-V-420.

FIG. 18. Photograph by William J. Dewey. Courtesy of Queen Victoria Museum, Harare. Acc.# ET1285.

FIG. 19. Photograph by William J. Dewey. Courtesy of Department of Library Services, American Museum of Natural History. Acc.# 90.0/1253.

FIG. 20. National Museum of Natural History, Smithsonian Institution, Washington, D.C. Acc.# 167447.

FIG. 21. Courtesy of Cambridge University Museum of Archaeology and Ethnology. Acc.# 1927.368b.

FIG. 22. Courtesy of The Trustees of the British Museum (Museum of Mankind), London. Acc.# 1892.7-14.151.

FIG. 23. Courtesy of Pitt Rivers Museum, Oxford. Acc.# 1968.23.43.

FIG. 24. Photograph by William J. Dewey.

FIG. 25. Photograph by William J. Dewey. Courtesy of Mutare Museum, Zimbabwe. Acc.# RHD 26/E.

FIG. 26. Photograph by William J. Dewey. Courtesy of Queen Victoria Museum, Harare. Acc.# ET4572.

FIG. 27. Courtesy of ©The Detroit Institute of Arts, Founders Society Purchase, Eleanor and Edsel Ford Exhibition and Acquisition Fund. Acc.# 1983.12.

FIG. 28. Palace Museum, Beijing.

FIG. 29. National Museum of Korea, Seoul.

FIG. 30. Courtesy of the Trustees of the British Museum, London.

FIG. 31. Suzuki Harunobu, Japanese 1724-1770, *Eight Parlor Views: The Returning Sails of the Towel-rack*, woodblock print, 1765, 28.6 x 21.6 cm, Clarence Buckingham Collection. Acc.# 1928.901. Photograph ©1992, Art Institute of Chicago.

FIG. 32. Bigelow Collection. Courtesy, Museum of Fine Arts, Boston. Acc.# 11.19733.

FIG. 33. Musée Royeaux d'Art et d'Histoire, Brussels, #5.

FIG. 34. Courtesy of the Freer Gallery of Art, The Smithsonian Institution, Washington, D.C. Acc.# 03.52.

FIG. 35. From Saulnier 1961:18, courtesy of Hamlyn Publishers.

FIG. 36. From Joppien 1985:219, courtesy of Yale University Press and Oxford University Press Australia. Original print in Staatsbibliothek Preussischer Kulturbesitz, Berlin, from J. R. Forster Journal, MS germ quart. 226, opp. f.65.

FIG. 37. From Joppien 1985:190, courtesy of Yale University Press and Oxford University Press Australia. Original print in British Library, MS 23920, f. 108.

FIG. 38. From Joppien 1985:189, courtesy of Yale University Press and Oxford University Press Australia.. Original print in British Library, MS 23920, f. 109.

FIG. 39. From Barrow 1979:16, Courtesy of Australia House, London.

FOWLER MUSEUM OF CULTURAL HISTORY

Christopher B. Donnan	DIRECTOR
Doran H. Ross	DEPUTY DIRECTOR
Patricia B. Altman	CURATOR OF FOLK ART AND TEXTILES
Patricia Anawalt	CONSULTING CURATOR OF COSTUMES AND TEXTILES
Millicent H. Besser	ACCOUNTANT
Daniel R. Brauer	DIRECTOR OF PUBLICATIONS
Guillermo A. Cock	DIRECTOR OF SECURITY
Roger H. Colten	CURATOR OF ARCHAEOLOGY
Henrietta Cosentino	SENIOR EDITOR
Cynthia D. Eckholm	ASSISTANT REGISTRAR
Betsy R. Escandor	ADMINISTRATIVE ASSISTANT
Christine Griego	RESEARCH ASSISTANT
Judith Herschman	LIBRARIAN
Sarah Jane Kennington	REGISTRAR
George Kershaw	GALLERY OFFICER SUPERVISOR
Anthony A.G. Kluck	ASSISTANT TO THE DIRECTOR OF PUBLICATIONS
Victor Lozano, Jr.	EXHIBITION PRODUCTION
David A. Mayo	EXHIBITION DESIGNER
Robin Chamberlin Milburn	CONSERVATOR
Owen F. Moore	COLLECTIONS MANAGER
Denis J. Nervig	PHOTOGRAPHER
Paulette S. Parker	RESEARCH ASSISTANT
Betsy D. Quick	DIRECTOR OF EDUCATION
Gene Riggs	EXHIBITION PRODUCTION
Daniel Shen	ASSISTANT ACCOUNTANT
Don Simmons	EXHIBITION PRODUCTION
David Svenson	PUBLICATIONS PROCESSING ASSISTANT
Polly Svenson	MUSEUM STORE MANAGER
Fran Tabbush	ASSISTANT COLLECTIONS MANAGER
Barbara Underwood	EXECUTIVE ASSISTANT
Bobby Whitaker	ASSISTANT DIRECTOR OF SECURITY
Patrick White	EXHIBITION PRODUCTION

PUBLICATION PRESENTATION

Judy Hale	PRODUCTION COORDINATION
Barbara Kelly	DESIGN
Leslie Jones	EDITING
Denis J. Nervig	PHOTOGRAPHY (unless otherwise indicated)

Editing and layout were accomplished on Macintosh computers using
QuarkXPress and Adobe Garamond and Stone Sans font software.